THE POLISH MAFIA

THE POLISH MAFIA

GUNS, DRUGS AND MURDER IN THE WILD, WILD EAST

CHRISTOPHER OTHEN

The History Press

First published 2024

The History Press
97 St George's Place, Cheltenham,
Gloucestershire, GL50 3QB
www.thehistorypress.co.uk

© Christopher Othen, 2024

The right of Christopher Othen to be identified as the Author
of this work has been asserted in accordance with the
Copyright, Designs and Patents Act 1988.

All rights reserved. No part of this book may be reprinted
or reproduced or utilised in any form or by any electronic,
mechanical or other means, now known or hereafter invented,
including photocopying and recording, or in any information
storage or retrieval system, without the permission in writing
from the Publishers.

British Library Cataloguing in Publication Data.
A catalogue record for this book is available from the British Library.

ISBN 978 1 80399 547 2

Typesetting and origination by The History Press
Printed and bound in Great Britain by TJ Books Limited, Padstow, Cornwall

Trees for Life

Contents

1	Death of a Polish Gangster	7
I	**THE WILD, WILD EAST, 1806–1992**	
2	The 15:10 to *Juma*	19
3	Enter the Goon Squad	27
4	Savage Youth from the PRL	37
5	Day of the Troglodytes	45
II	**WARSAW GOODFELLAS, 1993–95**	
6	Seks and Drugs	55
7	Rocket Man	63
8	'Get in the Van, You Whore!'	73
9	A Miniature Vietnam	81
III	**EMPIRE OF PRUSZKÓW, 1996–98**	
10	Making Friends with the Frog	93
11	The Sausage Butchers	101
12	We Are the Management Board	109
13	Unholy Trinity	117
IV	**THE POLISH GODFATHER, 1999–2000**	
14	Smuggling is Our Cultural Heritage	135
15	I'm the King Here	143

16	Planet Masa	151
17	Who Killed Pershing?	161

V POLSKA STRIKES BACK, 2001–03
18	Interpol Red Notice	173
19	A Moveable Beast	181
20	Here Come the Mutants	189
21	The Eagle Versus the Octopus	199

VI AFTER THE DELUGE, 2004–PRESENT
22	Ashes and Diamonds	209
23	Triumph of the Swill	219
24	Might is Right	229

Appendix: Gangsters of the Polish Mafia	235
Notes	237
Bibliography	251
Index	253

1

Death of a Polish Gangster

It was late in the afternoon and starting to get dark when they shot Andrzej Kolikowski in the car park of a Polish ski resort. The 45-year-old was stowing ski equipment in the boot of a silver Mercedes S500 when two men in goggles and winter hats came out of the December gloom with guns. The first man fired a sub-machine-gun burst into the air to frighten off other skiers, then the second gunman shot Kolikowski twice in the chest with a pistol as the big man turned around. Kolikowski fell back on to the snow and the gunman put two more bullets through his skull, before both attackers walked briskly to a green Audi and drove away into the Zakopane twilight.

Normally you have to pay for this kind of symbolism. Poland's best-known gangster had been chopped down in the dying days of the *Kolorowe Lata 90* (the colourful 1990s), a decade he and his friends had done so much to corrupt. Ten years earlier, the Soviet puppets and secret police who'd ruled Poland since the Second World War had been swept aside to be replaced by democracy, free elections and a 16 per cent unemployment rate. Inflation reached equally obscene levels and standards of living dropped through the floor, leaving many Poles to reflect bitterly that the daily grind in a capitalist paradise looked a lot simpler in Hollywood movies.

When every day was a struggle just to put food on the table, it became easy to admire those who'd unlocked the secret door that led to luxurious foreign cars, bundles of US dollar bills and expensive Western clothes. Some of Poland's new rich were film stars and musicians who made their money doing Slavic imitations of the American culture they saw on television; others were businessmen who negotiated the murky world of post-Communist wheeler-dealing to get rich and build themselves gaudy houses on land that had been farmers' fields a year before. But the wealthiest and most visible, rolling straight through the new Poland like a bowling ball that knocked over everything in its path, were the gangsters with gold chains and bulging muscles and a Kalashnikov within easy reach.

The men from the wrong side of the law weren't everyone's heroes. To those who embraced Western ideas of entrepreneurship, they were just degenerate Cro-Magnons brute-forcing their way into prosperity by preying on anyone smarter and more honest. To the power brokers hoping Poland would one day join NATO and the European Union, they were a noisy embarrassment who didn't understand the importance of keeping their violence out of the headlines. But to many Poles, the gangsters were textbook examples of how to outsmart the system when you came from the poorest rung of an already poor society and education was something that happened to other people.

Kolikowski claimed to be a car mechanic but that was only a plausible proposition to those who'd never met him in person. His flat-topped, bald head with its horseshoe fringe of dark brown hair sat on a muscular torso that would have given body dysmorphia to the gorillas at the zoo if it hadn't been zipped into a flashy tracksuit most of the time. A resident of Ożarów, a village just outside Warsaw, Kolikowski was smarter than he looked, and the car mechanic act fooled no one, especially not the skiers he mingled with at the Polana Szymoszkowa resort on his last day alive. Everyone knew he was 'Pershing', one of the leaders of the Pruszków Mafia, a gang named after their home town near the capital and the most famous organised crime family in Poland.

If any fellow skiers had somehow failed to hear about the life of sin that bought Kolikowski three homes, two with swimming pools, they'd still have found it hard to understand why a car mechanic had a pretty girlfriend half his age giggling beside him on the slopes. Patrycja was a 21-year-old marketing student from Szczecin – a colourful port city with a griffin's head on its coat of arms – who'd met her lover at a disco along the north coast. Kolikowski liked to dance but not everyone appreciated his uncoordinated jigging about to music. 'Baldy, you should take a dance class,' advised Andrzej Florowski, who served as driver and bodyguard.

Kolikowski didn't usually appreciate backchat from fellow gangsters but Florowski, known to all as 'Florek', was allowed occasional insolence as a reward for his dog-like devotion the rest of the time. That devotion had a price. A month before the visit to Zakopane, someone put a bomb under Florek's car, and he was lucky not to be shredded like lettuce. Another of Kolikowski's bodyguards was murdered at his flat in Warsaw's Wola district two weeks later. Despite the violence, no one could persuade the gang boss against taking his new girlfriend on a weekend away down south.

The Zakopane trip followed close on the heels of Kolikowski's return from a business trip to America where he'd met up with some important foreign crime figures and watched his boxer friend Andrzej Gołota lose to Michael Grant in Atlantic City. Kolikowski had seemed tense at the prospect of coming back to a Poland where a vicious gang war with rivals from Wołomin, on the other side of Warsaw, had been piling bodies high in the streets until recently. Even some members of his own gang seemed ready to turn on him. A superstitious man, he asked friend and professional clairvoyant Krzysztof Jackowski, who looked more like a punch-drunk streetfighter than a soothsayer, to predict the future.

'You will leave a hotel in Warsaw and two people will run up to you in the car park,' said Jackowski. 'One of them, with a weapon that fires very fast, will kill you.'

Zakopane was at the opposite end of the country from Warsaw and seemed a safe bet for the spiritually inclined. This tourist town of wooden houses near the southern border with Slovakia was famous for its skiing and Poles had loved the place for generations. Everyone had a souvenir photograph somewhere of a family member posing with a street performer in a white bear costume on the Zakopane main drag. The town was a neutral space for gangsters, who rarely settled scores within city limits, and Kolikowski thought he'd be safe there.

He and Patrycja arrived in Zakopane on Friday evening and enjoyed a weekend's skiing through the hard snow. On Sunday, 5 December, they were on the slopes above the Kasprowy, a red-roofed communist monstrosity of a hotel nestled among the forests only a few minutes' drive from the centre of town. The base of the ski lifts was conveniently near both the car park and the equipment hire shop, where Patrycja was retrieving their deposit when the gunmen struck.

A doctor who'd been loading up his own car tried to help Kolikowski as the gang boss lay in a darkening pool of arterial blood. Someone else called an ambulance but it was slow coming because an anonymous voice had put in a hoax call shortly before to report a major accident on the other side of town. The ambulance finally arrived and raced Kolikowski to hospital, but he died on the table as they tried to resuscitate him. The news was all over the media by the next morning. 'The alleged boss of the Pruszków gang, Andrzej K., alias "Pershing", has died,' reported the RMF radio station. 'He was shot yesterday in Zakopane. The police have not ruled out this being a professional hit.'

Professional was right: the phone call to distract the emergency services; the green Audi stolen from Kraków and soon to be discovered burned out near a ski jump; the way the gunman with the sub-machine gun had kept his weapon partly inside a bag to collect the used cartridges. But who ordered the killing?

There was an obvious candidate: for most of the 1990s, the Pruszków Mafia had been fighting rivals from Wołomin for control of every racket imaginable, from multimillion-dollar drug-smuggling networks, slot machine profits and protection rackets to political corruption, control of brothels and car theft on a massive scale.

Scores of gangsters had been shot, stabbed or blown apart in the gang war. Kolikowski had already survived at least three assassination attempts, including a bomb that collapsed a pub ceiling on to a crowd of gangsters playing pool in Warsaw's fashionable Saska Kępa district five years earlier.

A lot of people assumed the Zakopane hit had been ordered by the Wołomin gang leaders, but the few still alive denied involvement in Kolikowski's death fervently enough that a lot of well-informed people believed them. Other candidates existed, like the karate enthusiasts who robbed the wrong man and had their kneecaps probed with an electric drill by Pershing and his friends; rogue police officers frustrated at his apparently untouchable status; foreign gangs he'd annoyed over the years, including, it was rumoured, some Colombians; or even his own Pruszków friends, who had been noticeably unhappy about Kolikowski's expansive plans for the new millennium. Some observers suggested he'd already split from the gang to carve out his own territory.

And why had Patrycja's first action after the murder been to locate her boyfriend's mobile phone and snap its SIM card in half?

Live fast, die rich. In the *Kolorowe Lata 90*, you couldn't trust anyone.

Today, Pruszków is a small, quiet town full of people living their lives and bringing up families but, thanks to men like Kolikowski, it remains synonymous with organised crime for most Poles. A strange fate for a place first recorded in the eleventh century as a tiny village offering up nothing more spectacular than a few peasants and a fistful of mud. Over the coming centuries, it would remain an insignificant speck on the map while distant gangs of self-declared nobles fought to unify a sprawling chunk of Eastern Europe into what would eventually become the Polish–Lithuanian Commonwealth. Once achieved, the unity didn't last long. A grim period of political turmoil, foreign invasion and some truly incompetent leadership saw the Commonwealth collapse and its territory swallowed up by Russia, Austria and Prussia.

By then, Pruszków was a few hectares of arable land farmed by minor gentry and scarcely bigger than it had been 700 years earlier. No one objected when a Russian merchant dismembered the place and sold it off in pieces to any buyer with ready cash and a burning desire to build a house in the middle of nowhere.

As Poles struggled to retain some sense of national identity under three different empires, Pruszków adapted better than most and unexpectedly began to flourish. Nineteenth-century visitors from Warsaw found a small town with a railway station, an iron works and a home for the mentally ill. The First World War came and went, leaving rubble and death in its wake, but in the aftermath, Poland recovered its independence as the old partitioning empires crumbled to dust.

Marshal Józef Piłsudski took command of the resurrected nation in the interwar years, determined to keep it free of the Nazis and Soviets who were growing ever more threatening on the borders. He died with his homeland unconquered but still painfully underdeveloped. Much of the country remained a rural backwater of forests and farms where horse-drawn carriages were more common than anything with an engine.

Pruszków was a rare, industrialised exception. The 30,000-strong town now boasted a skyline of smoking factory chimneys, even if the men in charge didn't think the locals deserved luxuries like pavements, streetlights or a functioning sewage system.

The summer of 1939 brought German troops with swastika flags, who spent the next five years killing Jews, Roma and patriots of all kinds. A third of Poland's population died, with 2.9 million of them being Jewish. The country became a launch pad for an invasion of the Soviet Union that ultimately failed, but not before turning Eastern Europe into a slaughterhouse.

In the spring of 1945, the victorious Soviets invited Polish resistance fighters to a conference in Pruszków for a discussion about the future. Those trusting enough to turn up were arrested and hanged in Moscow three months later. Soviet dictator Josef Stalin wanted it known that Poland was now part of his drab, murderous Communist empire with self-determination no longer on the menu.

The promised collective prosperity of the Soviet system never arrived and the *Polska Rzeczpospolita Ludowa* (Polish People's Republic – PRL) remained a poor country with few private cars, overcrowded trams and the lucky ones riding bicycles. All those grey housing blocks emerging from the rubble were utilitarian and totalitarian, and seemed to have been designed purely to crush the spirit.

A puppet government dedicated its most enthusiastic efforts to political symbolism. Warsaw's historic *Stare Miasto* (Old Town) was rebuilt to the smallest detail after the Germans destroyed it in the dying days of the war, while the centre of the city boasted the *Pałac Kultury i Nauki* (Palace of Culture and Science), a Soviet skyscraper that looked like a brick rocket ship tinted the colour of stale champagne. Officially a gift from Stalin, the palace was finished the year after his death. The Poles hated it. A popular joke of the time:

Q. Where is the best view of Warszawa?
A. From the top of the Palace of Culture.
Q. Why there?
A. Because it's the only place in Warszawa you can't see the Palace of Culture.

Pruszków lost its freedom like everywhere else, but benefited from a new communist ruling class who were smart enough to see potential in the town and invest accordingly. Soon it became the manufacturing heart of central Poland. A place that valued manual labour and distrusted too much education fitted perfectly into a dictatorship that felt the same way, although Pruszków was never a model of socialist obedience. In the PRL, everyone had a job or a good excuse, but noisy urban spaces were hard to control and offered plenty of opportunities in burglary and black marketeering for a working man who didn't like to work too hard.

Only the truly hardcore criminals were in any danger of prison. In a system everyone knew was broken from first principles ('we pretend to work and they pretend to pay', as the old Soviet joke went), even the policemen of the *Milicja* looked the other way for a big enough bribe.

Up in the port city of Gdańsk, the car thief and smuggler Nikodem Skotarczak, alias Nikoś, became a popular hero in the 1980s for his criminal escapades. The *Milicja* barely pretended to care. For most Poles, breaking the dictatorship's laws seemed little worse than slacking off at work, cheating in exams or maintaining their Catholic faith with a ferocity that sent the official atheist line from Moscow yelping back into the steppes.

In 1989, the Soviet empire collapsed when the number of true believers dwindled to single figures and Poland had to deal with democracy – a system it knew more in theory than practice. The grey scum line of communism would remain visible across the country for years.

Russia had flooded its satellite with dreams of socialist equality for half a century, but that drained away to leave nothing except dirty tower blocks, cracked concrete and the defeated faces of people trudging between the two. A galaxy of new parties appeared but their mutually incompatible political dreams proved only that Poles couldn't decide whether they wanted their new country to be a capitalist utopia or a rest home for watered-down leftism. A lot of Poles didn't care at all, judging by the 43.2 per cent turn-out rate at the first fully free election.

Adverts and the free market livened up the country a little, but not enough. Early Western visitors found a broken, monochrome world where customer service was a purely theoretical concept and the men all seemed to be potato-faced drinkers with unflattering moustaches.

Polish women had the bone structure of a Hollywood starlet but the dress sense of a blind housewife with cruel friends. Everyone drank vodka like water and smoked as if lung cancer had never been invented.

With socialist subsidies gone forever, post-communist Pruszków fell harder than most. Jobs and prosperity vanished overnight, turning the already rough housing estates of the Żbików district into some of the most violent in the country. It was here that the Pruszków gang was born, even if the media sometimes forgot that not all of its members were locals. 'Pruszków Mafia' was always more a convenient journalistic term than a geographically precise fact. Some of the gang's most significant individuals came from very different backgrounds.

Jarosław Maringe was a dark-haired, good-looking young man from a run-down part of inner-city Warsaw, who got mixed up with Pruszków in the mid-1990s and just about lived to regret it. The product of an intelligentsia family – the closest communism had ever got to a middle class – Maringe's soul was a battleground between angel and demon in which the contestant with horns usually came out on top. In another country, in another time, Maringe would have been a respectable young businessman with his face in the newspapers, but this was Poland in the *Kolorowe Lata 90*, where the life of a gangster seemed the more natural choice. His path from entrepreneurial teen to street soldier to exiled, paranoid crime boss paralleled the rise and fall of Pruszków over the whole violent decade.

The gang he joined in the early 1990s had been formed by men like veteran jailbird and genuine Pruszków resident Janusz Prasol, aka 'Parasol' (Umbrella), with his Genghis Khan moustache and years spent in brutal PRL prisons. Parasol's crew had taken advantage of all the freedoms post-communist Poland had to offer by hijacking trucks, extorting businesses and destroying anyone who got in their way. The gang's numbers were swelled by younger disciples like Jarosław Sokołowski, aka 'Masa' (Mass), a walking wall of muscle with a head like a football, a drink problem and a misleadingly boyish smile. Together, they bribed politicians, corrupted police officers and terrified a population trying to enjoy itself for the first time in decades.

'We went on the dance floor and started to fuck with anything that moved,' remembered one gang member:

There were only two of us, but we caused a panic; there was no one strong enough to stop us [...] Let me tell you, that was Poland in a nutshell. This was the answer to the question why the Mafia so easily dominated the whole country. No one could stand up to us, everyone was shitting their pants. And they only dreamed that we would leave them alone. And honour? Fuck honour.

The criminal horizon widened with the arrival of gangster legend Pershing from Ożarów, which was about 8km from Pruszków but a very different place. He introduced gambling, debt collection and car theft on an industrial scale. Expensive vehicles were stolen from Germany, cocaine imported from Colombia and gangsters from Russia who challenged the status quo were shot dead in the street. Not even a gang war with Wołomin that littered the streets with bodies could slow them down.

It would all go wrong, as it always does, when egos got bloated and the money too big to share. The further Jarosław Maringe climbed up the gang's hierarchy, the more clearly he could see the brains of those around him breaking down under a diet of vodka and cocaine. Bad decisions began to seem like good ones and eventually Pruszków would collapse in a bloody round of murder and betrayal that saw Pershing shot dead and his colleagues on trial, in hiding or on a path to become Poland's unlikeliest celebrities. Other members of the gang cycled in and out of prison, retired or died; one even became head of Ukraine's International Legion after the 2022 Russian invasion. Bloody gang wars tore the Polish underworld apart as rivals fought for the vacant crown.

But when the going was good, it was very good. Pruszków gangsters went to Marbella and Phucket on holiday, wore athletic wear with designer labels, lived in new-build mansions, counted celebrities as friends and draped gold crosses around their necks. It was not an understated style and to Westerners and many fellow Poles they looked ridiculous, but perhaps that was always the point. They were just the latest in a long line of crooks who were not shy about broadcasting their wealth.

'Ninety percent of all mob guys come from poverty,' said 'Fat' Vinnie Teresa, a Mafia-made man in the Patriarca crime family of 1960s New England:

They grew up with holes in their pants, no shoes on their feet. They had rats in their rooms and they had to fight for a scrap of bread to eat. Now they made it. They got money, five-hundred-buck suits, hundred-buck shoes, ten-grand cars, and a roll of bills big enough to choke a horse. It doesn't do any good to just look at it. They want everyone to know they've made it.

The gangsters of Pruszków liked to show off just as much as Fat Vinnie's friends, even if 1990s Poland had a lot less to offer in the way of luxury than post-war America. No one ever mocked their fashion choices out loud.

They were violent, damaged people. Masa spent his childhood listening to his mother having sex with random men in the same room, while Parasol had been viciously tortured in jail by guards who laughed when he coughed up blood. A few rare exceptions, like Maringe, had a background in the intelligentsia, but they had to fight harder than most to be accepted into an underworld where man was wolf to man and the Kalashnikov just another tool.

Maringe's fellow gangsters called him 'Chińczyk' (the Chinese), even though his family had first taken root in Poland when a Frenchman met an Italian girl while a Corsican soldier ruled the continent from west to east. His family tree had some interesting branches.

I

THE WILD, WILD EAST, 1806–1992

2

The 15:10 to *Juma*

The people of Warsaw leaned out of their windows and cheered when the most famous Frenchman in the world came riding into their city in the early days of the nineteenth century. Napoleon Bonaparte had been rampaging across the continent at the head of his *Grande Armée* for the last two years, crushing enemies, dismembering realms and remaking the map of Europe. A few days before Christmas 1806, he arrived in what had once been the capital of Poland to regroup his forces before plunging east into the Russian Empire.

The Poles saw him as a liberator and seized the opportunity to petition for the resurrection of the old Polish–Lithuanian Commonwealth. They quickly discovered the emperor had no interest in their nationalist dreams. 'They have allowed themselves to be partitioned,' Napoleon told his generals dismissively. 'Today they are no longer a nation.'

Instead, his troops turned this quiet city of dirt roads and Dresden-style architecture into a swarming multilingual barracks, busy as an ant farm. Food was so sparse and rain so common that the French soldiers complained the only Polish words they needed were '*Chleba? Nie ma. Woda? Zaraz!*' ('Bread? Not available. Water? Right away!') In past centuries, Warsaw had been known as the 'Paris of the East', but the new arrivals concluded whoever thought up the title knew little about France and even less about its capital.

After a few months of bustling occupation, Polish nationalists had reason to be hopeful again. A seductive local girl succeeded where diplomacy had failed by persuading Napoleon to grant his hosts an independent state in the modest 'Duchy of Warsaw'. It looked good on paper but this sawn-off version of the old Commonwealth was never more than a vassal state.

The Duchy's Polish leaders were feeling more like puppets than partners in the summer of 1812, when Napoleon's horses finally rattled the wheeled cannons east for war with Russia. Soldiers of the *Grande Armée* managed to occupy Moscow for thirty-six days before falling back into a chaotic retreat that saw whole army corps killed off by snow, disease and Russian peasants with knives between their teeth.

As Napoleon's forces fled through the disintegrating Duchy, a Frenchman called Leonard Ludwik Maringe stayed behind in Warsaw to marry the 18-year-old daughter of a transplanted Italian architect. The marriage lasted, even as Napoleonic Europe collapsed around them, and the Maringes settled down to run a hotel in Warsaw, which had reverted to speaking Russian instead of French.

By 1973 the hotel was long gone, along with its legendary *befsztyk u Mareza* (Mareza Steak), and a bad apple was swinging from the Maringe family tree. A child called Jarosław Jerzy Maringe had come into the world with a French surname no one could pronounce properly and a sense of being destined for better things. He grew up in a city-centre household dominated by strong-willed, intellectual women who had survived a German occupation that killed off their men and were determined never to forget the past.

Maringe felt closest to the memory of his grandfather, executed by the Gestapo as a member of the resistance. 'One of his tasks was to liquidate informers,' Maringe remembered. 'He was basically a professional hit man!'

Maringe was less keen on his very much alive father, an electrical engineer with a drink problem who spent most days mourning the various opportunities for a better life that had slipped through his fingers. Jarosław was still young when his father finally did something right and got permission from the government to take a job in Paris arranged by distant relatives. Maringe's mother would eventually join him, kissing Jarosław goodbye with vague promises about a quick return. Instead, the Maringes fell out of love and soon separated, neither feeling inclined to return home or send for a son who had been abandoned to the care of his grandmother.

His life was turned further upside down when the government seized the family home under the guise of 'renovation' and moved everyone out to a bleak housing estate a few kilometres away in the Gocław district. Maringe found himself in an alien world where his foreign name, good manners ('being taught etiquette, told to kiss a woman's hand') and intelligentsia background were serious disadvantages. He had to toughen up and quick. 'In order not to be lost in the human jungle I had to become a predator,' he remembered.

Regular parcels from France made life easier. The arrival of an Amstrad personal computer in the mid-1980s opened a door into the growing subculture of software piracy – something the PRL government didn't understand enough to outlaw. At first, Maringe copied games for friends but soon realised there was money in his hobby and got a pitch at the Grzybowska computer market – one of the many centres of unlicensed weekend capitalism springing up around the city. He became a regular among the humming monitors and intense conversations on ulicia (ul.) Marchlewskiego Juliana, a huge avenue running through the city which local rumour claimed had been built specifically for Russian tanks to crush any uprisings.

Business was good. After changing his złoty profits into dollars, Maringe was making the huge sum of $100 a week. He didn't even need the money: his parents regularly sent enough cash from France that the teenager was better off than most adults suffering through a dysfunctional communist economy where petrol and chocolate were still rationed.

The real value of his market earnings was transformational: it changed him from an abandoned, lonely boy in a Gocław apartment block into a confident young entrepreneur. The teachers at school got a taste of the new Maringe when he forced them to get his surname right. 'It was something my grandmother taught me,' he said. 'My family died for Poland under that name. And I insisted it be pronounced correctly.'

As Maringe worked his market stall, the Soviet bloc was slowly disintegrating. In Moscow, Mikhail Gorbachev's liberalising *perestroika* policy chipped away at the authoritarian state while, closer to home, economic upheaval had forced the PRL government to work with its critics, the loudest of whom came from the 10 million-strong underground trade union *Solidarność* (Solidarity).

Created back in 1980 to protest communism, *Solidarność* had been immediately outlawed by Polish leader Wojciech Jaruzelski. The bat-eared and balding general was rarely seen without the sunglasses that made him look like a South American dictator and he went on to oversee a decade of martial law that did little except destroy the economy. By 1988, Jaruzelski had no option except to invite the *Solidarność* leaders for secret talks about the future of Poland.

The only issue being debated that meant much to Maringe was foreign travel. Well-connected types had always been able to go abroad, provided they could afford the two weeks' wages it took to purchase a single-use passport from the sour-faced bureaucrats at the Ministry. The paper trail thinned after that, thanks to a quirk of international diplomacy which granted Poles visa-free travel to a surprisingly wide selection of foreign countries. Even as far back as 1975, Polish travellers made 316,000 trips a year to non-communist nations, with West Germany accounting for 65,000 of those.

'A stocky worker in Warsaw said proudly that his doctor was visiting Paris,' noted a *New York Times* journalist at the time. 'His friend's doctor had returned from New York.'

The less well-connected found themselves stuck at home unable to get their hands on all the desirable foreign goods that international travellers routinely smuggled back. Cosmetics and textiles were popular in the sixties, digital watches and calculators in the next decade, but anything hard to source at home, from gold coins to lighter flints, was worth the risk.

As the 1980s economic crisis began to bite, smuggling became vital enough to the Polish economy that the government stopped even trying to police the black market. In 1987, the long-running *Centralnej Komisji do Walki ze Spekulacją* (Central Commission against Speculation) was shut down and the next year talks with *Solidarność* saw foreign travel regulations relaxed, among a host of other concessions. General Jaruzelski and his junta could no longer hold back capitalism.

In 1988, a 15-year-old Maringe took the money he'd earned from software piracy and got himself a passport. He set off for West Berlin on a packed train for the first step of a journey that would lead to a life of crime.

He was good boy, at first. In West Berlin, Maringe took his cash to the nearest Aldi and filled bags with chocolate, beer and canned drinks before dragging the haul back to the train station. After a few trips back and forth across the border, the teenager had enough stock to open two market stalls manned by friends from Gocław. The business expanded from food to selling blank video cassettes ('it was very important to our fellow countrymen,' he remembered, 'that they had this fucking inscription: Made in Japan') and then to a video rental library of pirated Western films for customers eager to get a window into a better life, preferably one involving Jean-Claude Van Damme.

Somehow Maringe managed to combine his life of guerrilla capitalism with decent school grades and might have built a legitimate career if other young Poles commuting to West Berlin hadn't showed him an easier way to make money. 'The biggest mistake of my life,' he said later.

His new friends were all involved in the *Juma*, a slangy Polish term for thieving abroad that took its name from the Berlin-bound train leaving the city of Zielona Góra at 15:10 every day, reminding everyone of the famous Western film *The 3:10 to Yuma*, where an impoverished rancher fights off circling bandits. Light-fingered young Poles justified stealing from Germany as reparations for the war and no one back home challenged them. It was hard to know what right and wrong even meant in the summer of 1989, as communism slipped away and the world flipped upside down.

That June, partially free elections were held in Poland for the first time since the 1930s. The communists had reserved 60 per cent of seats in the Lower House for themselves but *Solidarność* won the rest, along with almost all seats in the freely elected Upper House. A non-communist prime minister was chosen – the first to be democratically elected in the twentieth century who hadn't known Piłsudski personally.

The transformation into a genuine democracy was slow and Russian troops would remain on Polish soil for several more years, but the election result rocked the Eastern bloc. Gorbachev doubled down on *perestroika* by declaring the USSR would not stop countries leaving its orbit, igniting a chain reaction that brought down the Berlin Wall, reunited Germany and destroyed the Soviet Empire. To everyone's surprise, it all happened peacefully, except for a bloody revolution to remove the Ceaușescu regime in Romania that December. By the end of the year, only the USSR remained upright and even that was punch drunk and swaying, with multiparty elections scheduled for the next spring.

Maringe was too involved in the world of *Juma* to care much about the political changes around him. He'd formed a gang with other Warsaw boys on the train to shoplift electronic equipment, Gillette razor blades, perfumes, branded clothing, household goods, cigarettes, Absolut vodka and anything else they could smuggle past customs checks. Soon they graduated to stealing car radios abroad for a fence in Saska Kępa called 'Gruby Jurek' (Fat Jurek), who bought anything for cash with no questions asked.

Then, in 1990, the criminal life bit back when 17-year-old Maringe was arrested breaking into a car in West Berlin and spent three weeks behind bars in a young offenders institution. 'I was small, skinny, shit-scared,' he remembered. The place was run by Kurdish and Turkish gangs, all clearly older than their claimed ages, who took turns intimidating the Polish teenager. He learned to fight back, motivated by seeing a German boy carved up by a Turk in a row over a card game, and soon worked out the basics of prison life: 'You attack or you are attacked – the rules are simple.'

It was a grim experience, even for three weeks, but Maringe was too addicted to the easy money to think about going straight and stole car radios from the guards' vehicles in the prison car park on the day of his release. Soon, his *Juma* exploits expanded into stealing entire vehicles. At the time, foreign cars could be bought on the Polish black market for around $3,000, with some luxury brands going for as high as $25,000. That was a lot of cash for poor Poles, but nothing compared to how much they cost through official channels. By the time communism fell, thousands of 'unofficial' cars were estimated to be on Polish roads, most stolen from the West. 'Come to Poland!' joked the Germans bitterly. 'Your car is already here!'

Despite the crime wave, many well-off Westerners still trustingly left their vehicles unlocked with keys and documents in the glove compartment. Maringe and friends took full advantage to joyride choice models back through Europe with boots full of stolen car radios and apparently legitimate paperwork to show at the border. Gruby Jurek took the radios, and the cars got garage resprays and grateful new owners.

When the West finally began cracking down on car thefts, Maringe found himself pursued through foreign forests by police dogs, while helicopters chattered overhead, and searchlights blazed through the frothing treetops. It was nerve-wracking, but the racket remained too profitable to stop.

He made enough cash to buy a bachelor pad flat in Praga Południe, a rough area close to Gocław. His grandmother had given up trying to control Maringe and was glad to see him go – an attitude shared by an older relative called Stanisław who'd just been elected Mayor of Warsaw and could do without any scandal in the family.

Maringe was arrested several more times abroad and did short stints in adult institutions. Still young, he endured the grim realities of life behind bars that included gang fights between Poles and Romanians and fighting off rapists in a Luxembourg cell. He tried to cut his wrists in a Swiss prison, although how serious he was about dying was never clear to the authorities and perhaps even to him.

Back in Poland by 1993, Maringe couldn't face being locked up abroad again and abandoned his *Juma* operations. The hunger for easy money remained, along with some new-found resentment picked up in prison, and he targeted the market in Grzybowska, where he'd once had a stall. Maringe knew the place back to front and it was easy to sneak into the premises after hours and walk out with a haul of graphics cards and other peripherals.

Previously, his crimes had been socially acceptable, even vaguely patriotic to some, but robbing his own people was crossing a line. Maringe didn't even look back. He eventually hooked up with a young gangster working for a crew linked to the underworld in the nearby town of Pruszków.

A fixture at the Warsaw discos, Adrian Kołodziejek's handsome, well-dressed façade concealed an amoral thrill-seeker who was twisted enough to make a good corkscrew. He and Maringe palled around the capital, competing to see who could pick up the most girls, snort the most overpriced cocaine and do the most daring *skok* (heist). Once, they robbed a transporter in a car park and pepper-sprayed the guard dog; other times, Maringe conned the moneychangers in Saska Kępa by claiming to have a big wad of foreign currency and leading the victim outside to be robbed at knifepoint.

Maringe thought he and Adrian had become as close 'as two drops of water' and it didn't seem a big step to join Pruszków alongside his friend. Becoming a gangster was the easiest way to get rich in a country where law and order didn't mean much any more.

Adrian's Pruszków boss was less enthusiastic about the prospect of a new recruit. Marek Janusz Czarnecki was a hard case from Praga who went by the nickname 'Rympałek'(Crowbar) and had abandoned the life of an apprentice jeweller for crime. Only ten years older than Maringe, he looked nearly middle-aged with his slippers and beer belly, but the appearance was deceptive. Rympałek had trained as a wrestler and boxer before becoming a player in the underworld and now led a tough crew that included former policemen who'd turned their backs on the law for a bigger payday. It would not be easy to be accepted into their ranks.

Rympałek may have looked like a godfather to a street-level beginner like Maringe, but his bosses in Pruszków were the real powerplayers, and had been ever since an infamous shootout at a hotel near Warsaw, three years earlier. Adrian warned his friend that the gangster lifestyle was more death than glory and that the Hotel George incident was just the tip of a very big, very bloody iceberg. Maringe thought he could handle it. What was the worst that could happen?

3

Enter the Goon Squad

Back at the hotel, a man called Parasol had been shot through both legs, another known as 'Szarak' was dead with a bullet in his back and four other gangsters were in handcuffs. Outside, the traffic had pulled over to the verge of a two-lane highway so a wailing police car with a bloody officer laid out on the back seat could race past to the hospital. It was the afternoon of 6 July 1990, and someone had just shot up the Hotel George. The Pruszków Mafia was making its first headlines.

The hotel was a low-slung building of concrete rectangles painted an alarming shade of butter yellow on the road linking Warsaw with Katowice. No one in reception looked twice at the six tough-looking men who'd swaggered inside shortly before the shooting, searching for a Pole named Mirek. Their friend lived in West Germany but had recently come home to see what his country looked like without communism – a decision he'd regretted two days ago when the same men tear-gassed him in the George car park and stole his Mercedes. Now they were here to sell it back to him for $15,000.

Janusz Prasol, aka Parasol, led the gangster crew that day. Big, narrow-eyed and balding, with a drooping moustache 'like a Mongol warrior', according to a journalist, he was an amateur boxer from Żbików. Officially employed in a printing firm, his real career lay in imaginative combinations of robbery and violence. If he wanted something, he took it, and smashing someone's face in the process just added to the fun.

Parasol's father was a solid citizen who ran a place making electrical transformers, but his son took too much joy in breaking the law to ever go straight, no matter the cost. He'd been in and out of prison through the last decades of the PRL and earned a reputation as one of the *Git-Ludzie*: a convict elite who refused to bow down to the guards, no matter how many times they got beaten with a shovel handle or held under a scalding shower. Parasol took the punishment and still spat blood in their faces.

Only the toughest could hold on to the status of *Git-Ludzie* for long. Any disrespect from guards or other inmates, such as a punch, an insult or flicked water from a toilet brush, had to be punished with extreme violence or would result in an immediate slide down the prison hierarchy. Parasol and his friends had managed to stay on top through their many years behind bars and graduated from that Darwinian gladiator school transformed into what even fellow gangsters described as 'troglodytes'. Now they formed the core of a new criminal gang, taking advantage of the freedoms available in a democratic Poland. Extorting a visitor from Germany was the least of their crimes.

It never occurred to Parasol's crew that Mirek would alert the police about his missing Mercedes. During the PRL, law enforcement had been in the hands of *Milicja* paramilitaries who spent more time beating anti-communist protestors than solving actual crimes. If anyone had been handing out prizes for the most hated men in Poland, the gold cup would have gone to the *Milicja*'s notorious ZOMO riot police – a gang of bloodthirsty head-crackers who dished out the worst of the violence while their bosses shouted encouragement over the radio: 'Grab whoever you can and into the vans!' [static] 'Give 'em a nice, energetic kicking that they won't forget.'

In April 1990, the government tried to wipe away the stink of the old regime with a brand-new police force but lacked enough professionals for a truly fresh start and so was forced to rely on old *Milicja* veterans. Most Poles trusted this latest incarnation of law enforcement about as much as they would a chimpanzee with fine china.

Only an outsider like Mirek, familiar with the more orderly world of German law enforcement and desperate to get his car back, would have told the story of the stolen car to a roomful of chain-smoking officers. He got lucky. The men he talked with were that rare breed who were more interested in solving the crime than giving him a ZOMO-style kicking.

On the day of the meeting, armed police hid in the woods around the Hotel George and a helicopter buzzed tight circles in the summer sky. An undercover officer accompanied Mirek inside, posing as his bodyguard. It looked like overkill, but the police were in no mood to take chances, ever since two bodies had appeared beside the Warsaw to Katowice highway a month earlier.

Those deaths sprang from a row over a different Mercedes. On 29 May, a young Pruszków gangster called Wojciech Kiełbiński, known as 'Kiełbacha' (Sausage) to friends, had arranged to meet local fixer 'Bogdan' after a stolen car failed to meet expectations. The pair set up a rendezvous near Siestrzenia, a small town nestled in a forest where the skinny pine trees shot tightly packed and branchless towards the sky like the bristles of a giant toothbrush.

Bogdan arrived in an Audi 100 with two friends, both 'Russian' – which, back then, meant any nationality that used a Cyrillic alphabet, from Ukraine to Belarus – to find a large group from Pruszków blocking the road back to Warsaw with their cars. A man known as 'Słoń' (Elephant) and his violent, bearded friend 'Lulek', both just out of prison, piled into the back of Bogdan's car and ordered him to drive into the forest for 'a talk'.

As a shaky Bogdan turned the wheel, a gap opened up in the Pruszków barricade and he hit the accelerator, scraped through and went flying towards Warsaw. Kiełbacha and his friends chased the Audi as it zigzagged across the road while Słoń and Lulek fought for control of the car. Kiełbacha was almost bumper to bumper when the inside of the Audi lit up with gunfire. The rear doors opened and the bodies of the two Pruszków men ragdolled across the tarmac, one going into the uncut grass at the side of the highway and the other bouncing off the central divider. Kiełbacha screeched to a halt and the other Pruszków cars braked hard behind him. A furious Parasol jumped out. 'Why aren't you chasing them?' he shouted.

Kiełbacha pointed at their two friends dying on the road. The stakes had just been raised on Polish crime – an arena where disputes were normally handled with fists or knives.

Pruszków responded in kind by putting a price on the heads of Bogdan and his Russian friends, but it was never collected. One of the Russians died soon after in Chechnya when a deal went sour, while the other two escaped to Spain and an expat life of crime, until finally getting arrested twenty years later. Back in 1990, the police had no suspects and no reliable witnesses – just a firm belief that the events at Siestrzenia showed the cancer of organised crime metastasising under the new democratic freedoms. Crime figures that year would be 60 per cent higher than the previous year. When Mirek started talking about the Hotel George, the police decided to take no chances.

The six men didn't seem to suspect anything as they entered the hotel, but then it all went wrong very quickly. According to police, the men rushed the officer posing as a bodyguard and one pulled out a pair of nunchuks – a weapon choice that said more about the popularity of martial arts films at the time than the realities of street fighting. Either they recognised the officer or were planning to steal the cash from the start.

The policeman got cracked on the head so hard that the wooden nunchuk baton broke. He fell to the floor, woozily pulled out his gun and started shooting. Andrzej Ciężczyk, known to all as 'Szarak' (Hare), hit the floor dead as he tried to run. The others scattered as officers flooded the hotel and Parasol was shot through both legs climbing a fence in the hotel grounds. 'I felt a muffled blow,' Parasol remembered, 'and my heart was like a fluttering flag.' He woke up handcuffed to a hospital bed.

The police arrested the other four men, all old friends from Pruszków, most in their mid-thirties. Kazimierz Klimas, aka 'Kazik', was godfather to Parasol's son; Wojciech Budziszewski had the nickname 'Budzik' (Alarm Clock); Czesław Borowski, aka 'Dzikus' (Savage), was a well-preserved 45-year-old with shiny white teeth and kidney problems; and Krzysztof Ryszard Pawlik, aka 'Krzyś', was a dark, heavy-drinking bully who was regarded with dread even by other criminals. The dead man, Szarak, was a few years younger than the rest and well known in Pruszków for karate-chopping wooden planks near the open-air swimming pool until his hands and feet were bloody.

The men got out on bail in time to attend a vodka-soaked wake for Szarak and then their lawyers began arguing for a different narrative. In the Pruszków version, the policeman had started shooting without provocation, hitting Szarak in the back as he ran for his life; the nunchucks had been wielded by Mirek, not the men in court, although why the Mercedes owner wanted to hit the officer was never explained. It wasn't the most convincing story, but the judicial system remained distrustful of law enforcement after years of *Milicja* abuse and could easily believe some kind of entrapment had taken place. The judge acquitted all five survivors through lack of evidence.

Parasol was still denying it years later:

> They just set everything up. They came in, beating, kicking, the police shot me in both legs, they stole jewellery, everything. Szarak – Andrzej – they killed with a shot in the back [...] I'm happy about that acquittal, because I know that if there was even a shadow of suspicion that we were guilty, we would have received very long sentences.

Despite his name being all over the newspapers during the trial, Parasol was neither the brains behind the Pruszków operation nor its best-known member. Those honours belonged to two men who'd been absent from the Hotel George that day: 'Barabasz' and 'Ali'.

Every gangster had a nickname. Sometimes it was a corruption of their surnames, so Prasol became Parasol and Budziszewski was shortened into Budzik, while for others, it was a physical description. The huge Jarosław Sokołowski was known as 'Masa', although some braver types occasionally teased the talkative gangster with the nickname 'Kojber' (local slang for a pot), after the shape of his head. Wołomin speed freak Wiesław Niewiadomski was originally 'Dziad' (Granddad) for his habit of buying drinks for the old men in a bar, but he eventually passed that nickname on to his younger brother Henryk and adopted the more appropriate 'Wariat' (Lunatic). Other nicknames had more obscure origins: Wojciech Kiełbiński's slangy nickname of 'Kiełbacha' was somehow turned into the more formal 'Kielbasa' by proofreaders at the newspapers, although both words meant sausage; while Pruszków burglar and truck hijacker Zygmunt Raźniak was 'Kaban' to friends but called 'Bolo' by police officers, who'd confused him with another gangster for whom the moniker made more sense.

Ireneusz Piszczałkowski took his nickname from one of the darker moments in the Bible – an appropriately fire-and-brimstone source for a ruthless man who'd never turned the other cheek in his life. Calling himself Barabasz, after the thief freed instead of Jesus during the Jerusalem Passover pardons, reflected an almost religious dedication to crime, although few believed the Pruszków tough guy had ever read anything more biblical than the sports pages.

Barabasz had grown up hero-worshipping an even earlier, now forgotten, strata of local heroes with less-impressive nicknames like 'Grzyb' (Mushroom) and 'Śledź' (Herring), whose self-interested lawbreaking was routinely romanticised into mutiny against the communist system. He respected that older generation but refused to pretend crime was about anything more than making money using intimidating physical strength. In the 1970s, he and others created their own gyms in basements and garages using stolen rolling-stock parts for weights. 'Who said you can't get beautiful muscles pressing a steam engine axle?' noted Masa, then a young man growing up poor in Żbików, who hero-worshipped the local gangster as 'the embodiment of Zorro'.

Barabasz was a familiar figure around Pruszków with his bodybuilder physique, chatting up girls who didn't know or care that he had a wife and young son back home in a cramped apartment. Everyone recognised him as the front man of a gang who burgled houses, spent money like water and accepted regular stays in prison as an occupational hazard. The gang used to drink themselves stupid at the long, low Urocza restaurant in the town centre, where the local *Milicja* also hung out. The two groups would be clearly segregated at the start of the evening, but by the end, when the vodka had flowed a numbing river, everyone would be merged into one convivial, loud, sloppy party.

'I saw with my own eyes Barabasz pay the bill with a piece of gold ring,' remembered a witness. 'He simply cut off some of it with some clippers, because he calculated that it would be enough. The waitress didn't protest.'

Barabasz was the face of Pruszków, but the real power belonged to Zbigniew Kujawsk, known to all as 'Ali'. Tall, greying and almost distinguished despite the crude prison tattoos on his hands, Ali was just as tough as his friend but had more in the way of leadership qualities. He made a living stealing X-ray plates from factories and boiling out the silver, along with a profitable sideline pilfering ration cards from the local town halls. By the early 1980s, around 60 per cent of the products available in grocery stores required coupons and Ali sold them at a fraction of their face value.

His home life was less well organised, featuring an angry wife called Jadźka who intervened whenever he was prepping a job to declare that monkeys in the zoo would make better criminals than her husband's cronies. When Ali's thieving started bringing in decent money, Jadźka decorated their apartment in lavish, tasteless PRL style and would shoo visitors away from an expensive leather sofa in case they got it dirty. 'No one liked her,' Masa remembered, 'but she didn't care.'

Divorce was difficult in communist yet still firmly Catholic Poland, so the couple stayed together, but Ali spent most of his increasingly rare stretches out of prison with other women at what passed for upmarket places, like the Hotel George. He once drunkenly pulled a stranger's panties out of his pocket while getting undressed and Jadźka gave him hell for a week.

The gang's stolen goods were usually sold at Warsaw's Bazar Różyckiego, a century-old market east of the River Wisła. Its original incarnation had been destroyed during fighting against the occupying Germans, but it was rebuilt under Soviet occupation as 500 low, metal huts painted racing green, where housewives did their weekly shopping and grabbed a quick lunch at stalls that sold steaming *flaki* soup made from rubbery intestines. Hidden in the market's darker corners were crooks hawking stolen goods, pickpockets pulling wallets and conmen running games of *benkiel* (three-card monte) to separate the gullible from their money. The Bazar's criminal element socialised in the nearby Kassandra, a café so thick with smoke that regulars boasted you could hang an axe in the air. Cliques of illegal currency changers, silver dealers and professional burglars huddled around their usual tables, and any stranger who walked through the door would get a smack in the face, his wallet removed and be shoved back on to the pavement.

Ali, Barabasz, Parasol and the others could often be found in the Kassandra plotting with criminals from nearby Praga Południe, a rough district whose main claims to fame were a rare landscape of pre-war buildings and a criminal class dating back to the last century. The latest generation included tubby taxi driver Mirosław Danielak, a few years older than his Pruszków friends and known as 'Malizna' (Too Little – a nickname from his habitual response after snorting a line of drugs). He was the first outsider to penetrate the gang.

Malizna had a greying pompadour, a taste for string ties and a talent for sycophancy around those who could help his career, at least back then. He grew up among the old brick tenements of Praga, a slum of crumbling courtyards with plaster saints in plastic boxes where the old women lit candles and prayed. Once a law-abiding citizen, Malizna had morphed into an underworld villain, thanks to a talent for keeping quiet when passengers hailed his battered, boxy Polonaise taxi to escape a crime scene. By the late seventies, he'd become a professional getaway driver for local crooks, earning a slice of the take by staying cool as the engine throbbed and the minutes ticked away.

He saw promise in the tough guys from Pruszków and burrowed his way into their loosely organised gang by attending name-day parties (a birthday-like occasion held on the saint's day shared with the baptismal name of the person celebrating) where everyone drank vodka and friendships deepened. Ali began using him as a driver for silver robberies but the others, especially Parasol, were never quite sure they trusted a man who hadn't done any real time in prison and was trying a little too hard to be their friend. That might have been enough to keep him a permanent outsider, but Malizna had a trump card in his younger brother Leszek, known as 'Wańka', who everyone respected at the Bazar as a seller of contraband with international contacts. His reputation tipped the scales and the brothers were allowed into the embryonic Pruszków gang.

The criminal merry-go-round came to a grinding halt in 1978 and flung its riders when Barabasz, Parasol and other thugs targeted a woman whose family ran a greengrocer's, making her wealthier than the typical PRL family. The crew tortured her, nearly killed her husband and smashed out the eye of her son in an upstairs bedroom. All that violent, sadistic thuggery burst a lot of bubbles for those who had seen the crooks as romantic Robin Hood figures and sent the appalled authorities scrambling to punish the culprits. Finally caught, the men got heavier sentences than usual and would spend most of the next decade in prison.

Behind bars, their solidarity began to crumble. No one talked about it afterwards, but Barabasz was rumoured to have informed on other gang members out of revenge for some insult. The Mafia code of *omertà* meant nothing to Polish crooks and snitching was regarded as unfortunate but expected.

'Pruszków was not a town where such behaviour was judged harshly,' Masa reflected later:

> The old guys knew life and knew that there are no trustworthy people. And if there are, then only in the movies. That's why when someone sold someone out, it was swept under the rug and *frajerzy* [losers, i.e. non-criminals] had no right to talk about it […] The victim could insult the traitor, but that was the end of the circle of interested parties. Anyone else who passed moral judgments, and had no right to do so, was considered to be full of dick.

When these violent, back-stabbing thugs finally got out of prison, some barely talking to each other, they found Ali had consolidated his position as leader while they'd been away and introduced a new ingredient to Pruszków's criminal stew. The *Młode Wilki* (Young Wolves) were Pruszków youth like Masa and Kiełbacha, looking to make money by any means possible and just as ruthless as their older mentors.

4

Savage Youth from the PRL

Jarosław Sokołowski inherited nothing from his father except muscles and a taste for drink. He was 2 years old when Sokołowski senior, a struggling boxer who won more fights in the bars of Piastów than he ever did in the ring, left the family home and never returned. 'Masa's' mother moved to nearby Pruszków for a low-wage factory job and a life of grinding poverty. She loved her son, once saving for months to buy a pair of Polish-made jeans he wore proudly to school, but drunkenly brought men back to their tiny apartment most nights while he and two younger siblings pretended to sleep. After an endless parade of boyfriends and several more husbands, Masa would bitterly refer to his home life as 'a live sex show'.

He grew up in Żbików on the Kopernika estate, a place where the long, grey, four-storey housing blocks lay like beached whales. Masa remembered school trips to local factories that seemed to make only pencils or engineering parts, where the end of shift sirens went off at 14:00 and then again an hour later for the second wave. Workers poured out of the gates on foot, on bicycle or on *Komar* (mosquito) mopeds that got their name by whining like summer pests. Everyone seemed keen to get as far away from Pruszków as quickly as possible.

Real mosquitoes were everywhere when the July sun blazed down on the estate, but in winter the snow settled knee-deep and made for miserable trips to the outhouses still standing in the back yards of many pre-war tenements. Żbików was a rough place, where even ZOMO wouldn't go after dark, and Masa never saw many options ahead of him. 'As a boy, I could have been a bouncer, a gangster, or a truck driver,' he said.

He chose the second option by idolising the criminals swaggering around town and began lifting weights to look like them, helped along his journey by obsessive focus and good genetics. Masa was still young when he caught the eye of Barabasz at a town fair, where the gangster was showing off his muscles at a weight-lifting machine. The teenager easily outperformed him, and an impressed Barabasz visited the home-made gym that Masa and friends had built in a basement to offer some training tips. Soon, the 17-year-old Masa was big enough to work as bouncer at a local nightclub.

By the early 1980s, he was a young 20-something married man with a child, working various jobs as a car mechanic, plumber and locksmith. He avoided the usual compulsory military service thanks to a psychiatric diagnosis ('Category D'), which declared him unfit to hold a gun. Masa would later claim the doctor had been bribed, but most locals doubted the difficulty of identifying something scrambled in his brain. He had a lot of anger inside and alcohol flung open the cage door wide enough that friends learned to stay away during his two-day vodka binges or risk getting thrown through a window and welcoming a stack of broken ribs.

The drunken violence only enhanced his reputation among an admiring young fan club in Żbików. A teen called Mariusz, who would later join Pruszków under the name 'Szlachet' (Noble), remembered sitting with his friends in the heart of the Kopernika estate one day and watching Masa stroll past in a sleeveless T-shirt that showed off his biceps. 'In those years, it wasn't yet fashionable to go to the gym,' recalled Szlachet. 'And he was so muscular. One of the older kids bowed, then we all bowed. He laughed and said something like: Little kids, you'd better start exercising.'

Masa would have stayed a big fish in a very small pond if Wojciech Kiełbiński hadn't returned home. Known as 'Kiełbacha' in a play on his surname, the new arrival had a bland, oval face, light-brown hair already starting to recede and could have passed for the gormless son-in-law in a typical sitcom – except his eyes were as cold and dead as those of a shark. Kiełbacha came from a rare intelligentsia family in Pruszków, who should have been more understanding when the young Wojciech grew up sickly with problems learning to read and write.

Instead, his frustrated father turned to violence. 'When he saw that his father was getting ready to beat him,' remembered Kiełbacha's mother, a respected doctor, 'he got a constriction of the larynx, he could not make a sound. And it drove his father into a fury that the child would not beg for mercy.'

The beatings triggered epileptic fits that only went away when Kiełbacha's mother put him in a sanatorium; later, she arranged a place at an out-of-town technical school far from his father's fists. There, Kiełbacha discovered bodybuilding and came back changed. The weak, whimpering child was now a well-built, charismatic young man whose rotten childhood had given him a strong antisocial streak. He began burgling houses and hanging out with tough guys like Masa in the Żbików estates. At 17 years old, Kiełbacha was arrested, but wriggled out of any serious charges; by the mid-1980s, he was driving for Ali's silver robberies now that Malizna had graduated from wheelman to full-time gangster and considered getaway work beneath him.

Kiełbacha was drifting into the underworld and Masa, who'd become a close friend, was happy to accompany him. By the last years of the PRL, the pair were burgling factories and using the profits to trade dollars on the pavement outside Pewex shops – a PRL institution where rare consumer goods could be purchased for foreign currency. Everyone wanted dollars but the government kept the supply artificially low, so it wasn't hard for Masa to sidle up and make a better offer.

Money came in fast, and the pair became local heroes. When they bought bull terriers and walked them around the estate in the evening, all the other young men did the same; when they started wearing expensive German polo-neck jumpers and sports jackets, everyone went out and bought cheap local copies. To outsiders, they seemed like brothers. '[Kiełbacha] was my best friend,' Masa said years later, 'so maybe that's why I can only praise him, he had no bad qualities.' Few saw the occasional private tensions when Masa would complain angrily about his poor upbringing and make dark comments about Kiełbacha's luck in coming from an intelligentsia background.

Another bitter ingredient in the stew of their relationship was sexual jealousy. Having a fiancée didn't stop Kiełbacha sleeping his way through the girls of Pruszków and kicking them out the door with sadistic relish, watched enviously by the less smooth-talking Masa.

Relations between the sexes were always going to be difficult in a Poland that expected women to be simultaneously obedient housewives, devoted mothers, socialist revolutionaries and hopeless romantics, but Kiełbacha had darker impulses than most. In 1988, a friend asked the pair to recover a gold watch stolen at a party in Saska Kępa. The friend knew the thieves – two young men and a girl – were regulars at a club in a nearby town. Masa, Kiełbacha and an accomplice dragged the trio off the dance floor and away to an isolated road where they beat one thief with a baseball bat. He wouldn't admit to stealing the watch so Kiełbacha tied his legs to the car with a tow rope and began dragging the man along the tarmac. 'The girl shouted that they would give back the watch and she would do anything,' Masa remembered dispassionately a decade later. 'Then Kiełbiński went aside with this girl and forced her to perform oral sex. I saw he was standing and she was kneeling in front of him.'

Pruszków was a brutal place that divided the world into predators or prey, and many of the older men in the gang already had reputations as sexual abusers. Whatever emotions the girl was feeling as Kiełbacha gripped her hair by the side of the road meant nothing to the Young Wolves, and the whole scene was forgotten the moment they returned home to their wives and fiancées.

As the 1980s drew to a close, Kiełbacha and friends had become the official junior branch of Ali's team, then numbering no more than a few dozen men. Masa began providing protection for the businessmen who were springing up like mushrooms after rain as the PRL crumbled – an arrangement somewhere between a bodyguard and a $50 a week extortion racket. Kiełbacha got into the stolen car game, selling hundreds of vehicles and making up to $200 on each sale, for a profit of well over six months' wages for the average worker.

Then, in early 1990, Parasol and the others finally got out of prison after their most recent offences and things changed. The old guard had gone away poachers, but they came home determined to become feudal lords.

Free market capitalism landed hard on Poland. Shoppers who were used to queuing for hours to browse shelves groaning with potatoes and cabbage but not much else now had to deal with a surrealistic supply chain that vomited out Japanese television sets but couldn't provide basic necessities like toilet paper or sugar. Those had to be sourced from the unofficial street markets materialising across the country, where peasants clip-clopped in by horse-drawn cart to sell eggs and cheese, while young men on the *Juma* hawked stolen boxes of German washing powder, and Russian visitors fished everything from trainers to fur coats out of their square, apparently bottomless, plastic shopping bags. Nearby, penniless pensioners laid out family heirlooms and worthless communist trinkets on a blanket and begged passersby to buy something, anything.

Rampant inflation forced prices up quick enough to make Polish heads spin. The 30 złotys (zł) needed for a tram ticket in August 1989 had become 400zł a year later and no one was surprised when the government issued its first 50,000zł note, with a stern engraving of Warsaw Duchy leader Stanisław Staszic on the face. Soon, so many larger denominations were required that the Treasury was in danger of running out of national heroes to put on the money. Workers got used to receiving their wages in freshly printed, sequential notes and then heading straight to a *kantor* (bureau de change) to beat hyperinflation by changing them for dollars.

Those at the bottom of the economic pyramid lived in poverty unimaginable to Westerners. A primary school teacher asked a young pupil what she'd had for lunch and got the reply, 'a margarine sandwich'.

'Margarine with what?' he asked.

'With nothing, just margarine.'

The Pruszków troglodytes who got out of prison in 1990 had no intention of eating margarine. Ali's coupon robberies had become irrelevant with the fall of communism, but Malizna's market-trading younger brother had an idea that would lead to a better, more lucrative future.

A talented junior footballer who dropped sport to follow his sibling into the PRL underworld, Leszek Danielak, alias Wańka, had operated a stall in the Bazar Różyckiego for years, selling smuggled goods and distributing enough bribes to keep the *Milicja* away. A more polished product than Malizna, with intelligence behind the eyes and a touch of elegance to his appearance, Wańka had married young to a smart local girl who let her psychology degree gather dust to bring up two sons while he criss-crossed the Soviet bloc.

'I travelled to Germany, Hungary, Czechoslovakia, Russia,' Wańka remembered years later:

> Goods of all kinds were imported in bulk [...] It was a legal business, we paid taxes for those stalls where we sold trousers, wholesale shampoos, all chemicals. The trade was legal, but the goods were smuggled. Different things were transported one way, and other things back here; in those days it was silver from Poland, and gold and currency from abroad. It wasn't a criminal structure, it was a normal semi-legal structure.

Less semi-legal was the trade in stolen foreign cars run with Malizna, alongside a profitable line in underground casinos and amphetamine distribution. When communism finally slipped away, Wańka went searching for new business opportunities and found one in a cabal of corrupt PRL functionaries who were barely hanging on to their jobs under the new regime. They wanted to get rich while there was still time – an attitude shared with many fellow Poles. 'Nothing has ever lasted very long in this country,' a teacher told a foreign visitor in 1990. 'You get what you can while you can.'

Wańka's friends explained that the government had recently abolished its alcohol monopoly and introduced a 0 per cent tax on imports for personal use. Intended to help holidaymakers and small businesses, the loophole was being systematically abused by smugglers, who were driving lorryloads of cheap German medical-grade alcohol past heavily bribed customs officials who pretended to believe that the man behind the wheel planned to drink it all himself. One smuggler was able to import 797,000 litres in two months without paying a single złoty in tax. Once in Poland, the spirits were diluted in factories with questionable hygiene controls, rebottled as vodka and sold illegally on the domestic market at a competitive price. Poles were a thirsty people, with annual per capita adult vodka consumption at 8.3 litres, so profits were huge.

Wańka's cabal told him where to buy the spirits, which border crossings to use and who to bribe. All they wanted was a generous slice of the profits. This new business was soon making good money and Wańka earned extra cash on the side by filling any spare space in his lorries with German cigarettes, bought at 5,000zł per packet but worth twice that back home.

His brother's friends liked the scheme but had no intention of doing the hard work necessary to start their own businesses. 'Their method was not to build something,' said Masa, 'but to fuck it up.' Pruszków took the easier, brute-force path of hijacking rival smugglers and selling their loads to acquaintance and pigeon enthusiast Henryk Niewiadomski, who ran a lucrative black-market operation from a warehouse near Ząbki, a small town nestled into the eastern flank of Warsaw like a tumour. The reward was high and the risk low. Being criminals themselves, the victims couldn't risk going to the police.

The hijacking operation was disrupted by the murders of Słoń and Lulek that May, and then the Hotel George arrests. The Young Wolves were blamed for the first disaster, which had sprung from Kiełbacha acting as middleman for a $7,000 Mercedes deal that went wrong when the buyer dropped out and the thief refused to return the cash. Pruszków turned up in force to get the money back, but the afternoon ended with Parasol cradling a dying Lulek in his arms on the roadside grass.

Kiełbacha and Masa were brusquely ordered to wait for the police and give false witness statements as the others disappeared; later, a furious Kazik chased Kiełbacha around the yard of an apartment block with an axe for having got the two men killed. Ali smoothed things over, but the first cracks between Masa's friend and the older generation had appeared and would only get worse.

The Hotel George arrests delayed things for longer, but Parasol and the others used the time behind bars to dream up new hijacking variations. Decommissioned police cars were painted up and used to flag down drivers or gangsters would fake injury under a bicycle so the others could leap out of a hedgerow when the driver stopped to play Good Samaritan. Masa remembered doing apparently legitimate deals with smugglers then handing over a *kanapka* (sandwich) – a wad of newspaper wrapped in a few genuine dollars. By the time the target realised what had happened, a lorryload of spirits was already on its way to a Pruszków hideout.

The alcohol loophole closed at the end of the year when a political scandal erupted, which the media christened 'Schnappsgate', but the money was glorious while it lasted. The government lost somewhere close to 1.7 trillion złotys in alcohol taxes and another 16 billion złotys on cigarettes. A large chunk of that had been stolen by Pruszków, with

Masa later claiming to have earned the massive sum of $125,000 from his first two hijacks alone.

Malizna opened up a *kantor* in Warsaw to launder the money while Ali started an *alkohole* (off-licence) in Pruszków town centre alongside an American-style bar with pool tables and MTV blasting on satellite. The bar was ironically nicknamed the 'Marriott', after an ultramodern silver skyscraper of a hotel that had recently opened in central Warsaw, where it loomed over the city like the gnomon on a sundial.

The Pruszków mob was all smiles drinking together, but behind the scenes Parasol and his cronies had begun to resent Mafia godfather Ali. They sneered at his new-found affectation of wearing a tuxedo in the evenings like a gangster from an old Hollywood film and muttered that the gang would be better off with more ruthless leaders, like themselves. As 1991 came in, Ali remained in charge but a car accident near Nadarzyn was about to shuffle the cards and change everything.

5

Day of the Troglodytes

Masa had only been back on the streets for a few weeks when the gang asked him to wreck a nightclub. It was January 1992 and he'd spent the previous four months on remand in Białołęka prison after a late-night scuffle at a hamburger place turned nasty. The investigation dried up when both sides refused to talk and the gangster was released in time to settle into the leather passenger seat of Kiełbacha's Mercedes as they roared up the icy road towards Warsaw.

Their destination was Klub Park, a cavernous barn of a nightclub sitting among 73 hectares of public greenery in the Pole Mokotówskie district. Originally built for students from the nearby Warsaw School of Economics, the club's playlist of Western dance hits mixed with some classic Polish floor-fillers now attracted a wealthier and more dangerous clientele. An acquaintance of the gang known as 'Zbynek' – a well-groomed brute from Praga known for running Benkiel scams at the Bazar – had been drunkenly starting fights at the Park for months. The security staff initially held back because of his criminal connections, but one evening Zbynek went too far and got beaten up by a bouncer called 'Czaja'. By gangster logic, Pruszków had been disrespected and revenge was required.

Kiełbacha knew the club well and had even met his fiancée on the dance floor. A long-legged blonde with a temper, Małgorzata Mazur worked as a secretary but griped about becoming a model so much that Kiełbacha bribed the judges at a local beauty contest to give her first place. She went on to try her luck at the July 1991 Miss Poland contest in Sopot, a busy fleshpot on the Baltic coast. As Małgorzata slipped into an evening dress backstage, Kiełbacha and Masa had watched, amused, as veteran British hippie musician Donovan ambled on to provide the entertainment only to be visibly deflated by a crowd chanting for 'Jason', the Australian heartthrob-turned-pop star with the same last name.

Kiełbacha's fiancée hoped for the winner's crown, but the contest organisers cautiously explained that no bribe was big enough to make that dream come true. A typically blunt Masa agreed. 'It must be said that Małgośka did not sin with excess beauty,' he said. 'To be able to go on stage without too much embarrassment, an army of stylists and make-up artists was needed because in the uncooked version she looked pretty ordinary.'

The aesthetic views of a gym rat whose neck was getting thicker than his head were questionable, but Małgorzata seemed happy with third place runner-up. The winner got a tractor as a prize and the gangsters enjoyed themselves at the post-show party where unplaced beauty queens with teary mascara flirted frantically with anyone who could help their fading dreams of modelling stardom. A seed was planted that would later sprout into Pruszków buying the company that ran the contest; the original intention had been to launder money but no one should have been surprised when the veil dropped, and gangsters began treating contestants like prostitutes.

'Listen to how stupid these girls were,' Masa boasted years later. 'There were a dozen or so of us, and five or six girls but each of them had to "make us ice cream" [give oral sex]. If one of them didn't want to, we threatened: "Fuck you, you won't get a certificate [to participate in the contest]".'

The sexual abuse of desperate models was still far in the future that freezing January evening when Kiełbacha and Masa pulled up in a Pole Mokotówskie car park to find a huge crowd of gangsters waiting with baseball bats, pipes, chains and dumbbell bars. Some had guns.

The gang had scraped together a limited armoury after the deaths of Słoń and Lulek from hunting rifles, palm-sized 6.35mm Belgian automatics and a huge magnum revolver with laser sight that Kiełbacha acquired, but their firepower got a lethal upgrade in the summer of 1991 when hardliners launched a coup in Russia to roll back *perestroika*. Outraged Muscovites flooded the streets to foil the plan and a demoralised USSR officially voted itself out of existence at the end of the year. In the aftermath, Soviet troops abandoned their client states and left behind enough military equipment to start a few wars, with 2.5 million tons of munitions and 7 million weapons dumped in Ukraine alone. Anyone who wanted military-grade hardware could get it for cash with little trouble.

By the start of 1992, Pruszków was full of assault rifles boxed up in basements, wrapped in carpet at the back of garages or buried in plastic barrels behind houses. Masa once watched Parasol tuck a Kalashnikov into an Adidas bag to transfer it from one car boot to another in broad daylight.

The gangsters were more discreet outside the Klub Park as they approached the entrance looking like an ordinary crowd of clubbers. Czaja opened the glass door in welcome and barely had time to realise his mistake before a scrum of hands dragged him outside and the baseball bats came out. He broke free and ran but was dragged down trying to climb a fence and the beating began again. Czaja shook them off, sprinted around the side of the club and slammed a fire door behind him. The Pruszków mob were still waiting outside when he came back out holding a sub-machine gun and wearing a high-collared bulletproof vest that came halfway down his hips.

He started shooting and everyone scattered, but the gun jammed after the first burst and the gangsters began to shoot back. Czaja stumbled awkwardly towards the door, staggering left and right as bullets smacked into his vest, before getting inside. At the front of Klub Park, a gangster spotted the security team locking the main doors and fired off an entire magazine but missed with every shot, leaving the frontage peppered with bullet holes in white circles of smashed glass. The Pruszków mob ran to their cars and screeched out of Warsaw. Gangster honour had been avenged.

The incident was all over the city by the next day and Ali wasn't happy. Shooting up Warsaw over a trivial dispute was the kind of macho score-settling that could jeopardise the easy money rolling in from the gang's more low-key activities. Schnappsgate had ended the personal-use loophole but smuggling continued, and so did the hijacking business – an activity made easier when bootleggers began paying Pruszków tens of thousands of dollars simply to leave their operations alone. It seemed a natural extension to tax other criminals in Warsaw until it became impossible to operate in the city's underworld without paying a percentage to Ali's men.

Pruszków also expanded its operations into debt collection, nightclub security and protection rackets against local restaurants, while Kiełbacha and Masa had a new scam registering stolen foreign cars as legal second-hand purchases. Customers included a bishop who needed a fleet for his priests. The pair began importing cocaine from Germany on a small scale, mostly because Kiełbacha had developed a taste for the white powder and needed a constant supply. They sold the remaining coke through a network of dealers but an increasingly large portion went up Kiełbacha's nose to chill his already minimal empathy.

On the semi-legal side, Wańka had switched to buying domestic duty-free alcohol for export, getting the paperwork stamped at the border then turning the lorries around and selling his booze at home. The cash was flowing.

Ali's complaints about the Park shooting were ignored, which he failed to recognise as a warning sign. Pruszków was now an eighty-strong mob with Ali as the self-elected star on top of the Christmas tree, troglodytes like Parasol the next row down and street soldiers such as Masa and Jarosław Maringe's friend Adrian clinging to the lower branches. Cliques, sub-gangs and miniature armies were already forming, with Parasol and Krzyś jointly commanding a crew of twenty thugs who were loyal only to them.

Ali had no personal powerbase and didn't understand that when his Pruszków friends socialised without him every week over drinks and a game of pool at Wańka's company offices, they were discussing his failings as gang boss. A coup was stirring to life. The plotters would never have dared if Barabasz had still been alive.

Poland had changed since Barabasz was last a free man. Under communism, he excelled as the strongman of a burglary team, swinging fists and smashing down doors, but the wide-open spaces of the post-communist world were just too dazzling for him. The teens he'd mentored in Żbików a decade and half earlier were now adults rolling around town in a Mercedes, while his own peers talked more about exchange rates and border controls than housebreaking. Barabasz didn't fit into this new world.

Every night the television news revealed a different rogues' gallery of former communists and newborn capitalists who'd been caught siphoning millions out of the system. Banker turned bureaucrat Grzegorz Zemek diverted $1.25 million of Polish government funds to his private account in Aruba; the head of the National Bank was arrested for embezzlement; a strange company named Art-B reported huge profits but stole trillions of złotys before its owners fled to Israel.

The transition from communism to capitalism had become a wonderland for white-collar criminals who had no moral objections to fleecing their fellow Poles. Even Finance Minister Leszek Balcerowicz was being investigated for negligence after admitting he'd failed to warn anyone in advance about the inevitable tsunami of inflation and unemployment that would arrive after the transformation to democracy. 'Polish regulators acknowledge they are being overwhelmed by a horde of scam artists who bribe officials, bend Poland's antiquated business laws and outsmart the understaffed police,' observed a *New York Times* reporter.

Poles demonstrated their disenchantment with the new system when nearly 60 per cent declined to vote in the 1991 elections – the first fully free show of hands since the war. Those who did go to the polls abandoned *Solidarność* for 110 other parties, ranging from the enigmatic *Partia X* (Party X), whose activists were rumoured to be former PRL intelligence agents, and *Polska Partia Przyjaciół Piwa* (Polish Beer Lover's Party), a satirical effort with a more grounded economic policy than its supposedly serious competitors. Eventually, a minority government was cobbled together by nationalists and Christian Democrats, but the chaos of corrupt, democratic Poland did nothing but confuse Barabasz, who preferred simpler times when crooks robbed factories rather than owning them.

The others respected his street-fighting skills and Ali remained a close friend, but it was clear that Barabasz wasn't leadership material any more. He knew enough not to challenge Parasol and preferred to cosy up with a younger generation that still respected him. As an advisor-cum-mascot to Kiełbacha and Masa, he raised their standing in the underworld, even if his unthinking violence caused occasional problems.

The Polish Mafia

Asked by a friend to recover a stolen album of valuable stamps, the Young Wolves tracked it to a grimy tower block in Warsaw's Żoliborz district. They sent Barabasz to negotiate the album's return, but he smashed up the apartment instead and beat the old man living there until a grandson handed over the stolen goods. Back in Pruszków, the album opened to reveal 'just some shabby Polish stamps', according to an observer, 'with weeping willows and boats on Masurian lakes'. Barabasz had gone to the wrong apartment and terrorised an innocent family into giving up a worthless childhood stamp collection. After that, the Young Wolves never trusted him with any missions that required too much thought. 'Hitting was the only thing he really did well,' said Masa, 'so he beat people with all his heart.'

Reduced to a street soldier, patronised by colleagues and hanging around the junior team was bad enough, but further humiliation came when Barabasz worked the doors at a Wiatraczna disco that had been bought by gang members to launder money. One night, a guest spat in his face as revenge for being ratted out behind bars all those years ago. Things were quickly sorted out ('Ali and Dzikus told me to leave him alone,' remembered the man, 'because he had recanted and they forgave him'), but it was a reminder of how far Barabasz had fallen.

He looked on from the sidelines as old friends drove expensive foreign cars, wore expensive German clothes and boasted about the architects designing houses whose only reference points for luxurious living were reruns of the American soap *Dynasty*. The future of Pruszków held a lot of marble Jacuzzis and poorly designed sweeping staircases.

On the surface, Barabasz accepted his situation with good humour and seemed content to drunkenly race through town in a BMW Series 3 at speeds that terrified pedestrians. He was so unconcerned by his humiliation that suspicious fellow gangsters thought it might just be a front for secret plans to recover the crown. They'd never find out. In March 1991, the BMW was flying down the road from Pruszków to nearby Komorów when Barabasz lost control and crashed into a drainage ditch. The steering wheel crushed his chest and the ambulance crew arrived too late.

The Young Wolves mourned their thuggish mentor but the rest of Pruszków seemed relieved at the extinction of a PRL-era dinosaur. With Barabasz removed from the board, a prison-yard powerplay would unfold the next summer. A now 19-year-old Szlachet was sitting with cronies on the benches in Żbików when an acquaintance ran up, breathless and scared. Szlachet knew him from work at Ali's off-licence, where their pay included a bonus for keeping quiet when the price of alcohol increased by 20 per cent at 8 p.m. and only returned to normal the next morning. The *alkohole* was a prestigious job for young men looking to move into the underworld and Szlachet was keen to find out why his friend was so shaken up.

'Give me a cigarette,' the man said. 'I need to smoke.' The story only emerged when the tobacco had burned down to the filter. Ali had been thoughtful and quiet all day until a friend came to visit and the pair retreated into the back room for a long, muttered conversation over a bottle of vodka that seemed to resolve nothing. In the early evening, Parasol and Krzyś kicked open the off-licence door and shouldered their way inside, shouting threats; Ali came out of the back room, carefully placed his gold-rimmed glasses on the counter and went outside with them.

Szlachet's co-worker glimpsed the fight through a window ('Fuck, how they fucked him up!'), then escaped out the back door. Later Parasol admitted only to giving Ali 'a few slaps and that was it, the kind of thing that often happens in the backyard', while Masa pieced together a more brutal story of Ali getting his jaw broken from a sucker punch.

The attackers claimed Ali was a police informer – an explanation that made little sense in a town where intimidation or bribery had already put the authorities deep into the gang's pocket. One day, Dzikus and Parasol blocked all traffic in Pruszków by stopping their cars on the main road for a chat; a passing police car preferred to drive on the pavement rather than disturb the conversation. Locals rarely objected to their new criminal overlords, and not always out of fear. When a waitress at the U Frytki burger bar by Pruszków station made a few trips to buy cigarettes for gangsters idling away an afternoon, they tipped her so much that she took the next day off to buy a car. The only time anyone could remember Ali even noticing the *psy* (dogs – slang for police) was when he cleared the drunks off the street outside his *alkohole* after a mild warning about licensing conditions. Parasol and Krzyś' attack had been a leadership coup and they barely cared if anyone believed their cover story.

The Young Wolves waited to see if civil war would erupt, but Ali had no one to back him up after Barabasz's death and charging into battle single-handed would have been suicidal. The man once regarded as the brains behind Pruszków humbly accepted his beating and retired into the shadows while an informal coalition of Parasol, Krzyś, Dzikus, Budzik and other veterans took over, with support from Malizna and Wańka on the sidelines. Few of these new leaders would be getting a Nobel Prize anytime soon, but intelligence was never a primary concern for Polish gangsters.

'The boss didn't have to be an intellectual,' said Masa:

> It was enough that he knew people well and could judge who would stick with him in the future and who would be a flag in the wind. Who won't tell on their friends, and who will fly to the dogs with information. And he had to manipulate people in such a way that alliances would not form at the bottom of the group that could threaten the position of the ones at the top.

Ali's reign was over, and a new era had begun, but it would not unfold as expected. In late 1992, the gang began negotiating an alliance with a hardcore crew from Ożarów who were involved in debt collection, protection and gambling. The crew's leader was Andrzej Kolikowski, known to all as Pershing, and within two years journalists would be calling him the godfather of the Pruszków Mafia.

Parasol and Krzyś had got rid of one unwanted boss only to invite in another. Young intelligentsia Jarosław Maringe watched the resulting conflict between Pershing and the Pruszków troglodytes from his perch in the lower ranks of the Pruszków Mafia as he began his rise through the ranks of organised crime.

II
WARSAW GOODFELLAS, 1993–95

6

Seks and Drugs

Life was tough for girls who worked the brothels. They'd been lured away from their provincial backwaters by the bright lights of Warsaw only to find themselves trapped in a giant Venus flytrap of depravity with no way to escape the closing jaws. Now they lived in a world of sagging flesh, badly dyed hair and sex for money. The girls fantasised about going home one day, but Jarosław Maringe knew most were doomed to spend their lives in cubicles that smelt of cheap perfume and sweat, kneeling on kitsch Turkish rugs that got more threadbare every year.

The pimps who ran the brothels all seemed to be skinny men in dark glasses who radiated an aura of sleaze so strong that Maringe had to fight the urge to slap them around. Like most Polish gangsters, he regarded the *alfonsi* as unmanly decadents who would have been shunned by the underworld if they hadn't made so much money. Democracy had brought liberty in all its forms, and every free election in the new Poland was balanced out by a dank massage parlour and the hardest of hardcore pornography. His new bosses in Pruszków took advantage of the burgeoning *seksbiznes* by demanding $100 protection a month from every brothel owner in the city centre, with instructions to beat any pimp who dared talk back.

'Back then it was said that such types were "cunt fed",' Maringe explained later. 'A real criminal would not directly support himself from the exploitation of women. And we needed them for that so we didn't have to get our hands dirty and could keep to the unwritten rules.' He got into the brothel circuit after joining Pruszków in 1994 when Adrian introduced him to a girlfriend who occasionally slept with Kiełbacha. There was no initiation ritual, no burning paper icon held in cupped hands, no oaths of eternal loyalty, just some casual pillow talk that led to a position for Maringe in central Warsaw with Rympałek's crew. The new recruit was a mismatch from the start and found it disturbing to watch Rympałek routinely beat underlings for minor mistakes. 'I did not fit in with these fat primitives with their gold chains,' remembered Maringe years later.

He would have to adapt or die – not easy when Rympałek dismissed him as a pretty boy intellectual who'd only been engaged as a favour to Kiełbacha. The other gangsters nicknamed their new colleague 'Jąkaty' (Stutter) to mock his occasional stammer and Kiełbacha was too concerned with the growing influence of Pershing to offer any help.

Maringe endured it for a while then went for a tougher image by buying an illegal *klamka* ('door handle' – slang for pistol) from a prostitute. He regretted it the next year when police stopped his car, found the gun and put him behind bars for three months. The charges eventually went away and he earned some grudging respect from Rympałek for doing the time with no complaints.

Maringe's arrest was a byproduct of the crew's ongoing crime spree. In February 1995, two crooks disarmed a pair of officers who stopped them in a stolen vehicle, then took off with the police car and all its equipment. The next month, Rympałek held up a coachload of Polish tourists on the outskirts of Warsaw as they began the first leg of a trip to Turkey and stole 166,000zł – a more impressive haul than it sounded thanks to recent currency reforms having turned 10,000 old złotys into 1 new złoty overnight.

Four months later, the owner of a construction business emerged from a bank on ul. Puławska – a broad highway that split the city from north-west to south-east – carrying a bag that contained 250,000zł in cash for employee wages. A well-dressed 40-something man approached pushing a baby carriage, flipped back the cover to reveal a Kalashnikov and took the money with no resistance. The getaway was less smooth when the gunman's Seat Cordoba stalled and an unsuspecting passerby helped trundle it around a car park to get the engine started.

Police put the gang under surveillance as the crimes piled up, but Rympałek had enough corrupt contacts in the department to ensure only small fry like Maringe got caught in the net. The authorities never suspected the gang's biggest score was yet to come.

At 11:00 on 28 November, a security car pulled up outside a two-storey medical centre on ul. Zamiany, an isolated side road buried among apartment blocks and frozen fields where the city's southern edge bled into rural grassland. An Audi and a white transit van screeched up to block the car and four men in black boiled out carrying Kalashnikovs and Skorpion machine pistols. One security guard went for a weapon but was shot in the hand by a ZOMO thug turned gangster nicknamed 'Pinokio' (Pinocchio). A second guard, well known as a judo and karate expert, fainted after being forced to lie face down at gunpoint. 'Everything went white, then dark, and then I woke up on the road,' he told reporters later.

The attackers pulled a suitcase and travel bag containing wages intended for a string of healthcare facilities from the car and jumped into the transit. They peeled off down a narrowing road through more tower blocks, but crashed, and Rympałek had to lead his dazed team on foot to two getaway cars stashed nearby. Behind them, another guard was still playing dead and only opened his eyes when a colleague said disgustedly, 'Get up, they've already left'. The gangsters escaped with 1.2 million złoty: the largest ever cash robbery in Poland.

Maringe didn't have the skills or temperament for armed robbery and the gang never even considered him for the job. He remained with the brothels and escort agencies, but enjoyed it less and less every week, feeling increasingly depressed that some of the most abusive pimps were women and hoping other gangsters never heard about his occasional moments of kindness.

'I met a girl who had only been working for three days,' he remembered:

> It turned out she had been a virgin the week before, but the boy she'd done it with for the first time had made it known throughout the neighbourhood. I think she suffered some kind of psychological breakdown, so that because of this grief she came to work in a brothel, although she didn't have to because she had rich parents. When I met her, she was in a really terrible condition. With wounds in intimate places.

The resident pimp refused to let her leave, so Maringe beat him up in the front office and helped the girl pack a bag. Afterwards, he felt almost ashamed at being so soft-hearted. 'Don't think, however, that I had suddenly become a missionary who rescued damsels from the clutches of prostitution,' he warned anyone who heard the story.

Rympałek's crew just laughed at his sentimentality. Their interest in women who worked the brothels was strictly financial. When a rival gangster slashed a prostitute's face as part of a misguided plan to divert protection money, they burned his clothes off with a makeshift flame-thrower and beat him with metal pipes until he was lying a puddle of his own faeces. The attack was videotaped so it could be shown to anyone else thinking of trespassing on Pruszków territory.

Away from the brothels, Maringe worked a sideline as a car thief, stealing expensive models for Kiełbacha, until an opportunity arrived to feed the growing hunger for cocaine among the capital's clubbers. A friend from Grodzisk, a nondescript town that had been destroyed by various fires and foreign invasions over the centuries and then rebuilt with increasingly less enthusiasm each time, knew a minor-league smuggler who imported cocaine direct from South America. Maringe inserted himself into the supply chain and built up a distribution network in Warsaw with Adrian's help. They were smart enough to recruit dealers who were fine-tuned to different strata of society: 'Someone sold to celebrities, someone else to doctors, and someone else to politicians.'

Drugs brought in good money and for the first time the crew began to take his criminal aspirations seriously. As a teenager, Maringe had boosted his self-esteem with cash from the *Juma* operations and now the process repeated itself on a larger stage as the coke money saw him adopt a cocky young-man-about-town persona with a loud line in non-stop chat and a colourful wardrobe. He bought a sports car, went clubbing every night and invested some of the drug money into opening a shop selling Paco Rabanne designer wear on the same block as the Marriot Hotel.

Maringe was a new kind of criminal, very different to the older Pruszków types who preferred to waste every dollar of profit on weeks of dissipation at fancy Warsaw hotels, living as if saving money was a sin. Troglodytes proudly told the story of Malizna ordering a 100-egg omelette, delivered by room service, to where he lay in bed with two prostitutes, then deciding one egg had gone bad and throwing money at the bellboy for a repeat order. Maringe preferred to spend his earnings flying to Paris for licensing negotiations with clothes designers.

His new role as an up-and-coming entrepreneur of crime was reinforced when his social circle expanded to include some recent arrivals from the east. The Russian Mafia was in town.

The Stadion Dziesięciolecia was a shoddy concrete bowl on the right side of the River Wisła that had hosted football matches, athletic events and a lot of ceremonies celebrating the glories of socialism from the 1950s onwards. In the PRL's last years, the concrete began to crumble and the stadium was abandoned – an ironic bit of symbolism that was not lost on the Poles. Under democracy, the site became home to a lawless bazaar where hundreds of plastic-roofed stalls sold cheap clothes, pirate CDs, Chinese shoes, fake visa stamps, tattered old books, bootleg software, stolen electronic equipment, household goods and piles of old Soviet military gear. Pistols could be bought openly for around $600, while regular visitors swore they'd once seen an entire fighter jet towed in on a trailer for sale to the highest bidder.

By the time Maringe joined Pruszków, the stadium had been officially renamed *Jarmark Europa* (Europe Market) but was known to all as the 'Russian Market' because most vendors seemed to be visitors from the former USSR. Poles observed their eastern guests with bemusement, unable to understand why any foreigner would voluntarily move to a country where unemployment had reached 16 per cent for the second year running. At the last polls a disillusioned electorate voted in a leftist coalition of former PRL loyalists, hoping to slow the runaway train of capitalism but instead introducing a hypocritical new regime that privatised a swathe of state-owned companies and put its friends on the board.

Crime was so out of control that in August 1994 shop owners in Warsaw's *Stare Miasto* staged a symbolic weekend strike over the extortion rackets plaguing the district. More than 150 restaurants, cafés and antique stores closed their doors in protest at the $500 to $7,000 demanded every month by armed men who followed them home and threatened their families. The shopkeepers issued an open letter demanding action. 'If the authorities allow this to happen only a few hundred meters from the Presidential Palace, what does that say about the rule of law in this country?' asked one restaurateur.

The complaints were tactfully ignored by a government that was aware that half the police force and more than a few ministers took bribes to look the other way. No one seemed to care about the crimes taking place a few kilometres away in the Russian Market, where gangs from Ukraine, Belarus, Georgia and all points east prowled the labyrinthine alleys looking for easy prey. 'There were crowds of people, it was dark, especially in the mornings in winter, and all you could hear was the squeaks and screams of Russian women being robbed,' remembered a market trader.

The loot got squandered on girls, leather jackets and cocaine. Maringe soon had a crowd of regular customers in the *Jarmark*, who told him, between chopping out lines, that the émigré crime scene was not the monolithic 'Russian Mafia' reported by the media, but instead a squabbling mess of rival gangs divided less by nationality than generation.

The older crooks were tattooed convicts known as *Vory* ('thieves-in-law'), whose culture had been forged in the Gulag prison camps after the Russian Revolution. Bosses of the Soviet underworld for decades, they now found themselves challenged by a rising generation of young thugs who scarcely remembered communism and had crossed into crime from the world of martial arts.

The two types barely tolerated each other and, in 1994 alone, over 1,500 people had been murdered in score-settling gang hits across the former USSR. Exiles from both groups found sanctuary in Poland but brought the rivalry with them. 'They were from a different world,' said a Warsaw-based Belarusian kick-boxer about his *Vory* competition. 'They despised us and we did not respect them. We lived according to our rules, and they had their exotic rules that we thought were silly and pathetic.'

Maringe gravitated towards the younger group, with their shaved heads and automatic weapons, helping some settle into his old neighbourhood. His connection with the coke-snorting eastern mobsters earned him respect among tyro criminals who thought all 'Russians' were stone-cold killers – but not everyone was impressed. In late 1995, a group of Polish thugs cornered Maringe in a disco and threw punches.

It looked like a typical gangster row over territory and money, except the man who'd sent the attackers was Masa and they were all supposed to be on the same side.

The reasoning behind the antagonism was never clear to anyone except the main protagonists – and perhaps not even to them. Maringe's usual line was to claim the older gangster wanted a percentage from his drug network and was prepared to get physical to achieve it. Masa insisted the trigger had been Maringe brutally knifing another drug dealer with important friends over some trivial dispute.

Occasionally, Maringe blamed sexual jealousy for their rivalry. He was a 'slim guy with pretty nice looks', in his own words, who was successful with girls, even if he callously abandoned them soon after, while Masa was a hulking married man. The big man returned serve with claims that Maringe 'beat his girls in my presence [...] for the smallest offences', and defended his sex appeal with a grim story about travelling up to the seaside resort town of Sopot for a *balet* ('ballet' – slang for party), where friends convinced a female hitchhiker that Ali was a film producer who would give her a movie role in exchange for being 'nice' to him. A meeting in a hotel room degenerated into group sex as more and more gangsters joined the action, including Masa, who left his wife and kids asleep in another room. He blamed it all on the girl's 'stupidity' and never cared if her naivety had turned to acquiescent terror when confronted with a roomful of thugs unzipping themselves.

Ultimately, all that mattered was the two men didn't like each other, and Masa was the more powerful gangster. Friends suggested Maringe use his Russian contacts to send a message, but Masa was no small-time vulture to be scared away by an eastern accent and the flash of a Kalashnikov. The Russian Mafia looked tough but outsiders who openly challenged the Polish underworld rarely lived to regret it, later proved when a kick-boxing Belarusian Jew called Wiktor Fiszman carved out a niche as crime lord in the coastal city of Szczecin and was machine-gunned to death by local gangsters as a warning to others. Only a crew of easterners working for Pershing had managed to penetrate the local scene but they were tolerated solely because of their boss.

Maringe dug deep into his understanding of human nature, flipped the script and launched a strategic charm offensive. He publically lavished praise on his opponent as a local hero, underworld mentor and close friend. '[He was] an extremely entertaining and open guy,' Masa was forced to admit after a torrent of manipulative compliments.

Photographs from a group holiday in Tenerife showed them with matey arms around each other's shoulders, the camera catching Maringe in expensive sports casual while his new friend stomped around the resort like a human tank in baggy T-shirts and shorts. Their rapport was ultimately fake as a Potemkin village, but a truce was easier than war.

Finally secure, Maringe could settle back to enjoy his new position as a rising prince of Warsaw. 'The gates of paradise opened for me,' he said, 'but it was by no means biblical. My paradise was the land of easy money, beautiful girls ready to jump straight into my bed, fame.'

Some paradise. The bloody iceberg Adrian had warned about held robberies, beatings, rapes and worse. Maringe had joined just as war was breaking out between Pruszków and some former friends from the other side of the River Wisła. Misunderstandings and greed had snowballed into a violent conflict that would put dozens underground, turn Warsaw into a battlefield and force police officers to deal with a new reality where Kalashnikovs and plastic explosives were the weapons of choice.

It had all begun a year ago with a series of attacks that saw Pershing's house blasted with automatic fire and blood splattered all over his Mercedes.

7

Rocket Man

During the long, grey days of the PRL, anyone looking to find genuine social unity could do worse than head down to Służewiec racetrack, where proletariat, socialist elite and *kulak* all came together to watch the rippling horseflesh thunder past. Moustached workers in cheap suits packed the stands alongside senior party officials with faces like buckets of mud. At the paddock, farmers fresh off their tractors studied the odds next to older punters sporting ghostly reminders of a lost aristocracy in their tattered pre-war cashmere scarves and silver horse-head walking canes.

Even Andrzej Kolikowski was made to feel welcome, despite the balding truck driver looking like a gorilla with a gym pass. The Służewiec gates would always be open to anyone with a gambling problem severe enough to earn the nickname 'Pershing' for the way he sprinted from bookmaker to bookmaker, fast as a ballistic missile. More refined Służewiec regulars mocked Kolikowski's frantic betting, but never to his face. Even then, he was clearly a dangerous man.

By the next decade communism was dead, but the racetrack lived on. A chauffeur drove Pershing there three times a week for the big man to gamble the day away among a new generation of entrepreneurs and politicians. Winning was easier now jockeys could be bribed to take the favourite out of contention by the first bend.

Pershing paid well to fix races, but demanded results or retribution. One distracted jockey forgot to lose until the finish line was in sight and had the crowd gasping in disbelief as he yanked the reins so hard the horse was practically stationary as the rest of the field caught up. An enquiry voided all bets. Pershing cornered the jockey in a changing room and force-fed him a wad of losing betting slips before slapping him around. The violence was strictly business. When the jockey received a two-month suspension from the racing authorities, Pershing supported his family and paid the bills.

That mix of brutality and sentimentality appealed to the tabloid reporters, who'd begun writing about Warsaw's growing gangster scene. Their stories made Pershing's gambling addiction seem dashing; they glamorised his huge physical bulk ('at first glance, you could see the results of frequent visits to the gym,' said an admiring journalist), and tried to believe the large-frame glasses implied an intellectual side. He was newsworthy enough that a trivial story about two teens extorting a cigarette kiosk gloried in the headline, 'They Tried to Imitate Pershing'.

The truly brutal stories from the gangster world never made the newspapers. Readers would have been horrified to hear about the revenge taken on a gambler in the city of Łodz who refused to pay back a loan and made the mistake of drunkenly attacking Pershing with a chair. He was dragged off to a remote house and beaten with baseball bats for three days.

Chauffeur-cum-bodyguard Andrzej Florowski, aka Florek, got the order to drive the man home and was shocked by what was carried into the back of his car. 'I thought I would throw up,' he said. 'In front of me stood a blood-dripping mass that resembled a human only in parts. The head looked as if it had been kept in a hive full of angry bees for several hours. It was an inflated balloon. No eyes, no mouth.'

In 1994, the man who beat debtors to a pulp and titillated tabloid readers was 40 years old and a long way from the cramped apartment of his childhood by the railway tracks in the small town of Ożarów, near Warsaw. Back then, school had been an annoying distraction from friends and sport, and the subsequent vocational college that turned him into a car mechanic was only tolerated for extracurricular opportunities like wrestling practice and the chance to become a useful footballer with the local side. Pershing eventually found a job driving lorries for Transbud, a state-run logistics concern supplying the construction industry, and got a taste of the criminal world by smuggling goods home from Germany and Hungary to sell on the black market.

Pershing married young and had a daughter he adored, but gambling was the true love of his life. When the racing season finished, he spent long hours behind the steel doors of anonymous Praga apartments that concealed underground casinos with roulette wheels, long rows of foreign alcohol from Pewex and pretty girls hired to distract the players. Pershing won more than he lost but the real money only arrived when some thugs tried to extort a friend's place and he beat them senseless. After that, his name alone was enough to frighten away the jackals seeking protection money. Warsaw's illegal casinos fell over themselves to bring him on board as co-owner.

In the mid-1980s, crime became a full-time occupation when the big man lost his Transbud job, his marriage collapsed and he stopped pretending to care what decent people thought. Pershing was soon making enough money to buy a new house with a tennis court and swimming pool. He lived with his new girlfriend and her daughter, in an attempt to recreate the family dynamic he had already lost once.

As Poland pupated into democracy, he assembled a group of hard, hungry men to plunder the new freedoms. At the gang's core were some young Belarusians he had first encountered in the casino at Minsk's Hotel Yubileiny, a towering slab of neon-lit concrete across the border. They brought muscle, but Pershing's most loyal lieutenants were Poles like Paweł Miller, aka 'Małolat'(Youngster), who liked to tell grim stories about bodies dumped in the Wisła but knew how to launder cash through front companies; the fanatically loyal chauffeur and bodyguard Florek, product of a vicious orphanage who'd worked protection for *benkiel* scams in the Bazar before finding a father figure in Pershing; and chubby right-hand man Robert Bednarczyk, nicknamed 'Bedzio', with his bad haircut and obvious crush on the boss's daughter.

The gang ran illegal casinos, laundered money, collected debts of $10,000 or above for a fixed fee of 50 per cent, lent money at equally extortionate rates, did some deals with the corrupt Art-B company before it went under and recovered stolen goods. Anyone whose car went missing in Warsaw knew Pershing as the figure wearing a loud floral shirt in the Marriot Hotel casino who could arrange the vehicle's return within half an hour. More than a few victims assumed he'd also arranged the theft, but there was no point complaining when the official police clear-up rate for stolen cars was only 2 per cent at best. Contacts with the celebrity gangster Nikoś on the Baltic coast were friendly enough for Pershing to be a guest at his wedding and for them to jointly own a casino with a powerful electromagnet under the roulette wheel to prevent customers winning too much.

Off duty in Warsaw, the gang drunk themselves stupid on vodka every night and were protective of their boss to point of psychosis. At a place called Nite Club in ul. Chmielnej, a drunk once staggered too close. 'We didn't think about it,' said Florek:

We moved the tables. The furniture was flying but it didn't matter to us. There was only one goal – to eliminate the threat. He got hit hard. Fists, elbows, feet were going in and when that wasn't enough we broke the table on him, under which he'd crawled with the last of his strength. The bodyguards had to drive him to the emergency room themselves so that there'd be no blowback. He was a sack of meat.

Pershing's gang first connected with Pruszków while doing club security work alongside the Young Wolves. An informal alliance solidified into something more permanent at a meeting with the troglodyte leadership, where it was agreed 'there is enough honey for everyone'. At first, the Ożarów gang was just the largest of various groups from across the country who'd merged with Pruszków, but very soon Pershing's disciplined thuggery and charisma began to dominate those around him. Younger gangsters abandoned their own crews to join his team and even those who stayed loyal began to look at their own chiefs differently. 'Parasol and Krzyś would get fucked up half the night outside the *alcohole* and yell at the whole neighbourhood,' said Szlachet dismissively. 'That's what the bosses of Pruszków were like.'

When tabloids began referring to Pershing as the Pruszków Mafia's leader, the troglodytes realised too late they'd invited a cuckoo into the nest. Nothing could be done: Pershing was no Ali to be beaten prison-style in the street. A fragile unity was presented to the world, often through gritted teeth on the part of Parasol, until someone declared war on Pruszków and any internal squabbles were shelved for the duration. A large chunk of Warsaw real estate was about to get blown up because of a long-simmering dispute over a few hijacked trucks.

Players were leaning over the pool table lining up a shot when a bomb exploded in the exposed ventilation shaft snaking across the ceiling and blasted the entire glass frontage of the bar out into ul. Meksykańska. The explosion was so loud it could be heard across Warsaw. When the echoes died away, the only sound left was the slow crunching of broken glass as stunned, bleeding gangsters shambled outside covered in plaster dust.

The Multipub in Saska Kępa had been just another grotty bar during the PRL days, but capitalism transformed it into a sleek den of Western-style wood and steel with a price list to match. Richer members of Poland's budding middle class occasionally dropped by for a beer, but the only regular customers were members of the Pruszków Mafia, whose daily breakfast meetings usually took place there around midday, thanks to a punishing late-night schedule of extortion and violence.

On 30 March 1994, the gangsters rolled in as usual, nursing hangovers and bruised knuckles, all wearing the typical underworld uniform of track suit, trainers, cropped hair, a signet ring on the little finger and a gold chain with a crucifix around the neck. The bartenders poured beers and the usual ritual of handshakes, collecting money and assigning duties began.

Business was quiet enough that staff did any cooking required at a small electric hob in the kitchen without bothering to turn on the gas. That lack of a secondary gas explosion meant no one died when the bomb detonated at 12:30 and destroyed the place. 'If the gas had been on,' said a member of the fire brigade at the scene, 'bits of the pub would have been found on the other side of the River Wisła.'

Violence in the Polish underworld had been steadily escalating in past years as ruthless men squabbled over a pie that could only be cut into so many pieces. Expat crook Zbigniew Nawrot was blown apart in a Hamburg car bombing over an alcohol-smuggling dispute, and a 21-year-old barmaid with underworld connections was shot dead in the northern city of Szczecin. Closer to home, a nightclub waitress was executed along with her gangster boyfriend in his Warsaw apartment, and stories circulated about Pruszków thugs beating a market vendor to death with bricks and dumping his body in the sewer.

The noisiest killings occurred when two of Maringe's Belarusian friends working the Russian Market, one of them a 23-year-old kick-boxer and former soldier, were bundled into a car at gunpoint in the Ochota district and driven towards the nearest forest. The kick-boxer made a desperate move at a red light:

> As the driver hit the brakes and the car rocked, I quickly snatched the gun from one of the tormentors. It was an act of absolute desperation. I knew my chances were slim and trying to save my skin might end in the worst possible outcome, but what did I have to lose? What's the difference: now or in a few minutes?

His friend grabbed the other gun and both opened fire, killing two kidnappers before the light turned green.

A shooting in the centre of Warsaw was hardcore enough to make the front pages, but trying to wipe out an entire bar full of gangsters was on another level. Things were changing.

The fuse on the Multipub explosion had been lit back in the autumn of 1992 when two hijacked lorries carrying German spirits took a wrong turning on the road to Ząbki. The drivers were following Kiełbacha's Mercedes through the winding streets to Dziad's warehouse when the coked-up gangster turned left instead of right at a vital crossroads. Neighbours peered out their windows at the noise and confusion caused by large lorries turning around in a small residential road.

Parasol and other members of the gang arrived to check on the delay and a row broke out. Kiełbacha and Masa were sent home in disgrace as angry troglodytes took over the job of manoeuvring the vehicles back towards Ząbki.

Someone must have called the authorities because police had the warehouse under observation the following night when three gangsters drove up to finalise the deal. A searchlight lit up the car and someone inside tossed a gun out the window into nearby bushes as armed officers swarmed forward. The man in the passenger seat was the small, neat Andrzej Banasiak, a sharp-featured 40-something crook better known as 'Słowik' (Nightingale), whose life had changed forever when he absconded from prison on Christmas leave and pushed his way into Pruszków's upper ranks. His friend Marek Medvesek, aka 'Oczko' (Eye, named for his glass eyeball) – a Pruszków associate usually found in western Pomerania who'd borrowed his wife's Croatian surname to confuse the police – sat in the backseat.

The driver of the car had the most to lose because the warehouse was registered in his name. Henryk Niewiadomski was a crook and pigeon fancier with dark-blond hair, green eyes and unfashionable sideburns, whose outsized beer belly made him look more like a backwoods farmer than a Mafia godfather. He'd inherited the nickname 'Dziad' from his older brother Wiesław, who was currently imprisoned in newly united Germany, and that criminal call sign suited a man who relied more on cunning than education.

The family home had been 20 square metres of wooden hut in northeast Warsaw with no running water or electricity and a kitchen whose roof was left unfinished when their tubercular, alcoholic father died young. Their mother worked as a cleaner, bringing home minimum wage and constantly fighting off suggestions from well-meaning friends to put her eldest sons into an orphanage. Henryk and Wiesław used to listen to the conversations crouched outside the front door, trembling with fear that she might agree one day. She never did.

Every home in the Targówek district seemed to have a pigeon loft stuffed with cooing racing birds and Dziad shared that passion until the council moved the family into a Praga apartment with plumbing and lights that actually worked. It was a major upgrade. As late as 1985, a government survey revealed that every third Polish household lived in crumbling pre-war accommodation and 40 per cent of Poles collecting a pension lacked an indoor toilet. Dziad appreciated the modern conveniences but felt heartsick at leaving his birds behind.

He dropped out of school early to work on Warsaw construction sites as a skinny 15-year-old, mixing concrete by hand before drifting into what everyone called *Kombinacja*, that wheeler-dealing grey zone between socialism and crime where rules were broken, and favours exchanged. In the PRL, it was how people survived a broken system. An investigation at the time found that well over 80 per cent of Poles felt their fellow citizens obeyed the law only to 'a certain extent' or 'not at all', as items disappeared from work, queues were jumped and workers moonlighted at other jobs for better money. 'The State robs me, I rob the State, and it all comes out even,' explained a worker.

Dziad watched his older brother cross over into outright crime in the 1970s to become a pickpocket and currency trader before graduating to amphetamine distribution. Later came an association with Nikoś up on the coast, selling stolen cars. Wiesław was drunk, impulsive, violent and usually wired on his own pharmaceutical products. If Pruszków were troglodytes, Wiesław was a Neanderthal swinging a club so wildly that everyone had to duck, often including his younger brother.

Dziad was a more controlled and wily man, who did his national service as a marine and then opened a *flaki* stall at the Bazar Różyckiego and started a profitable sideline transporting coal around the city by horse and cart. It all looked respectable enough, but behind the scenes Dziad was fencing a regular flow of stolen goods. The money, legal and illegal, was good enough to buy a two-storey property in Ząbki with enough space for pigeon lofts and a family that now included two sons.

Dziad and Wiesław joined a criminal network based around Wołomin, a small town to the north-east of Ząbki known for its pre-war pickpockets and not much else. Their new colleagues were hard, cold-blooded men like 'Ceber' (Czesław Kamiński), 'Kikir' (Andrzej Czetyrko), 'Lutek' (Ludwik Adamski) and 'Maniek' (Marian Klepacki). They controlled most of the crime in the area but then the *Milicja* cracked down hard and Wiesław had to flee abroad, spending time in Canada before ending up in a West German prison for possessing a fake passport. Dziad took over his brother's rackets until communism fell and then the real money began when Wańka offered him the opportunity to buy the contents of lorries hijacked by Pruszków.

The arrest outside the Ząbki warehouse in September 1992 brought a landslide of legal troubles into Dziad's life, but strategic lying and wholesale bribery eventually made the problems go away. He blamed Kiełbacha for attracting the police with his wrong turn and talked angrily about all the money that had been lost. Pruszków leaders pointed out they'd been forced to pay 300 million old złotys in bribes to free Słowik after the police realised he'd absconded from prison. Tempers flared, other grievances escalated and soon Wańka was demanding Dziad pay $300,000 'compensation' for the loss of the lorries.

When the pigeon-loving gangster refused to pay up, a convoy of Pruszków cars headed to his kantor in Ząbki. 'Dziad did not want to settle down,' said Masa laconically. 'As a result a bomb landed on the roof of his office.'

A financial compromise was eventually reached that soothed gangster honour. It might have ended there if his brother Wiesław, soon to acquire the nickname Wariat, hadn't come home to Poland, crazier than ever and seemingly determined to avenge his brother's humiliation.

The first shots were fired when a group of gangsters including Florek were sitting outside the Hotel Polonia, a French-style building opposite the Palace of Culture that looked like a solid block of melting vanilla ice cream. Wariat drove past in his huge American truck and shouted abuse at a group. They took the bait and chased him into a nearby tunnel, where they were ambushed with a Kalashnikov. Florek's party barely got out alive.

Then the kidnappings began. A senior member of Pruszków was dragged off the street by Wariat's men and Pershing baffled his fellow gangsters by hiring a professional psychic to locate him.

8

'Get in the Van, You Whore!'

Having a free and independent press reduced the chances of secret police kicking the doors in but introduced Poland's journalists to a whole new set of problems. In the free market, circulation was king and newspapers had to sell or die. The editorial staff at *Życie Warszawy* (*Warsaw Life*) took the true-crime route and opened a telephone hotline for anyone to ring in with anonymous tips about mob activity. With the city rocking to more gunfire than at any time since jackbooted Germans marched through the streets, it made sense to feed the growing hunger for stories about the gangsters turning the city into a warzone.

Gunfire was something the *Życie Warszawy* knew all about. Its first edition had rolled off resistance presses in November 1944 at one of the few buildings still standing in a capital smashed to rubble. Two months earlier, Poland had risen up against the occupying Germans hoping for Soviet help that would never arrive. Instead, the Red Army waited patiently on the east bank of the River Wisła until the Poles had lost the battle. Few resistance fighters were surprised at the betrayal. In the first days of the war, Soviet troops had slaughtered 22,000 members of the nation's elite in the Katyn Forest, looking to decapitate a country with an inconvenient passion for independence, and they were happy for their German foes to finish off the job.

The Soviets had few friends left in Poland after that, but *Życie Warszawy* was realistic enough to express no great objections when rigged post-war elections brought in a communist dictatorship. It toed the party line for three decades until *Solidarność* came along, and the editorial policy became a little more independent. By the time communism fell and monuments to the Rising were appearing on every street corner, reporters from *Życie Warszawy* were finally ready to report the uncensored truth about life in the capital.

The newspaper hoped its telephone hotline would bring in juicy gangster gossip, but it was instead deluged with calls from crooks informing on and insulting each other. The results could be deadly but were sometimes just ridiculous. Someone claiming to be a friend of Kiełbacha rang in to suggest the gangster's real nickname was 'Penis' and *Życie Warszawy* was brave enough to run the story, until the man himself placed a call. 'We spoke on the phone once,' remembered journalist Piotr Pytlakowski. 'He threatened to kill me: "You are dead for this 'Penis'!".'

Other gangsters had different uses for the media. Some welcomed reporters into their large, kitschy mansions and claimed to be legitimate businessmen who had been unfairly libelled by corrupt police officers and fame-hungry politicians. Few believed them, but that was unimportant when being branded a gangster in the press could be professionally useful for anyone who made a living intimidating others. Dzikus, now in prison after being caught with a stolen lorry, had a pet reporter on the outside who was paid to write flattering articles about his Pruszków friends. 'Journalists helped us a lot,' said Masa. 'They wrote how dangerous we are, how bloodthirsty. We had good press.'

In early 1994, tips poured into the *Życie Warszawy* hotline about a titanic battle between Pruszków, led by Parasol, west of the River Wisła, and the Wołomin mob, taking orders from Dziad in the east. A senior member of Pruszków had been kidnapped off the street by Wariat's men and hotline callers were claiming he wasn't even the first.

The snatched victim was a short 40-something man with thinning, dark hair teased into the early stages of an unflattering comb-over. Ryszard Szwarc, known to all as 'Kajtek', was standing at the Rondo Wiatraczna when a minivan pulled up and an assault rifle poked out the side panel. For a moment he considered running: the roundabout was a busy D-shaped space in east Warsaw criss-crossed by roads and tram tracks, with plenty of scope for escape. Then a finger tightened on the trigger. 'Get in, you whore,' said the gunman.

As the kidnappers wrapped a blindfold around his head, Kajtek wondered why he'd been chosen. The Pruszków man was more peacemaker than warlord, a veteran thief who was under the thumb of his hard-nosed wife and an unlikely candidate to have offended anyone powerful enough to risk a street snatch in broad daylight. A lot of motives flashed through his head but Kajtek missed the obvious one: he was an easy target.

A few weeks earlier, Wańka had dropped into the restaurant at the Marriot Hotel to pick up some food and was heading to the door when he registered a selection of young men in tracksuits looking as out of place as tarantulas on a wedding cake. Among them was Wariat, scanning the room with the hard outline of a gun in his pocket. Wańka only got away because the speed-freak gangster hadn't seen him since the PRL days and failed to recognise his prey behind the jowls and glasses. The Pruszków man called out, 'Long time no see!' as casually as his nerves allowed then pushed fast through the door and sprinted for his car.

Wariat didn't realise the snatch had failed until one of his gunmen cautiously asked if the plan had changed. He wouldn't make the same mistake with Kajtek, who was tough enough but lacked Wańka's nervy sense of self-preservation as he strolled out into Rondo Wiatraczna and a date with a minivan.

A telephone call from one of Wariat's men demanded $120,000 for the gangster's release. Pruszków soldiers ran around town trying to discover where their man was being held until Pershing announced a foolproof way to find Kajtek. He would ask a clairvoyant.

For all their fervent Catholicism, many Poles found space by the Bible for a belief in psychic powers and mysticism. In the early days of the transformation, Soviet sage Anatoly Kashpirovsky had been all over Polish television healing the ills of viewers with only a piercing stare and a hypnotic voice. With the old certainties buried beneath the rubble of socialism, it wasn't difficult for many to believe that a Ukrainian-born weightlifting psychiatrist with a bowl haircut might be a psychic healer who was able to 'tap the inner resources of the body'. Kashpirovsky soon faded from view to be replaced by home-grown talent like Zbigniew Nowak, who claimed the ability to remotely charge glasses of water placed by the television set with his healing 'bio-energy'.

By the mid-1990s, another name was getting attention on the psychic scene. Krzysztof Jackowski was a metal worker from a small town in the north of Poland who'd reinvented himself as a *jasnowidz* (clairvoyant) and was disarmingly honest enough to admit that not all his visions came true. Jackowski had been a married 27-year-old whose only sign of otherworldliness was a collection of UFO books when he began experiencing visions that seemed to predict the future. Word spread and people visited his apartment for information on the fates of missing children, the success of business ventures and anything else whose answers lay beyond the veil of everyday reality. Jackowski's reputation grew until clairvoyance became a full-time job after the fall of communism.

He entered Pershing's orbit by correctly predicting that an expensive foreign car belonging to a friend would be stolen – a vision not everyone regarded as otherworldly in a country where car theft was now endemic. But the gangster was impressed and began peppering the clairvoyant with questions. Who took the Mercedes from outside the hotel in Minsk? Was that Russian girl really pregnant with his baby? The answers pleased him enough to adopt Jackowski as a psychic mascot, treating the crumple-faced seer to drinks at the Hotel Polonia and private parties where Słowik's girlfriend jumped on a table and stripped for guests.

They made an odd couple. Pershing was big, bald and wore his floral shirt open at the neck to show off a gold chain with a boxing glove emblem instead of the usual cross; Jackowski was shorter, blond and looked like a bulldog melting in the heat. A good Catholic, the clairvoyant occasionally probed Pershing on his religious beliefs and was surprised to discover an occasional churchgoer whose deterministic view of Christianity held God at least partly responsible for his own crimes. 'I'm a believer,' said Pershing, 'but if I do what I do then He knows about it, so why should I be false to Him?'

Jackowski was equally surprised that the gangster's requests for psychic visions usually involved women rather than crime. For all his violence, Pershing was a romantic who fell for most women who crossed his path and pursued them with flowers, chocolates and expensive meals. His girlfriend was unimpressed and the ex-wife even more so, but Pershing's heartfelt tomcatting made a refreshing change from the vicious abuse of women undertaken by his Pruszków allies. 'I know that Polish gangsters liked to brag about their erotic conquests, including ones taken by force,' observed an unimpressed Belarusian gunman. A number of girls were paid to make sexual assault charges go away, but that wouldn't stop Masa being arrested for rape in August 1994, with

Parasol and Krzyś facing similar charges later. Most women regarded Pershing as a saint compared to them.

A similar gap in attitudes materialised when Pershing asked his psychic friend to locate the kidnap victim. A sceptical Pruszków crew drove around Warsaw checking out the visions but were unsurprised to find nothing. 'Pershing was simple-minded and believed in miracles, he believed in a soothsayer,' Masa scoffed. Eventually, the ransom was paid and Kajtek stumbled home, shaky from having spent days roped to a basement bed with a hand grenade tied to his leg.

The gang were planning their retaliation when Wariat got hold of some dynamite and showed how crazy he could be with the attack on the Multipub. They'd barely recovered when a more targeted strike was launched at Pershing.

Late one April evening in 1994, a clique of Pruszków gangsters led by Pershing were drinking hard at the capital's Hotel Polonia. As the night started to wind down, Florek was ordered to drive over to a small town called Ożarów outside the capital and accompany the boss's girlfriend to a party she insisted on attending. The Multipub bombing was only a few weeks old, and Pershing wanted his loved ones protected at all times.

Florek, the heavily built, eternally loyal chauffeur, would have preferred to go home and sleep but faithfully set off on the long drive. His destination was a two-storey house full of thick carpets, gilded trimmings and furniture chosen for its price tag rather than aesthetic value. Journalists described his boss's taste as 'tacky' but expensive.

Agnieszka was kind enough to cook Florek dinner before they left and he ate by the kitchen window, looking out into the dark of the street and wondering when Pershing would cut down the bushes that obscured the end of the garden. The pair were climbing into the black Mercedes when men with guns came running out of the night. 'Get the fuck out of here or they'll shoot you!' Florek shouted to Agnieszka as automatic fire shattered the windscreen.

Callers to the *Życie Warszawy* hotline would describe this latest attack, like the other bombings and kidnappings, as being carried out by members of the 'Wołomin Mafia', but that wasn't quite correct. The network had never been especially coherent and by 1994 had splintered into distinct groups with little loyalty to each other. Dziad led a crew based in Ząbki along with Ceber; Maniek controlled the Łomianków-Wołomin faction, best known for the Old Town extortion rackets that had the shop owners out on strike; his ally Lutek had a group in Praga smuggling drugs; and Kikir led a gang in the small town of Marki that hated all the others. To confuse reporters further, most of the factions were happy to do business with Pruszków, individually or collectively, as long as the money was good. Even Dziad tolerated his partner Ceber retaining some discreet contacts with friends on the other side of the river.

It was the Ząbki faction that had declared war on Pruszków, and the motivating force behind the attacks was the recently returned Wiesław Niewiadomski. Dziad's sibling had finally been released from a German prison and come home looking to rebuild his gangster empire. Brother Dziad privately predicted chaos but welcomed him into the gang with the gift of a Russian rouble-forging scheme and the largest amphetamine factory in Europe at an anonymous two-storey house outside the capital. It wouldn't be enough.

Physically a darker-haired version of his younger sibling, Wiesław had the same air of cunning but with more blankness in the eyes. He soon picked up the nickname 'Wariat', for his habit of making violent, speed-fuelled decisions with little thought for the consequences. The war on Pruszków was a prime example.

No one knew exactly why he'd started the attacks. Some thought him motivated by rage at Dziad's treatment at the hands of Pruszków, but others knew the brothers were not as close as generally assumed, especially after a row over some gold coins Wariat had entrusted to the younger man before prison and probably wouldn't be seeing again. Equally plausible motives included Wariat aiming to remove any competition for his own criminal ambitions or him acting as frontman for a cartel of smugglers who were sick of having their transports hijacked by Masa and friends. No one would ever know for sure, and not even Dziad seemed entirely certain why his elder brother was dragging him into a full-scale gang war. Perhaps Wariat's brain had scrambled into psychosis after years of amphetamine abuse.

Whatever the reason, he followed up the Multipub bombing with a more targeted strike at Pershing's home in Ożarów that caught Florek in the crosshairs. The chauffeur was shot in the hand when the hit team opened fire and fell bleeding into the driver's seat of the Mercedes. A screaming Agnieszka crawled underneath the vehicle.

Florek was half slumped over the wheel when the attackers got close and shot him again in the chest and stomach. 'Almost no pain,' he remembered later. 'It's like someone put a hot wire in and out.' They tossed a hand grenade into the car to finish him off and ran back into the darkness. Florek tried to get out but collapsed with his legs still in the vehicle and the metal egg of the grenade somewhere around his feet.

After long seconds, it failed to explode. He told Agnieszka to go inside and call the boss, then lay there in a puddle of blood wondering if this was what it felt like to die.

Masa and Kiełbacha got a call and raced out to Ożarów, where they found the car riddled with bullet holes and Florek face down on the gravel, weakly waving them away from the grenade. They were still waiting for the ambulance when Wańka and Słowik arrived and ordered them to drive the bloody chauffeur directly to hospital. He would flicker between life and death, but he survived.

The attackers had mistaken the bodyguard for Pershing in the dark, just as they had wrongly believed Florek's boss was in the Multipub before thumbing the detonator. Wariat was trying to decapitate Pruszków by killing the man who had risen to become its most important member.

Things began to escalate. In late April, someone called the police one evening after finding Słowik and a group of Pruszków soldiers camped outside Wariat's apartment block in Warsaw. Officers arrived to find the men quickly discarding pistols and hand grenades into a nearby bush. Słowik explained he had only gone 'out with friends for an evening walk'.

Early in the morning of 5 May, a Wariat crew blew up the Escada restaurant in Saska Kępa, which was a frequent hang-out for Pruszków and owned by a businessman linked to the gang. The police searched Dziad's offices the same day, resulting in little except a complaint that they'd scratched his Mercedes, then raided a Pruszków birthday party looking for illegal weapons with apparently equal lack of success. 'The police used to be far more polite about it,' said Dziad. 'Now they just barge their way in, demanding to be bought off.'

Dziad went into hiding that May, but three of his men were kidnapped and beaten into revealing the location. Betting big to finish the war,

Pershing obtained a battlefield rocket launcher from a corrupt contact at Warsaw's Military University of Technology; the contact was already well known in Pruszków for allowing gangsters like Masa and Kiełbacha to test their guns on the university range while his soldiers obediently brought them sausages and vodka. The rockets punched holes through Dziad's windows but failed to explode.

On 24 July, Pershing's car was blown up at Służewiec racetrack. The big man and Florek were on the other side of the stables when they heard the bang and raced over to find the car windows shattered and the tyres melting. A bomb placed under the engine had exploded prematurely. Pershing blamed it on a broken fuel line and tried to have the Mercedes towed, but a police technician found bomb fragments and was unimpressed by the gangster's stock answer about being a legitimate businessman without any enemies. An officer asked to see Pershing's identity card. 'If you don't know who I am,' said Pershing contemptuously, 'then we have nothing to talk about.'

Important people in the Warsaw police force began to wonder if all the bribes coming their way were worth the chaos boiling over in the city. Some kind of a stand had to be made. Pershing didn't know it, but he had only a few more weeks of freedom left.

9

A Miniature Vietnam

The gang had clogged every parking space in town with their convoy of Mercedes and taken over a pub with a nice view of Sopot pier, where the sea stretched out flat towards infinity or Sweden – whichever came first. In August 1994, Pruszków had braved the pot-holed inter-city road to Sopot for a confrontation with local warlord Nikoś, a handsome car thief-turned-gangster with a winning smile and an endearing lisp. Pershing had once been a good friend but the gang's steady expansion across the country required the absorption of regional rivals through consent or violence. Nikoś' stubborn hold on the coastal *Trójmiasto* (tricity) area of Gdynia, Sopot and Gdańsk was a problem; typically for Pruszków, intimidation was the answer.

Nikoś arrived at the gangster summit with a team of bodyguards, looking suave as ever but clearly surprised by the size of the Pruszków delegation. A short, sharp discussion about territorial boundaries ended with the cowed Gdańsk gang boss retreating and leaving the visitors to their vodka. He recovered his composure later that evening and tipped off the local police to raid the pub. Everyone was dragged to the station, but events quickly dissolved into farce when the arresting officers ran out of handcuffs, and became more ridiculous when Wańka bribed a jail orderly to deliver boxes of chocolate bars to the hungry prisoners.

The next morning, a magistrate refused to believe the men sitting around in expensive leather jackets and Adidas sportswear were all hitchhikers who'd met by chance but he didn't have enough evidence to hold them. Back at Sopot pier, they toasted their release with more vodka and went home to nurse a bitter grudge at Nikoś for bringing the police into underworld business.

One gangster remained behind bars. At the request of the Warsaw police, Pershing was being held on charges that included the extortion of $40,000, document forgery relating to a stolen vehicle, kidnapping and tax evasion. Senior Pruszków members didn't seem too bothered at leaving behind the man who newspapers still claimed was their leader. 'The bile between [the troglodytes] and Pershing was noticeable,' observed one of Masa's cronies.

Pershing had been arrested at a time when the crime lord had seemed untouchable. Even Dziad's business partner Ceber had begged the big man for help when his 22-year-old son was kidnapped and an anonymous voice on the telephone demanded $300,000. Pershing offered the services of his pet psychic Jackowski, who failed to pinpoint the missing man (to no one's great surprise), and managed to negotiate the ransom down to $100,000. Ceber Jr was released but, in the aftermath, his father split from Dziad after a bitter quarrel over whether the pair should have sold their joint businesses to meet the kidnappers' demands. There would be no more sightings of the pair trotting around Warsaw together in expensive imported track suits and trainers, with Ceber hanging on the older crook's every word. Now they were rivals, or worse.

After Sopot, the authorities put together a basket of charges against Pershing, with the most serious being the revenge he'd taken on a vicious gang of karate enthusiasts-turned-criminals who'd robbed the house of a friend. Two of the robbers were snatched off the street and held in a cellar where Pershing beat them for days with a baseball bat. One who refused to talk had an electric drill ground through his knee cap. The pair eventually confessed to everything, and the stolen items were returned by their terrified friends. 'I practised karate for eighteen years,' one said later, 'but when I saw the men from the Warsaw Mafia I was afraid. We were all afraid. They had guns, baseball bats, explosives. They were well organised. In the event of a confrontation, they would kill us.'

At first, Pershing assumed bribing his way out of trouble would be easy. The corruption that had always been part of the PRL had spread like damp under democracy and now 95 per cent of adult Poles regarded it as a serious problem, with 20 per cent claiming to have been forced to pay at least one bribe, usually to police or doctors.

A fish rots from the head downwards and, back in 1993, Słowik had been able to buy a pardon from the Polish president and former *Solidarność* leader Lech Wałęsa for $150,000 to erase the consequences of his prison break. It was later claimed that someone in Wałęsa's entourage had slid the pardon among other state papers waiting for a signature without him noticing, but that didn't explain why the bushy-moustached president had granted an average of two pardons a day for five years: more than any other president in Polish history. Pershing's confidence that he could benefit from similar treatment seemed more than feasible when the authorities refused to even acknowledge that organised crime existed in Poland.

'I remember press conferences where we, as journalists, asked the then interior and justice ministers about how they intended to fight the Polish mafia,' said Magda Roszkowska, looking back on the period. 'For years, their only answer was surprise: what are you talking about, our mafia? The mafia is in Sicily or the United States. We have crude bandits, back alley thugs who just attack, rob, and nothing more than that'.

Despite the denials, things were slowly starting to change. In 1994, senior police officials had finally agreed to the creation of a department specialising in organised crime and the following July saw the *Sejm* (Polish parliament) grant officers increased powers, including more weapons, electronic surveillance and investigative tools wide ranging enough to alarm Poles traumatised by memories of the PRL secret police. Corruption and incompetence would remain a serious problem for years to come, but those with their ear to the ground could detect the distant hoofbeats of a genuine attempt to fight crime.

An oblivious Pershing didn't notice the world shifting beneath his feet. He spent the rest of the year more concerned about the lack of luxuries behind bars: no more lunches at the Baszta restaurant near Służewiec racetrack, where traditional Polish cuisine was served in an atmosphere of white tablecloths and fake rustic charm, and the wild deer cost 250,000 old złotys; no more hanging out with friends like Andrzej Gołota, a talented boxer from Warsaw with a Cro-Magnon brow who'd won bronze at the 1988 Seoul Olympics before turning professional; no more drinking until the early hours at the Klub Go-Go in the Hotel Polonia and insisting the slow, dreamy track '*Miłość i Ja*' by Bajm be played over and over for hours, with no one allowed to complain.

As the months rolled on, some of his gang faded away but many remained loyal. 'He was like a father to me because I didn't have one of my own,' said Florek, who would soon spend a few years in prison himself for theft, 'and he determined what was right and what was not.'

Some thought Pershing fortunate to be in prison. As he sat behind bars, the conflict between Pruszków and its enemies east of the river was ramping up and bodies were hitting the floor.

The gangs killed each other but sometimes turned the guns on themselves. Budzik was an old-school troglodyte from the Hotel George shooting with a vicious temper made worse by an amphetamine habit so bad that his hair was falling out in handfuls. On 5 September 1995, he pulled a gun on a guest in his apartment overlooking ul. Kubusia Puchatka, a narrow Pruszków street of green trees and grey blocks whimsically named by the local council after an internationally famous bear who loved honey. There was a struggle, a shot and then the police found themselves investigating a murder on Winnie-the-Pooh Street.

Local gangsters weren't surprised to hear Budzik had finally tipped over the edge. Along with other veterans of the gang, like Dzikus and Kazik, his talents were less and less in demand as Pruszków changed from a local gang into a nationwide Mafia. Budzik felt the new leaders like Parasol were sidelining him and he tried to shoot his old friend in the foot outside the Hotel Polonia during a drunken argument, but the bullet went through the shoe's leather upper and into the pavement without hitting anything vital. The next day, Budzik was beaten into a bloody mess by a punishment squad headed by Krzyś and kicked out of the group. Friends pleaded for his reinstatement but Parasol refused to listen.

The exiled gangster's mental state was swinging hard between self-pity and rage that Monday night, when a 30-year-old guest called Maciej talked too much and got shot in the throat. Police were at the apartment within minutes but Budzik had vanished, leaving behind a body in the kitchen and shocked guests still holding glasses of vodka. They said the row had begun when Maciej jokingly referred to his host's amstaff (American staffy) as 'a cow in the meadow'.

Insulting a dog seemed a trivial reason to kill someone, but the war between Pruszków and Ząbki was turning increasingly rabid as it escalated into what Dziad drily called 'a miniature Vietnam'. The murder on Winnie-the-Pooh Street was just the latest pointless loss of life in a year-long streak of violence.

By the mid-1990s, some colour was finally coming back to into Poland's cheeks after the long, grim decades of communism. Western-style marketing was in bloom and Warsaw natives hungry for a Big Mac could stroll past a giant inflatable Ronald McDonald sat cross-legged in the city centre like a fast-food Buddha. The chain was so popular that when the city's first Metro line opened that year, a graphic design team came up with a cheerful red-on-yellow colour scheme that mimicked the burger giant's logo.

Elsewhere in the capital, a home-grown funfair spun thrill-seekers around the Palace of Culture car park, while corporate workers in the newly built skyscrapers looming overhead talked knowledgeably about a stabilising economic situation. Inflation was down 8 per cent, gross domestic product up 28 per cent, and 100,000 fewer people were unemployed than the previous year.

The crime rate expanded just as fast as the economy. On 10 January, important Pruszków figure Zygmunt Raźniak, aka 'Bolo', opened his apartment door after the buzzer sounded and a bomb attached to the outside handle dropped the lift shaft, three floors, a staircase and eight apartments into the snow below. The block at Ostrobramska 78 was a communist-era lump of concrete that looked like a giant row of filing cabinets, but it proved more solidly built than most PRL structures when it stayed upright as grey dust clouds billowed out across the neighbourhood. Bolo's sturdy front door deflected enough of the blast for the gangster and his neighbours to miraculously survive.

Soon, news crews were swarming across the rubble and the incident was all over the media – a special humiliation for the muscular crook who liked to keep a low profile and had criticised Pershing for appearing in the headlines so often. Bolo had been equally scathing about fellow troglodytes with a taste for the limelight, like Parasol and Krzyś who decided to promote their club, Kaskada, with newspaper adverts featuring their jailhouse faces and the unlikely slogan: '*U nas najbezpieczniej*' ('You're safe with us').

That campaign hadn't been going long before a woman accused them of raping her in the club car park, which triggered a long investigation that petered out without any charges. Bolo was too much a thug to care about the alleged victim but the publicity had been unwelcome. Now Ostrobramska 78 was on the nightly news programmes and everyone in Warsaw knew his name.

Few people doubted Wariat had been behind that attack, but a February bombing on the leafy boulevard of ul. Białostocka in the centre of town had no obvious perpetrator. The target was Zbynek, the well-groomed gangster who'd been the reason for Pruszków invading Klub Park a few years back. After the raid on Dziad's warehouse, he sided with Ząbki, despite maintaining friends on the other side of the river, and was now working with Ceber collecting protection from local car thieves. The residents of Białostocka 11 were watching the evening news when a car bomb exploded out front and caved in their windows. Zbynek walked away unharmed but with no idea who had tried to kill him.

The answer arrived a month later at a large house in Marki, a small and unimpressive town near Ząbki. Its previous owner had been a market trader who took a loan from Ceber to buy a generous amount of stock. The gangster handed over the money with a smile, watched the trader store the goods in a garage, then came back at night and stole everything before demanding the house as repayment on the defaulted loan.

Buyers were showing interest in the property when Ceber received a phone call on 13 March from a police contact advising that someone suspicious had been seen nosing around the neighbourhood. The gangster turned the key, opened the front door, and two electrical contacts sparked an explosive device that fireballed Ceber and his bodyguard across the front garden. Another bodyguard was urinating behind a wall and lived. The blast aimed at Zbynek had been a warning, but Ceber hadn't listened. His killer was an old friend.

The bomb solved a problem which had begun when Ceber discovered the real identity of his son's kidnapper. Short and muscular, the Wołomin gang leader Maniek had been in and out of prison during the PRL for various warehouse robberies before taking advantage of the transformation to establish himself as a big-league boss on the east side of the river. Profits from alcohol smuggling bought him a huge villa in Wesoła with an automatic gate, a giant television and an army of porcelain cat figurines that no one dared joke about.

Ceber had helped some old friends from Pruszków hijack one of Maniek's lorries and the kidnapping was payback. The gang boss had taken particular pleasure in pretending to search the city for Ceber Jr, even as the kidnap victim was being brutalised by underlings in a distant villa.

Somehow, Ceber uncovered the truth and demanded his money back. Maniek refused, and things had been getting nasty between them until the explosion. Pershing might have been able to broker a deal, with or without Jackowski's psychic powers, but in March 1995 was otherwise occupied being on trial for various offences. The case collapsed when the main witness was too scared to attend court and sent an endless stream of doctor's notes claiming crippling depression before disappearing entirely.

The prosecution kept Pershing behind bars while rustling up some new charges and managed to convict his sidekick Małolat for possession of the rocket launcher used in the attack on Dziad's house. Pershing gave interviews from jail trying to persuade journalists that he was a businessman being unfairly treated, without ever convincingly explaining the source of his wealth. 'My company just collects debts,' he told a reporter. 'It's good that you asked about it, because this is – which I forgot at first – the most important source of my income.'

The next trial involved a car stolen in Paris and resold in Warsaw with false documents, but this time the witness testified incognito – a first for Polish law that caused some muttering among lawyers who remembered the PRL's use of informers and entrapment. Pershing got four years and a heavy fine, to the astonishment of those who assumed powerful men never went to jail, and stomped off angrily to his cell. Bedzio and others kept the Ożarów gang going and promised to stay loyal.

As the prison gates slammed shut, the daisy chain of violence continued. On 14 April 1995, police found three men shot dead at a pigeon loft near Dziad's home. Two worked for him and the third was a fellow pigeon enthusiast who wandered over at the wrong moment to investigate the noise. A hit team from Pruszków lined them up against a wall and pulled the trigger after failing to locate their boss. 'The war was always there,' said Masa. 'Parasol complained that he'd been lying in drainage ditches with weapons for so long, because they wanted to get Dziad, that rheumatism caught up with him.' No one had any evidence Parasol had been involved in the murders, but the Pruszków leader raised a glass of vodka to toast the news all the same.

In August, a bomb destroyed the Pruszków-affiliated Amadeus pub on Warsaw's ul. Żeromskiego 27. A month later, someone informed police about Wariat's amphetamine factory and officers kicked in the front door of a modern lab that leached electricity off neighbouring houses to produce export-quality speed for the more discerning drug abusers of Scandinavia.

On 30 October 1995, two hooded figures shot Cezary Dresz outside his apartment. The son of important Pruszków man Jacek Dresz, aka 'Dreszcz' (Shiver), Cezary was believed to have murdered his own father in an apartment stairwell not long before, although no one seemed to care that the old pervert was dead. Masa claimed Dreszcz had picked up a taste for men in prison that was so vicious that he once went into a brothel looking for a girl but saw a young, pretty, male customer waiting his turn and raped him in an unused cubicle instead. After that, the racketeering and violent bullying of his son seemed trivial.

'I want to make you realise that the Pruszków group was largely, not to say 100 per cent, composed of psychopaths and degenerates,' said Masa. 'People whose nightmares mixed with reality, who functioned in a parallel world. Compared to them, a septic tank is like the gardens of Versailles.'

For this and many other reasons, Cezary had switched sides to Dziad's gang and occasionally acted as bodyguard for the older man despite being permanently wired on drugs. 'He snorted coke like a vacuum cleaner,' remembered a colleague. Once, he nearly killed a pack of homeless men camped in an abandoned building with a burst from his Skorpion machine pistol after mistaking the red dot of a burning cigarette for something more sinister.

A Pruszków hit team took him out that autumn near an apartment block in the leafy Warsaw district of Żoliborz. They'd been after Cezary for weeks and managed to fix a bomb to the underbelly of his car but it fell off as he accelerated along the capital's badly tarmacked roads. The coked-up young gangster barely registered the threat, just as he failed to notice the two men with guns waiting as he strode towards the block.

Cezary's last act was to look at his wife framed in a window high above and wonder why she was opening her mouth to scream.

The bloody, violent year ended with Budzik being arrested on 12 December at a flat in the Mokotów district after an early morning raid. Police rushed inside to find him half asleep among piles of weapons and forged dollar bills. The interrogators got the gangster to admit that the murder had been triggered, not by insults over a dog, but by Maciej sleeping with Budzik's wife during a prison sentence. He hadn't wanted to hurt the younger man, but 'my eyes went dark'. The court gave him twenty-five years.

As the city celebrated New Year with parties and fireworks, Warsaw's inhabitants hoped that 1996 would bring peace. Instead, Rympałek's crime spree of the previous year briefly made him the most powerful gangster in the capital, Pershing would continue to rot away in prison and Kiełbacha paid the price for angering his elders. The New Year would be bloodstained.

Jarosław Maringe tried to stay above it all from a new position in the Polish drug business, but the iceberg was getting bigger and bloodier.

III

EMPIRE OF PRUSZKÓW, 1996–98

10

Making Friends with the Frog

The glass on Jarosław Maringe's moral compass had fogged badly over the last few years. He'd gone from being the kind of man who rescued girls from vicious pimps to a drug dealer who went clubbing every night with a man known as 'Kuba Gwałciciel' – Jack the Rapist. Maringe didn't recognise the face looking back at him from the bathroom mirror these days, but all the money coming in took the edge off that particular moral dilemma.

His descent had begun in late June 1996, when a handover outside the Macro Cash & Carry on aleje (al.) Jerozolimskie went bad. Someone had come up with a plan to lure a rival dealer with a large amphetamine stash and a trusting nature out somewhere remote for a beating. Maringe was part of the crew who dragged the dealer 'Bączek' out of his car in the forest and battered him with iron bars among the tall trees.

Bączek refused to reveal the stash location even as his teeth were smashed out, and only the trilling of his mobile phone stopped the beating turning to homicide. On the other end of the line were friends who quickly agreed to ransom the dealer for $20,000, to be handed over at the Macro, a huge Dutch-owned store in the Ochota district of Warsaw with a car park the size of an airfield.

Maringe's crew got there at 15:00 and located colleagues of Bączek waiting with angry faces outside the neat brick building of a recently opened KFC fast-food restaurant in a far corner of the car park. Oblivious restaurant workers were sweeping up around them. Two Pruszków men called 'Kotlet' and 'Matyś' swaggered over and for a moment it looked like the kidnapping might work – then the cleaners dropped their brooms, pulled out Skorpion machine pistols and opened fire.

Both Pruszków men went down bleeding and a boxy old East German Trabant screeched up to drag Matyś inside. The communist-era car was ugly as a wart and even less likely to vanish quickly, but the engine in this model had been swapped for something that belonged in a Grand Prix and easily outdistanced Maringe's sports car through the Warsaw traffic. 'Probably the first such case in the history of the automotive industry,' said Maringe, still angry years later, 'when a good car lost a race to such an old shit-box'.

The Trabant's getaway ended at a routine police stop on the other side of the city. Officers got a quick glimpse of Matyś in the back seat bleeding from open wounds and barely had time to grab at their holsters before being disarmed and dragged into nearby bushes. They were lying face down in the dirt praying when a police helicopter flew low overhead and the spooked gangsters jumped back in their car. They left behind Matyś, who'd got a door open during the confrontation and was stumbling around the road in bloody circles.

Back at the Macro car park, Bączek had also escaped and was banging on taxi windows trying to find someone brave enough to take the fare. Everyone ended up in the same hospital, refusing to talk to the police, and a mushroom picker would later find the souped-up Trabant abandoned in the woods. No charges were ever brought after a corrupt policeman wiped the tapes of all security cameras sweeping the Macro car park.

The chaos only made sense when the Pruszków crew discovered that Bączek was a dealer for Wariat and they'd walked into the crossfire of an ongoing gang war. They'd been lucky to get out alive. The others talked tough about revenge, but Maringe – a lone wolf ever since his friend Adrian had to flee the country after some unspecified 'trouble' – saw the shootout as a sign from God to switch to a less dangerous sector of the gang. 'I had become very much aware,' he said, 'of what might happen when you went flying round the city without strong back-up.'

Maringe needed someone who could provide both protection from the violence and a ladder to climb the gangster hierarchy. He found the perfect candidate in Jerzy Wieczorek, aka 'Żaba' (Frog), an advisor to

Rympałek who'd picked up the amphibious nickname when a childhood illness made his eyes bulge for long enough that no one would ever call him anything else.

The 50-year-old Wieczorek grew up in Praga and started his criminal career, like so many others, at the Bazar Różyckiego, with a clothes stall that provided cover for stolen goods and a *benkiel* game. His earnings went into trading dollars outside a Pewex shop and, by the last years of the PRL, he'd become a supplier of German work visas through a corrupt contact at the embassy.

The veteran crook was big, surprisingly respectable-looking and a hopeless alcoholic. Underlings who phoned to talk business might find a drunk Żaba babbling incoherently and have to cancel anything planned for that day. Other times, he forgot to show up for big meetings and would be located at the racetrack stables amusing vodka-soaked cronies by punching horses hard enough to knock them down into the straw.

His crop-haired, sour-faced wife Baśka took care of the money and allegedly ran things when Żaba was too drunk to give orders. They'd married young then divorced in the last days of the PRL to save some joint property from a *Milicja* confiscation order. Since then, they'd lived and raised children together as a couple but pretended to be virtual strangers in front of anyone who worked for the government.

Their complicated relationship perched at the tougher end of love. Baśka once hit her husband round the head with a frying pan at a party when he wouldn't put down the vodka bottle. 'Żaba would drink himself to death without Baśka,' observed a friend.

Despite the alcoholism, he was a much more important figure in the gang than a tyro like Maringe. As a childhood friend of Kajtek, the troglodytes trusted him with the twin roles of consigliere to Rympałek and breaking Pruszków's bad-luck streak in the drug business.

The gang had taken a big loss back in February 1994, when a scheme to break into the cocaine trade by importing 1,190kg of the stuff into Europe failed and left everyone a lot poorer. Wańka organised the affair through old friends who'd moved to Colombia and formed connections with the Cali Cartel: psychotic cocaine wholesalers who made $20 billion a year exporting their product around the world.

The British authorities became suspicious when the Polish freighter *Jurata* docked in Birkenhead carrying a cargo of tiles and glue that would have been cheaper to buy locally than overseas. They tore the ship apart and found the drugs. Wańka and friends lost at least $1 million, and the Colombians a lot more, but a police sting went badly wrong when the ship finally docked in Gdynia and, somehow, no one was charged.

Żaba adopted a more cautious approach to drugs by focusing on the domestic market. Investing the proceeds from Rympałek's healthcare robbery into bricks of cocaine made a 120 per cent profit and proved the existence of a widespread Polish hunger for more sophisticated highs than just cheap speed and *Kompot*, a homemade heroin substitute boiled down from industrial chemicals. Plenty of ambitious gangsters wanted to work with Pruszków's new drug baron, but Maringe got his attention by offering up a well-designed plan to exploit an obscure loophole in sugar taxation. They made 200,000zł together and Żaba was impressed enough by the young man's business brain to recruit him into a different kind of white powder.

Maringe used the larger stage to demonstrate his talent for organisation. He arranged drug buys, storage locations, enlisted more coke dealers and made sure Żaba got his cut. Talented chemists were recruited straight out of school to oversee amphetamine factories in remote houses where the cooking stench wouldn't alert neighbours. Ecstasy required only a tablet press, a private apartment and a few bug-eyed testers to ensure a quality product. Heroin came through Kuba Gwałciciel (a nickname Maringe initially thought was a joke) and was known for its purity. Other dealers' heroin turned to brown or black paste when melted in tin foil but his product was pure enough to retain its colour.

No one with a steady supply of high-quality narcotics would ever be lonely and Żaba's crew became so popular that Polish celebrities greeted them like old friends. Maringe's shop at the Marriott became a hangout for models, actors, singers and athletes to smoke dope and flick through his racks of designer clothes. He snorted rails of cocaine with players from Legia Warszawa, the country's biggest football club, and thought it funny to dose a pair of them with LSD the night before a big match. They lost 2–0.

Selling drugs brought in so much money that Maringe began abandoning any car with engine trouble in the street below his apartment and buying a new one rather than visit a garage. Żaba had found a bright, young gangster with a talent for logistics; Maringe had found the father figure he didn't know he needed. 'Żaba had charisma and the ability to win over people,' Maringe said. 'He talked, patted backs, smiled. Such a charmer, but effective. He was trusted, I trusted him too.'

The trust between the two men would evaporate over time, but in those early days they felt like family. A drunken, dysfunctional criminal family.

Being a gangster meant not caring about the opinions of ordinary people. On a Tunisian holiday, Maringe watched his new boss drink fourteen bottles of wine every day without once leaving the hotel. In Warsaw's Promenada shopping centre, he accompanied Żaba through the stores, picking out the most expensive clothes and leaving without paying. No one tried to stop them. In the best restaurant the capital had to offer, they urinated against an interior wall because the toilet was too far away. Other customers looked on in disgust but the staff pretended not to notice. Maringe's intelligentsia upbringing seemed a long way in the past.

He tried to widen the boss's horizons with a trip to Thailand, but first had to prise the Frog, dead drunk, out of a brothel, where he'd beaten several of the girls into tears and was splayed out naked in the sauna, refusing to pay. Threatening to call Baśka provided no moral leverage since she'd long ago stopped caring where her husband got his cheap thrills as long as the girls involved were paid by the hour and didn't linger. Żaba had been careful never to cross that line, ever since Baśka had enlisted members of the gang to shave the head of a mistress to whom he'd got too attached.

The Frog only agreed to crawl out of the sauna when police sirens began to wail in the distance. He was still drunk when the plane took off from Warsaw Airport. In the air, Żaba attacked a flight attendant and punched the pilot. All the other passengers had a long, unpleasant journey to Bangkok, where Thai police in riot gear stormed the aircraft and deported him straight back home. Contacts in Warsaw immigration managed to keep the affair quiet.

Maringe and the other members of the gang stayed on to explore the city until Kuba Gwałciciel inadvertently picked up a transgender prostitute and a fight broke out when his hands wandered far enough south to discover the truth. Local gangsters came running with meat cleavers, the prostitute sliced off most of Kuba's ear with a broken bottle and Bangkok police officers turned up with guns.

Maringe had to bribe his friends out of prison with $5,000 in cash. 'Me, a boy from a respectable family,' he said in wonder, looking back at the period, unable to understand how he'd been happy to wallow in so much sleaze.

The sleaze got thicker and dirtier when he discovered Kuba Gwałciciel's nickname was not a joke. His heroin supplier was a rapist who attacked girls in nightclubs and dragged them outside at knifepoint, unnoticed in the booming bass and flashing lights. Maringe was so drugged up most evenings that he didn't even care:

> It turned [Kuba] on, the fear in the eyes of the girl that he fancied. I was the stupid bastard who watched it passively. Maybe this will shock you, but I will tell you something else – I enjoyed it. My brain, drained of higher feelings, was unable to generate any empathy or sympathy.

His moral sense only came crawling back one night when Kuba tried to bundle a fresh victim into a car, but she screamed so hysterically that someone called the police, and the rapist ran away into the night. Seeing the girl shaking with fear in the flashing blue lights awoke something approaching a conscience in Maringe.

Any difficult decisions about the logistics of heroin supply were solved soon after when Kuba's obsessive quest to see terror in a woman's face led him to attack a pretty young clubber drinking alone at the bar. He didn't realise she was Bolo's daughter. 'Finally, the scythe hit a stone,' noted a fellow gangster. A Pruszków hit team blew up Kuba Gwałciciel's car, but the rapist survived and disappeared. No one knew if that meant he'd skipped the country or been driven into the forest and forced to dig his own grave.

An alternative heroin supply was sourced by Maringe during a trip to Bulgaria, which opened up contacts with some expat Albanian drug barons. Initial talks about importing 50kg of brown powder a month destined for the West fell through when Pruszków proved gun-shy after the *Jurata* affair, but Żaba did a deal to feed Poland's 20,000 heroin addicts and pull a few more into a miserable life of chemical dependence.

The donkey work was carried out by traders who visited Bulgaria to sell electronic goods and returned with heroin (known as *sól* [salt] to junkies) hidden among bundles of cheap clothing destined for Polish street markets. Maringe's Bulgarian connection was the first glimmering of Eastern Europe as a stop on the 'Balkan Route': a smuggling network that would eventually supply around 80 per cent of the heroin consumed on the Continent.

Maringe had no moral qualms about dealing death in powder form, but he was less keen on the brutality required to expand Żaba's territory. When local dealers in the town of Olsztyn refused to give up their patch to the Warsaw crew, a mass brawl with telescopic batons, baseball bats and brass knuckles was arranged in a night club. Maringe was there with the rest of them, leaping out of his sports car and kicking open the club doors as the adrenalin pumped, but the excitement drained away when he saw his friends get to work with calculated, professional violence.

Torturing Bączek in the forest had been little more than a business decision and slashing the rival dealer an act of passion, but this was a very different kind of sustained assault carried out by men who knew the fine line between killing their opponents and making sure they would never walk straight again. 'I witnessed ripped stomachs, shattered heads, eyes popping out, mutilated limbs,' Maringe said. 'And that shrill screaming […] A scream of pain, despair, fear. For a moment I felt like I was in hell.' By the time it was over, the Olsztyn crew would never again pose a threat to Pruszków's power. Maringe numbed any finer feelings with endless rails of coke and some local club girls who happily dropped their old gangster boyfriends to party with the victors.

Back in Warsaw, he continued to throw away money on luxury sports cars and expensive clothes, top restaurants and exclusive clubs, and holidays in the West, where he barely even cared that some of the coke-snorting girls in his bed were almost-famous models or actresses. The white powder dialled up a paranoia that he tried to tame by smoking dope in his flat with the curtains drawn for days at a time, puffing away the fear that this life could not last. Arrests for drug dealing had doubled or tripled over recent years and were already thirty-five times higher than in the last days of the PRL. The police were cracking down, the prison sentences were getting longer and Maringe was convinced the same cars were passing below his windows every day.

He couldn't share his fear with anyone. Civilians wouldn't understand and his fellow gangsters lacked the imagination to empathise. The horizons of Żaba's crew rarely stretched further than vodka and pickled cabbage and a summer holiday by a mosquito-infested Masurian lake. 'A lot of people rave in various interviews that gangsters were "kings of life", Maringe said later. 'Indeed, the fun went on thick, but when I remember those simpletons, the word "kings" is the last one that comes to mind. It was at those moments that I felt like a foreign body in the group.'

He clamped down the paranoia and kept his feelings of superiority hidden from the others. Life in the underworld could be brutally short for those who refused to keep their mouths shut. The troglodytes had spent the last few years punishing anyone who challenged their authority and Maringe did not want to end up like Kiełbacha, another promising young gangster who thought himself smarter than his fellow crooks. They came for him with a Kalashnikov.

11

The Sausage Butchers

It was January 1996 and Masa was strolling broad-shouldered through the evening cold towards the entrance of his grey concrete apartment block on ul. Kopernika when a bomb exploded under a nearby car. 'At first I thought that [my driver] was joking around and had set off some fucking firecracker,' he remembered later. Then parts from a neighbour's Ford Escort began raining down and the bonnet slapped against his back on its way across the road.

When the noise and flames died away, Masa was standing, bleeding, by the block entrance holding the handles of two shredded shopping bags that had been full of cold meats from the delicatessen a few seconds earlier. He was only alive because his young shaven-headed driver, Dariusz Bytniewski, aka 'Bysiu', had parked the Lexus further back than normal, forcing Masa to take a different route to the front door. A metre to the left and the paramedics would have been removing him with shovels.

This was the third attempt on his life since he got out of prison the previous year when the authorities dropped the rape charges. Two of Wariat's men had rented a neighbouring apartment to organise a hit but failed to realise Pruszków was too small a town to hide themselves and were spotted within days. Masa's bodyguards cornered one would-be assassin and slashed his face into steak tartare with a straight-edge razor.

Then a defective bomb was found under his car just before Christmas. It seemed obvious to everyone that the latest attack had been organised by Wariat, but Masa disagreed. He blamed his best friend. 'Masa was 100 per cent convinced that Kiełbacha was behind the attack,' said

Szlachet, who had graduated from Ali's *alkohole* to working as a driver in Masa's entourage. 'That was his first reaction. Jarek vowed that he would not forgive Kiełbacha for this. He was absolutely convinced.'

The pair had once been as close as brothers, but things had unravelled. Kiełbacha had a talent for annoying people more powerful than himself and had proved it a few years back when a paranoid Pershing accused a minor Pruszków man of involvement in a shadowy, possibly entirely fictitious, assassination plot. Kiełbacha saved the man's life with a sneering demolition of the evidence but annoyed Pershing's crew enough in the process that they murdered a friend of the accused just to prove a point. Not long after, an explosive device was attached to the gates of Kiełbacha's house, shots were fired at a rear window and one of his cars was sabotaged. Pershing didn't like being contradicted.

Kiełbacha asked the troglodytes to intervene but the days when he'd been groomed for a top spot in the gang were long gone. Parasol had never forgiven him for the 1990 deaths of Słoń and Lulek, while the others considered the Young Wolves leader an unreliable coke fiend whose wrong turn on the road to Ząbki had started the gang war. They told Kiełbacha to deal with the problem himself.

Ultimately, Masa showed an unexpected gift for diplomacy and smoothed things over with everyone, but his friend saw the wisdom in hiring a trustworthy bodyguard. He gave long-time subordinate Rympałek the job.

Kiełbacha's new head of security had started his criminal career leading an independent crew who burglarised their way across the city until a more established group of thieves pulled guns and demanded a share. Only the shadow of a bigger beast could scare away the vultures, so Rympałek arranged an introduction to Kiełbacha through friends working in club security, and his crew was absorbed into the Pruszków Mafia. The new arrival was initially regarded as more irritant than comrade.

'Rympałek commanded his boys, but for us he was just a soldier,' remembered Masa:

> When he came to the Telimena café in Warsaw, where Kiełbacha and I had our office [i.e. would hold lunchtime meetings with underlings], he would not sit at our table. He waited politely by the stairs for one of

us to nod and invite him to talk. And sometimes he had to wait a really long time, especially since we didn't let him into all the group's secrets.

He took his new role seriously and rented an apartment in Pruszków along with the tougher of his gangsters, but then the balance of power changed in a way no one could have predicted. Pershing went to prison and the ul. Zamiany medical centre heist with its massive score turned Rympałek into a major gangland figure overnight. The man who had waited patiently at the Telimena café to be summoned now swaggered around town in colourful shirts open to the navel, demanding respect like the Italian Mafiosi he'd only ever seen in movies. He had more money than God, a tough crew and the ambition to stamp his mark on Warsaw.

Kiełbacha's relationship with Rympałek moved from boss, to equal, then rapidly to subordinate. He coped with the demotion by snorting long rails of cocaine and nagging Masa to join Rympałek's group as a much-needed ally. Masa wasn't keen on giving up a senior role in the Young Wolves to start again, and only joined under pressure from the troglodytes who wanted a double agent inside what was increasingly looking like a rival group.

The two men wouldn't be together for long. Kiełbacha was spiralling ever deeper into a snowstorm of cocaine addiction and sadism. He enjoyed torturing people who failed to pay back debts, taunting them about coming agonies on the drive to the forest, where the baseball bats and pliers came out. He wasn't much more protective of his friends, once casually pulling the trigger on a pistol dangling from his hand and sending a bullet ricocheting around a room of chatting gangsters before burying itself in the floor. Kiełbacha just laughed, the same way he did when shooting dead a stray dog on the outskirts of town to try out a new pistol.

Inevitably, Kiełbacha fell out with Rympałek, who had an even lower tolerance for sarcastic intelligentsia than the troglodytes, and retreated behind the high, white walls of a converted farm building in Pruszków with his family to become fat on a diet of drugs and alcohol. He lived at night, emerging only to buy coke at the gate or pace the garden chatting endlessly on a mobile phone. Rumours circulated about him being indiscreet with journalists and spending time with a car thief in the orbit of Wariat, to the disgust of some important people in Pruszków. He was dancing on the edge of a volcano and didn't seem to realise it.

Masa drifted away from his friend. He got on well with fellow gym rat Rympałek, was earning good money and had the approval of the Pruszków troglodytes as their inside man, all of which gave him little incentive to follow Kiełbacha out of the gang and into a druggy, nocturnal lifestyle. Their once-close relationship stretched to its limits, then broke.

Disputes about money may also have played a part. The division of some cash entrusted by Jacek Dresz before his death had caused problems, and Kiełbacha was rumoured to be stubbornly holding on to a stake in the Dr Witt company established by Masa and an entrepreneur friend to sell an ordinary fruit juice at inflated prices in the guise of a luxury foreign brand. By 1996, the company had grown into a 50 million złoty household name, with Pruszków's involvement kept carefully hidden. The truth would emerge years later, once the company had passed into more respectable hands.

'I admit it surprised me,' announced a pop culture blogger when the company's origin story finally became known:

> One – I had no idea. Two – I got screwed. At the time, these juices stood on the top shelf of the stores and, in addition, were sold in such fancy (for the '90s) bottles that I seriously thought of them as a premium brand. And three, it turns out my [Dr Witt-drinking] grandma financed the Mafia.

By the time a bomb at ul. Kopernika flashfried a neighbour's car into four melted seats on a metal frame, the former friends had become something closer to enemies and Masa was so wired on vodka, steroids and hurt feelings that it was easy to believe Kiełbacha had been behind the attack. He refused to listen to anyone who suggested the Niewiadomski brothers as more likely suspects.

The two Pruszków men ran into each other at a disco one night, where Kiełbacha begged his old sidekick to accept that someone else was responsible. 'Jarek, I know that it's not like it used to be between us, but I swear on my kid and God, that I would never, never do something like this to you.' Masa pretended to believe him, but privately his opinion hadn't changed.

On 19 February 1996, passing cars were churning the snowy roads of Pruszków into freezing slush and Kiełbacha's bull terrier sat patiently in the passenger seat of the small, white Nissan waiting for its master to come back. It was a cold and gloomy lunchtime and Kiełbacha had parked outside a grocery shop in the centre of town to pick up some shopping.

Witnesses would be unable to remember if the maroon Ford Mondeo and the white Mercedes were already lurking on the street or had been trailing the victim through Pruszków. Kiełbacha seemed unconcerned as he left the grocer and was picking his way across the road when a man stepped out holding a Kalashnikov in a professional stance. Kiełbacha dropped his shopping and ran for the car but was brought down by a burst of fire that popped holes in the Nissan's skin and spun him around. '[He] was surprised when he saw them,' said a witness, 'and then his skull blew out.' The gangster fell backwards on to the road with his jumper riding up over a bloated belly and a look of disbelief on his face. The bull terrier howled inside the car as its master bled out on to the road and the assassins accelerated away.

Police arrived to cordon off the scene but cautiously left the frothing dog in the Nissan until a shell-shocked Małgosia could be summoned to lead it docilely home. Kiełbacha's doctor mother watched from among the crowd on the other side of the police tape, denied permission by detectives to see her son up close for the last time before the morgue boys arrived. Journalists were already flocking to the scene to write stories that claimed a gangster called 'Sausage' had died, but placed the murder outside a butcher's shop to extract maximum irony.

Masa claimed to have heard the news while in the gym with Rympałek and a crowd of witnesses. 'At the time, I didn't know who killed him, because Wojtek had many enemies,' he said. Later, he dropped the pretence of innocence and boasted about having organised the hit himself, which surprised no one in the underworld, who'd heard the rumours about a bulky figure with thinning hair hacking a hole through a frozen lake to dispose of a Kalashnikov. The police never took any action, which didn't surprise anyone much either.

Years later, Masa reversed course and revealed he'd been lying about his involvement in the shooting to make himself look like a tough guy and impress other gangsters. 'You don't mean anything in this town if you're not in the murder club,' he complained.

Many Pruszków gangsters accepted the retraction. Masa looked about as compromising as an anvil but plenty of fellow thugs regarded him as lacking that vital ice chip in the heart that made a human capable of murder and had openly doubted his involvement from the start. So, who killed Kiełbacha?

Some thought senior Pruszków figures had ordered the hit out of fear he would cross over to Wariat, others that the killers had been former ZOMO riot police from Rympałek's crew, seeking revenge for recent arrests. Police had raided Kiełbacha's home looking for illegal weapons and found nothing, but he failed to pass the news on to other gangsters. A subsequent raid caught their main armourer with a house full of guns.

Rympałek's subordinates dismissed any rumours concerning their boss. At the time of Kiełbacha's murder, he was otherwise occupied with almost daily robberies, including carefully planned operations against businessmen heading abroad at a time when everything was done in cash and a briefcase full of dollars could be snatched at gunpoint from a rammed car near the airport.

Foreign territories were also up for grabs following a deal with some Ukrainian gangsters from the Donbas, led by a 50-something woman who looked 'like a lightly beaten Playboy kitten' in Masa's opinion, to distribute large quantities of cocaine in their homeland. Sales were initially poor because the Ukrainians, for all their flashy cars and homes dripping with marble and gold, were inexperienced dealers. Rympałek thought his men could do a better job and had become preoccupied with planning a territorial expansion out to the Russian border. Kiełbacha was a footnote to a potential criminal empire and barely worth the bullets.

All the chaotically conflicting storylines meant no one was ever charged with Kiełbacha's death. The police had too many suspects and too little evidence to even think about making an arrest, so the dead man became just another victim of the gangster violence tearing Poland apart, unavenged and mostly unmourned. He wasn't the first and wouldn't be the last. 'It was not a war,' said Wańka later. 'It was a hopeless game of people who didn't know how to talk to each other. If they could, they wouldn't shoot and they wouldn't plant bombs'.

The bombing of Masa's car remained a mystery for years until a member of Dziad's gang, hiding behind the English-language pseudonym 'Golden', claimed to have organised the attack as the latest strike in the ongoing war. He'd watched in surprise as the blame was laid elsewhere, things escalated and Kiełbacha was murdered by persons unknown. Afterwards, a delighted Dziad threw a party in Ząbki where the champagne flowed like tap water. 'The sheep of Pruszków will kill themselves,' someone triumphantly announced at the party.

That prediction would prove to be very wrong. Instead, the troglodytes would consolidate their authority, reorganise the gang and erase the competition with ruthless efficiency.

12

We Are the Management Board

The Kasprowy was seven storeys of white walls, red hall carpets and pointy-legged wooden furniture in the snowy slopes just outside Zakopane, a dilapidated ski resort of old wooden houses lurking below the jagged mountain peaks of the Tatras. Decades of underinvestment had given the hotel little incentive to upgrade its once-luxurious PRL-era fittings, but the Kasprowy still remained the destination of choice for anyone wanting a touch of luxury in southern Poland, providing they could survive on a diet of *pierogi* and pork knuckle with the inevitable side dish of cabbage. Before the transformation, only the communist elite had access to its 288 rooms and indoor swimming pool, but these days a different kind of powerplayer was banging the reception bell.

Pruszków bosses had been holding their annual New Year's Eve parties at the Kasprowy since the start of the decade. The gangsters would arrive at the hotel clutching suitcases stuffed with dollars to pay for their pleasures and were greeted like nobility. 'In front of the entrance, a delegation of highlanders waited with torches, bread and salt, or something like that, singing, dancing,' remembered Masa. 'An obligatory daily sleigh ride. And if there's a sleigh ride, there's music and drinking. And fucking girls non-stop, not only in the hotel, but also in the sleigh!'

Pruszków had good reason to celebrate as 1996 departed. Eight months earlier, they'd been in danger of losing Warsaw to an increasingly influential Rympałek. Confirmation of the power shift had come when Parasol and friends turned up at a nightclub with the intention of reminding their subordinate who ran the city. They had barely begun shouting threats when the other patrons of the club swivelled around and pulled out weapons. Rympałek had packed the place with his crew. Smirking, he told Parasol that Pruszków didn't give the orders any more. The gangsters slunk home.

Rympałek's reign as King of Warsaw was short lived. In March 1996, gang member 'Remek' crashed a car and received a beating from the boss – something that humiliated him enough to make him become an informer for the police. Rympałek was arrested the next month, initially for assaulting two students in a row over a pool game, but then for armed robbery when Remek began to talk.

The gang boss hired the best lawyers to try to avoid prison and someone would shoot dead a crook testifying for the prosecution in the pedestrian subway near the Marriot Hotel during the trial. The same gunman also took out an innocent 18-year-old getting his hair cut after mistaking him for the dead man's bodyguard. None of it would stop Rympałek from being found guilty, along with twenty-one fellow gang members.

With Rympałek behind bars, the remains of his crew tried to preserve their territory in Praga, but the borders soon crumbled as other crooks sensed weakness and moved in like sharks on a seal pack. The troglodytes saw their opportunity and activated double agent Masa to collect Rympałek's 'orphans' and bring them back under Pruszków's control.

Jarosław Maringe now found himself working directly for a man he only pretended to respect, and he disliked the experience enough, especially after the Macro shootout, to seek out Żaba. Others stuck with their new boss or slipped away to start independent careers in crime.

A reborn Pruszków required a new command structure. The gang had grown from a tightly constructed hierarchy into a sprawling nationwide concern hundreds strong. Parasol and the others lacked the interest or ability to impose the American Mafia's strict structure of Boss–Underboss–Caporegime–Soldier–Associate that made it so easy for FBI agents to draw neat diagrams back at headquarters. Instead, a 'management board' was created from Parasol, Kajtek, Bolo, Wańka and Malizna, in which all decisions were made collectively to ensure everyone got an equal taste of risk and reward. Some suggested Słowik was also on the board but that was never proved, at least according to the lawyers.

As the top men closed ranks, they loosened the reins on the rest of the gang and allowed it to devolve into a network of semi-independent crews united by occasional socialising and the obligation to pay the board anywhere between 15 and 50 per cent of their income every week. That tithe bought Pruszków's gangsters the use of a name which terrified most civilians and the understanding that a criminal army would back them up in times of need. Legitimate businessmen would probably have called it a franchise deal, even if the real purpose was to ensure no one would ever build a big enough power base to challenge the new bosses. Life was good, the money flowed fast and it was time to celebrate at the Kasprowy.

The Pruszków crew staggered around the hotel as 1996 ended, drunk and loud, with one hand kneading a pretty girl through her thin dress and the other clutching the novelty of a mobile phone to check up on subordinates back home. They were thirty strong that year and led by Parasol, Słowik and the rest, with a few promising younger members like Masa and Maringe tagging along as invited guests. Money was thrown around, vodka drunk for breakfast and an entire restaurant rented out night after night because Parasol liked the baked piglet served up with an apple in its mouth.

The freshly constituted management board orchestrating the debauchery had supposedly equal authority, but Malizna liked to throw his weight around more than the others. His once-deferential attitude to the others had vanished when the money started coming in and had been replaced with an arrogant edge that only got sharper after a rail of cocaine. 'Although he didn't offer his paws for kissing like some people,' said an observer, 'he acted like a fucking emperor.'

Officially head of the Gredbug construction company, Malizna had built up a private army of Praga thugs who loved him like brainwashed cultists and some troglodytes were already regretting allowing the former taxi driver to climb so high. 'He became unpredictable, he had praetorians ready for anything,' said Masa:

And no one was sure when they would fuck shit up. During Mafia meetings, Malizna attacked other board members, gave them orders, threatened them, especially when he snorted coke. Everyone had had enough of him, but in this corporation it's quite difficult to get rid of shareholders [...] They had to endure him patiently. Even his brother, Wańka, had difficulty getting along with Malizna.

The management board kept these kinds of internal issues quiet to avoid damaging their reputation as a Mafia machine, and even the observant Maringe caught only glimpses of discord in Zakopane. Masa owed his greater insight to landing the job of bagman, who funnelled tribute from the various crews up to the board. He received a percentage for his trouble but had to endure continuous abuse from Parasol, who still held him responsible for Słoń and Lulek's deaths. Every encounter stung, but Masa could console himself with getting a useful overview of an increasingly compartmentalised gang and bragging rights to the criminal version of a middle-management role, even if others regarded him as little more than an errand boy.

He was still a significant enough figure to be invited along to Zakopane to watch the management board indulge themselves. Wives and children had been ordered to stay at home, but a few exceptions to the no-family rule were allowed, like Żaba's 12-year-old son, who ran around insolently threatening top gangsters while his drunken father laughed himself sick. Słowik had brought along his new wife Monika, who liked to dance on a table at the end of the evening and 'show everyone her ass', in Maringe's unusually puritanical words, although he grudgingly appreciated the couple as the only other members of the gang who enjoyed exotic foreign travel. By the end of the gang's stay, Kasprowy's staff were serving them with fixed smiles.

When the hangovers wore off after New Year's Day, the gang bosses left Zakopane feeling as violent and greedy as ever. Working on the principle that the world contained a lot of money and very little of it was nailed down, they set about getting richer. Their only real concern was being shot up by their rivals from across the river. Everyone knew the police lacked the resources or desire to stop them.

The law-abiding citizens of Poland wanted guns. By early 1997, increasing numbers were demanding firearms for personal protection even as the authorities made themselves unpopular by stubbornly refusing permits.

With only five months left until a general election, white-haired Interior Minister Leszek Miller shamelessly pandered to voters by posing with his own pistol and admitting he'd illicitly owned the weapon for two years before getting it legalised. 'In a democratic country, every citizen should have the right to possess something that he thinks is necessary for his safety,' said Miller.

Voters weren't convinced and would replace Miller's government with a conservative coalition when the election came that September. The crime rate kept racing upwards, with 1,093 murders recorded in Poland that year – substantially more than the 778 committed in Britain, which had a population 20 million souls larger. The bullet storm had become so thick that even Maringe's friends in the Russian Mafia began drifting back towards the eastern borders. Some didn't drift fast enough.

On 22 January 1997, the Belarusian gangster Wiktor Fiszman was machine-gunned by Oczko's Szczecin gangsters as he returned home from the gym one morning. Six months later, two men in sportswear approached Russian Mafia boss Andrei Isaev – a genuine Moscovite for once – and his Polish bodyguard near a petrol station in Poznań, exchanged a few words, then shot them both dead. The killers were Wołomin men doing a favour for a local godfather. Isaev's body was transported back to Moscow in a $20,000 coffin and buried beneath a 2m-high Orthodox cross.

Gangland murders were front-page news, but most Poles experienced organised crime through the sordid everyday reality of protection rackets. The management board leant on everybody and even Pruszków locals would find young men they'd known since childhood entering their shop with a baseball bat to demand tribute. A restaurant in central Warsaw paid $500 a month; a cheese wholesaler in the leafy nearby town of Milanówek paid $1,000; and a shoe warehouse in Ursus $1,500.

Other gangsters caused trouble in nightclubs then forced the owners to employ their friends as security just to keep the peace, only for the new door team to take a percentage from ticket sales and steal fur coats from the cloak room.

Sometimes, the extortion was more subtle. A business owner having problems getting money from a creditor might confide his problems to a market trader; a recommended and friendly seeming thug would quickly recover the debt but demand a share of the business as payment.

Now the business owner had a silent partner who hired friends for jobs they never attended, used the company as a front for illegal activities and milked the cash cow into bankruptcy.

Other takeovers were even more direct. Wańka and Słowik simply walked into the Dekadent nightclub and informed its management that they had new co-owners. That bit of business turned into a scandal when Wańka hosted a boozy party there for the staff of *Teleexpress* (the main news programme on the government-run TVP channel) and a senior reporter was heard drunkenly advising guests not to embarrass the gangsters by taking photographs.

Poles couldn't even escape the extortion by leaving the capital, now that Pruszków's influence had spread across the country like an oil slick. Nikoś remained independent in his Tricity kingdom on the Baltic Sea, but elsewhere gangs that tried to resist the management board went through a familiar ordeal. Their leader would be forced into a car boot and driven to the forest where Pruszków men, all looking like bodybuilders or martial artists, waited around drinking vodka and eating sausages. The hostage was given a shovel and told to dig his own grave then forced to lie in it as guns were fired into the earth around him. 'All right,' a Pruszków man would say when the shots had died away. 'Enough fun. If you and your guys want to play in our area, then you will pay for the privilege. Half of what you earn goes to us.' Then the gangster stumbled home with pissed pants and terror on his face to tell colleagues they'd been demoted from lords to serfs.

Neither civilians nor crooks could depend upon the police to protect them. The crackdown on crime promised by the arrests of men like Pershing and Budzik had failed to materialise so far. Law enforcement numbers rose to 95,700 police officers in uniform – a big increase over the 62,276 *Milicja* members who were active in the last year of communism – but new recruits were rarely of the highest quality. The average starting salary was 800zł a month (about $190), well below the Polish average, and only increased to 1,200zł after eleven years on the force. The talented and driven preferred to find employment elsewhere.

When one in every four police families lived below the poverty line, it was easy for gangsters who routinely carried fat rolls of $100 bills to bribe officers into supplying information or looking the other way. In 1997, it was estimated that 4.5 per cent of Poland's police officers had been disciplined for 'misconduct', although the true number of corrupt cops was much higher. Masa had his own tame dog in the 'kennel' (the law enforcement apparatus) who was so unconcerned about their relationship that the pair once had a meeting in the police station canteen.

Even when officers arrested lawbreakers, the prison sentences handed out were obscenely low: a legacy of the PRL system which had balanced brutal conditions behind bars with a naive belief in the reforming power of Marxist Leninism. By the late 1990s, only 10 per cent of those convicted of aggravated assault would serve any time. Budzik may have got twenty-five years for murder, but a trio of 18-year-olds from 'respectable' families who killed a homeless man for fun got only three years each.

Those who went to prison found recent reforms gave them better medical treatment than on the outside and even allowed 'intimate visits' from wives and fiancées, or prostitutes posing as such. 'It was a summer camp, not a severe punishment,' sneered a hardened criminal.

Cracking down on organised crime required a political consensus that was impossible to reach in a corrupted society. Taking bribes was a banal, everyday activity in the *Sejm* and only occasionally became too blatant to be ignored.

Senior leftist Ireneusz Sekuła was under investigation for his links to the management board and Christian Democrat politician Tadeusz Kowalczyk only escaped charges by dying in a car crash. Jacek Dębski barely scraped into the post of Minister for Sports & Tourism after his Pruszków connections were exposed and the reputation of Donald Tusk's *Kongres Liberalno-Demokratyczny* (Liberal-Democratic Congress) party was badly damaged after an attempt by some members to set up a crooked *Zielone Bingo* (Green Bingo) lottery with Pruszków, supposedly to benefit environmental causes but really to divert money into their own pockets. Media attention saw the lottery shut down before it even opened.

Other deals stayed under the radar and made politicians rich, although some took payment in different forms. 'One minister asked the Mafiosi if the workers on the construction site of his house could be beaten, because he didn't like the way they worked,' remembered journalist Artur Górski.

By the end of 1997, Pruszków had a monthly revenue stream that outsiders estimated at anything from tens of thousands of dollars to millions. The management board laundered the money through bars, security firms, domestic and foreign real estate, sports clubs, stables, import/export companies, a large fruit juice concern, a chain of tanning salons, construction businesses, the stock market and escort agencies. Often the front companies were run by supposedly respectable businessmen who'd first encountered gangsters back in the money-changing days of the late 1980s and saw an advantage in remaining close. One had the wit to name his money laundering front '*Finansowe Biuro Informacyjne*' ('Financial Bureau of Information' – FBI).

Pruszków gangsters could look just about respectable when posing as shareholders in an apparently legitimate company or when photographed with a chummy arm around an establishment politician, but violence on the streets was never far away. Słowik and Monika barely survived a bomb attack at their apartment block when TNT hidden in a plastic bag detonated as they returned from a shopping trip. The blast shattered every window in the block and a doctor spent hours picking shrapnel from their bodies.

The following July, a drug trafficker connected to Pruszków called 'Kręciłapka' was killed by a car bomb near central Warsaw, three months after escaping death in a similar attack on the same street. In November, only good luck saved Wańka in an attack on his apartment.

In 1998, three important men from both sides of the law would be assassinated, ending the gang war and establishing dominance. The gentlemen from Pruszków took credit for the first, pleasure in the second and denied any involvement in the third, despite an avalanche of conspiracy theories.

13

Unholy Trinity

At 21:30 on 6 February 1998, a white Chevrolet truck pulled out of the traffic on ul. Plowiecka, a busy eight-lane expressway running through Praga, and the driver got out to hurry into the brightly light interior of a late-night delicatessen. Wiesław Niewiadomski, known to the underworld as Wariat, had stopped off on his way home this cold evening to buy some food. He was climbing back into the truck with a shopping bag when a passing car slowed and the barrel of an assault rifle slid out the passenger-side window.

They'd found him through the telephone company. Someone working at a mobile provider was taking regular payments to track Wariat's phone and pass the location to his enemies. Mobile devices were still a luxury for most people but gangsters had been using them extensively after a recent scandal about a Polish Army chief's landline being tapped by counterintelligence agents. The spies recorded nothing worth prosecuting but the story sparked a mass underworld exodus to digital technology under the impression that it was harder to intercept. Mobile networks cashed in on their sudden notoriety. 'There were stories circulating that the Polish mafia switched to [mobile network] GSM because of the affair,' a spokesman for the company boasted to the press. 'And it is true. All kinds of people suddenly became very concerned about the security of their conversations.'

Secure or not, Wariat's phone got plenty of action. Officially, he ran a construction company based in Russia, owned several restaurants in Poland and had a debt collection service on the side. His Confetti Club near the River Wisła was one of the capital's top nightspots and had become the favoured location for record companies to present their acts with gold discs at champagne receptions. Unofficially, Wariat cooked the best methamphetamine in Poland and ran a violent organised crime gang with brother Dziad.

Both men had been in and out of prison over the last few years on various charges, which were either mysteriously dropped or ended in a quick release on the grounds of dubious doctors' certificates. Neither Niewiadomski enjoyed being locked up much, but at least they were safe behind bars; back on the streets, the brothers were just another target in the Pruszków shooting gallery.

Early 1997 had seen numerous grenade and bomb attacks on Dziad's properties, while Wariat had barely escaped death the previous Christmas after an ambush by the Pruszków management board in the small town of Zakręt. That hit team had opened up on his vehicle with automatic weapons from behind some bushes and left convinced they'd killed their prey. Regrouping at a restaurant in the capital, the Pruszków men warned the bartender, 'Remember, we've been here since noon and we've been drinking all the time', and then got royally wasted as they laughed about Wariat's minivan, peppered with bullet holes, reversing frantically down the road.

The laughter died when a phone call brought the news that Wariat had been rescued by his bodyguard, Apoloniusz Dąbrowski, aka 'Poldek', after the shooting and was still alive. Poldek paid for his loyalty at the start of the next year when his body was discovered rotting in the boot of a frost-covered car. He wouldn't be around to help his boss when the bullets started flying on ul. Plowiecka in February.

Pedestrians outside the delicatessen ran for cover when the man in the passenger seat of the passing car opened fire. It was tough to aim while firing from a moving vehicle, but the shooter managed to blast out the side windows of the Chevrolet's cab and two bullets ricocheted around the interior before burying themselves in Wariat's chest. He died at the scene. Typically heartless jokes about his death quickly spread around Pruszków.

'Żaba also told me that [another gangster] had said Wariat was shot in the testicles,' said Masa. 'He said, "They shot him in the ball sack". It was very funny for everyone.'

Dziad turned up to observe the bloodstained Chevrolet from behind police tape, although no one could tell if he was mourning his brother or regretting that the authorities had found a notebook in the glove compartment containing contact details for important politicians, law enforcement officials, businessmen, journalists and prosecutors. All would later deny knowing the dead gangster.

The funeral Mass was held at a small wooden church in Bródno a week later. Police stood outside the cemetery gates noting down the number plates of cars parked along nearby roads while 250 people followed the coffin into the church, most of them shaven-headed young men in leather jackets. Afterwards, their suit-wearing bosses stood around the tombstones talking business. The few journalists present were contemptuously ignored but one who tried to film the mourners had his camera taken away and the cassette ripped out.

A wake was held at the Confetti nightclub, where Dziad drank too much and shook his head sadly for most of the evening. On the other side of the river, Pruszków held their own mock wake to toast the death of an enemy.

Wariat's widow, Ewa, the sister of Dziad's wife, allegedly took over the drug business with the help of a nephew and swore revenge against the killers. Dziad tried to make her understand that the gang war was over and they had lost. Ewa wouldn't listen. She closely followed news reports that Pruszków management board member Kajtek and 31-year-old street soldier Michał Pawłowski had been arrested for the murder then released through lack of evidence. Dziad was trying to talk her out of a revenge hit when the Polish underworld was turned upside down by another murder that April. The dead man had known Wariat and shared the same enemies.

Gdańsk was a red-roofed port city on the Baltic coast that had passed between the Poles and Germans like an infectious disease for decades. The first shots of the Second World War were heard there in September 1939 when the city was called Danzig, but it entered the post-war world flying the Polish flag after the victorious Soviets reworked the map of Eastern Europe.

Communist investment turned this busy port into a major shipbuilding centre, but the locals were independent enough to remain unimpressed by socialist revolution. In 1980, the city became the birthplace of underground trade union *Solidarność*. Dissidents across the country rallied behind future Polish president, Lech Wałęsa, as he gave stinging speeches in the shadows of half-built cargo ships about Soviet repression and the need for free elections.

As Wałęsa manned the barricades, another Gdańsk native called Nikodem Skotarczak was undermining the system in his own self-interested way by robbing foreign sailors blind in crooked currency deals, smuggling forbidden goods and running a stolen car ring. Nikoś was a handsome man by Polish standards, with the black hair and bright teeth of a discount Elvis impersonator working undemanding audiences in provincial towns. He'd started off running security for local nightclubs back in the 1970s before transitioning into the bodyguard of a local fence who soon recognised the criminal potential lurking beneath the surface of the cheerful young man with endless self-confidence. Under the guidance of the more experienced crook, Nikoś crossed into the underworld full time and began making good money smuggling contraband and currency from Budapest: the criminal crossroads of the Soviet bloc, thanks to Hungary's conveniently lax border controls.

By the start of the PRL's last decade, Nikoś was posing as a successful businessman with the spare cash to sponsor local football team Lechia Gdańsk. The act was convincing enough for the city's communist authorities to present him with an award for public spiritedness, but Nikoś soon dropped the façade and moved to West Germany, where he formed a gang shipping stolen cars into Poland. He did some jail time in Berlin but enhanced his growing Robin Hood reputation by switching clothes with his visiting brother and walking out the front gate.

Back in Poland, as democracy dawned, Nikoś added some tough guys to his gang and introduced organised crime to the fleshpots of the Baltic coast. The public loved his powerful brand of twinkle-eyed, Porsche-driving, roguish charm. Closer up, the celebrities in Gdańsk nightclubs found it thrilling to hear him trot out live-fast, die-young clichés like, 'It's better to live a year as a tiger than a hundred years as a turtle'.

Nikoś got on the wrong side of Pruszków by siding with Wariat and Dziad when the gang war started, but his Baltic kingdom was strong enough to resist the consequences. For all the charm, he was as ruthless as any Polish gangster. In May 1997, a former subordinate with backing from Pruszków was shot dead after attempting a coup. Not long after, a bloody war with gang boss Zbigniew Mikołajewski, aka 'Carrington', over alcohol smuggling on the Polish borders left fifteen in the morgue and many more buried in forest graves. Cinema audiences still cheered in recognition when Nikoś made a brief cameo in the 1997 action-comedy film *Sztos* as a casino patron.

On 23 April, the Nikoś gang celebrated the name-day of senior member 'Kura' at the Marco Polo restaurant in Gdańsk, where the vodka flowed and food circulated late into the next morning. Ordinary locals were heading out to work when Nikoś, Kura and their wives moved on to a private afterparty at the nearby Las Vegas escort agency. Deserted except for a barman and few exhausted prostitutes, the gang boss ordered drinks to be brought to a private VIP room furnished with black leather furniture and accessed through a discreet corridor. Bodyguards arrived at the agency at around 09:00 to protect their boss but had little to do except lounge around the reception area under the potted palms meant to give the place an exotic appeal. Three hours later, Nikoś' party was still there, slowly winding down from the celebrations and waiting for breakfast to be delivered.

Just after 12:00, all of the bodyguards and staff left the agency for reasons that no one ever convincingly explained, and shortly afterwards, two masked men came through the front doors. They headed straight for the VIP room with guns. 'Good morning,' said one cheerfully as Nikoś looked up in surprise.

The two women slid under a table as the bullets started flying and escaped injury. Kura was shot in the legs and groin but lived. Nikoś was hit six times in the head and chest and died at the scene with his body pressed against a wall. He was 43 years old.

Within weeks, a bootleg video taken from the police walkthrough was available for any gangsters with $50 spare to gawp at high-contrast footage of Nikoś lying on the floor of a Gdańsk brothel with his black jeans and T-shirt soaked in blood. Detectives didn't know who'd pulled the trigger.

Some suspected that Carrington had taken revenge for the alcohol war or the increasingly powerful *Łódzka Ośmiornica* (Łódź Octopus) gang had carried out the shooting as revenge for interference in a lucrative kidnapping. Others blamed the murder on clashes over drug distribution in Katowice, issues with Russian Mafia figures or a coup by Nikoś' shaven-headed subordinate Daniel Zacharzewski, alias 'Zachar'.

The underworld was an endless merry-go-round of feuds and murders and usurpers. No one doubted that a replacement for Nikoś would arrive and the violence continue as before. 'It's like weeds,' said a Gdańsk police officer. 'You pull one up and another springs up in its place. It cannot be eradicated.'

The police may have had no firm suspects, but fellow gangsters were sure Pruszków had been involved. Masa had managed to stay friends with Nikoś despite the conflict and was soon spreading stories about being summoned to Warsaw's Holiday Inn by the management board a few months earlier and overhearing someone mutter, 'This whore from Gdańsk is going to die soon'. He got word to Nikoś, but the gang boss didn't take the threat seriously until the two hitmen walked into the Las Vegas escort agency.

Afterwards, Masa became paranoid his warning had been intercepted. During a gang party in the Marriott Hotel where everyone drank an ironic toast to Nikoś' health and some hard stares came his way, Masa was paranoid enough to make an 'English exit' (a Polish expression meaning to leave without telling anyone) and spent long weeks lying low and wondering what to do next.

Not everyone believed Masa's story, especially after his lies about Kiełbacha. Cynics noted that if Pruszków had killed Nikoś to absorb his territory, they did a poor job, because Zachar took over the Baltic coast and seemed, initially at least, ready to defend the territory just as fiercely as his old boss.

True or not, the rumours kept circulating and only enhanced Pruszków's reputation as mad dog killers. Wariat's widow seemed to accept that revenge was pointless, especially after an even higher-profile murder was attributed to her husband's killers that June.

Marek Papała was a sombre-faced 38-year-old who'd recently been dismissed as Chief of Police for Poland. A *Milicja* veteran who'd signed up when the hammer and sickle still flew over the Kremlin, he'd clawed his way up the ranks in the unexciting backwater of traffic control but attracted endorsements from important figures by earning a PhD in law. He dodged any purges when communism ended and in 1996 was made Deputy Chief of Police – a political appointment by a leftist government which viewed Papała's long *Milicja* service more favourably than those on the right of the spectrum.

He did well enough that early the next year, Leszek Miller gave him the top job. Papała wouldn't hold it for long. Miller's government lost the elections and, by January 1998, Papała was unemployed, spending his days learning English and looking for a fresh direction.

In the evening of 25 June, he drove out to the apartment of a former PRL secret service brigadier general who had become a businessman after the transformation. The two men were long-time acquaintances and Papała was hoping for career advice but forgot it was the brigadier general's name-day and was surprised to find the apartment full of friends and neighbours drinking vodka. He stayed for a while, chatting with a businessman friend called Edward Mazur, who had immigrated to the USA from Poland decades ago and got rich. They discussed potential career paths for Papała, including moving to America for immersive English lessons before becoming a police liaison officer in Brussels.

At about 22:00, Papała drove off to pick up his mother at the Central Railway Station but the train was severely delayed so he returned to his apartment in Mokotów's ul. Wincentego Rzymowskiego. Someone shot him in the head as he sat in his Daewoo Espero in the block car park. A Vietnamese man living on the sixth floor was having a cigarette on his balcony and saw someone running from the scene with a pistol, possibly modified to either muffle the shot or catch the spent cartridge. The general's wife was walking their dog nearby and found her husband's body moments later.

The murder of a former top policeman horrified Poland. Few officers ever died in the line of duty: in 1998, only eight would be killed doing their job, compared to the twenty-five who died by suicide.

Efforts to find the killer were hampered by the crime scene being left unsecured by shell-shocked police in the vital early stages and evidence subsequently trampled by onlookers and journalists. The investigation then derailed when detectives convinced themselves Papała's wife had been involved and bugged the coffin during the funeral in case she made a guilty last-minute confession to the corpse. They recorded nothing except broken-hearted sobs, and after that the leads dried up.

No one knew who had shot Papała or why, although the official story would eventually resolve into a carjacking gone bad. That made sense in a city where car theft was an epidemic and violence everywhere, but the Poles were a conspiracy-loving people who refused to accept the official line on most things. They'd grown up in a communist state that insisted the wartime massacre at Katyn had been carried out by Germans when everyone knew the Red Army was responsible. It was hard not to suspect that the real truth of any event could only be found by digging deep beneath a crust of lies. Papała's death was no exception.

Elaborate and often contradictory theories were soon circulating, which connected Papała's death with professional assassins as part of some shadowy plot cooked up in Warsaw or possibly Gdańsk by an expat Polish businessman or perhaps a cabal of corrupt cops covering up their misdeeds. Public pressure would soon make the police reopen the investigation and within a few years there would accusations, counter-accusations, statements from informers, badly compromised trials and intervention from an American District Attorney. By the end of it, the police would be more confused than ever about the motive behind Papała's death.

But that was all in the future. In the summer of 1998, many people were convinced the former Chief of Police's death was the third in an unholy trinity of murders committed by Pruszków. In the aftermath, gang members flaunted their money and muscles in the clubs and gyms and bars of Warsaw, enjoying the notoriety too much to keep a low profile. A few knowledgeable outsiders, aware of how quickly things could change, saw only pride and the inevitable fall. 'In general, it seems to me that the Polish *ludzie z miasta* [city people, i.e. gangsters] attached too much importance to the facade, from the toned body to the grotesquely lavish lifestyle,' said a Belarusian gangster living in Warsaw. 'People were begging to be caught and jailed.'

The next two years would prove him right when the authorities finally established an effective plan of attack against organised crime. Jarosław Maringe experienced it all first hand when police walked into his apartment one day with handcuffs and an arrest warrant.

1. Gang boss Andrzej Kolikowski, aka 'Pershing', was shot dead at a Polish ski resort, leaving behind a puddle of blood and a rented Mercedes. *(© PAP SA)*

2. A decade earlier the Pruszków Mafia had announced itself to the world when two members were murdered during a chase triggered by a disagreement over a stolen car. *(Policja.pl)*

3. Pruszków was founded by Ireneusz Piszczałkowski, aka 'Barabasz', a cheerful bodybuilding thug who wouldn't live to see his gang become the country's biggest crime family. *(Author's collection)*

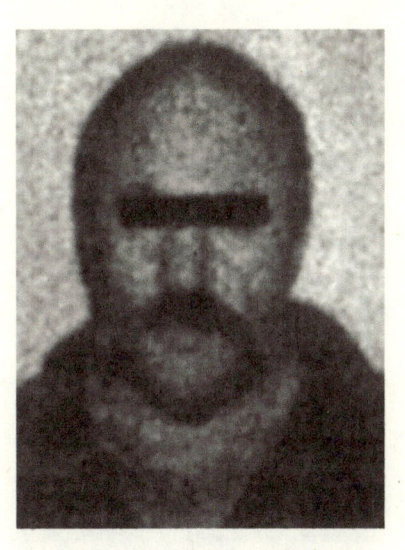

4. The tough and ruthless Janusz Prasol, aka 'Parasol', lacked much in the way of education but became one of the gang's most effective leaders after Barabasz's death. *(Policja.pl)*

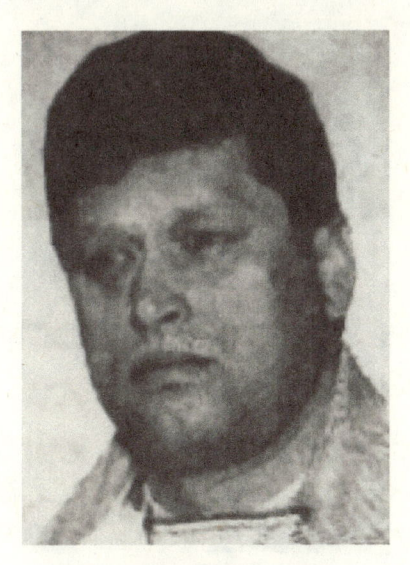

5. Important Pruszków figures included Parasol's thuggish sidekick Krzysztof Ryszard Pawlik, aka 'Krzyś', who was in and out of prison through the gang's glory years. *(Policja.pl)*

6. Mirosław Danielak, aka 'Malizna', was a former taxi driver whose skill as a getaway driver saw him earn the trust of senior gangsters and eventually join the leadership. *(Policja.pl)*

7. The gang's youth division was run by Wojciech Kiełbiński, aka 'Kiełbacha', a cocaine-addled wiseguy with more enemies inside the gang than on the outside. *(Policja.pl)*

8. Jarosław Maringe, aka 'Chińczyk', started his criminal career as a car thief but became one of Pruszków's biggest money-makers by applying a sharp business brain to the logistics of international drug smuggling. *(Policja.pl)*

9. Alcoholic Jerzy Wieczorek, aka 'Żaba', ran the gang's drug operations and mentored Maringe in the cocaine trade until their dysfunctional relationship fell apart. *(Policja.pl)*

10. Senior Pruszków gangsters invited Pershing to join them but soon regretted it when his charisma earned him a leadership position and threatened their authority. *(© PAP SA)*

11. Originally a friend of the gang, Wiesław Niewiadomski, aka 'Dziad', and his brother declared war on Pruszków after a row over a stolen truck spiralled out of control. *(Wikimedia Commons/Kordiann)*

12. Ryszard Szwarc, aka 'Kajtek', was a senior Pruszków figure but less violent than the others, although that wouldn't stop him being kidnapped by Dziad's men and ransomed for $120,000. *(Policja.pl)*

13. The gang's violence sometimes took out its own members, as Kiełbacha discovered when someone gunned him down in the street and left the police vainly looking for clues. *(© PAP SA)*

14. Gdańsk car thief and smuggler Nikodem Skotarczak, aka 'Nikoś', was a popular hero for his criminal escapades but made the mistake of siding against Pruszków in the Mafia wars. *(Wikimedia Commons/Edyta Skotarczak)*

15. Many people blamed Pruszków for the mysterious murder of former Police Chief Marek Papała, although the gang denied any involvement. *(Policja.pl)*

16. Gang member Andrzej Banasiak, aka 'Słowik', would eventually be charged with organising Papała's death but proved his innocence in court. *(Policja.pl)*

17. Promising young businessman-turned-gangster Ryszard Bogucki was the man pulling the trigger when senior Pruszków figures decided to eliminate their comrade-turned-rival Pershing. *(Policja.pl)*

18. Robert Bednarczyk, aka 'Bedzio', vowed revenge for the death of his boss Pershing but eventually had to accept the war was lost. *(Policka.pl)*

19. Politician Ireneusz Sekuła was one of many politicians in bed with Pruszków, but in his case pressure to repay huge loans led to suicide. *(SEJM)*

20. When the gang's leadership went on trial, Jerzy Brodowski, aka 'Mutant', took advantage of the power vacuum to try to take over the Warsaw underworld. *(Policja.pl)*

21. The psychotic Robert Cieślak, aka 'Cieluś', went out in a bloody firefight when law enforcement stamped out the last significant organised crime gangs. *(Policja.pl)*

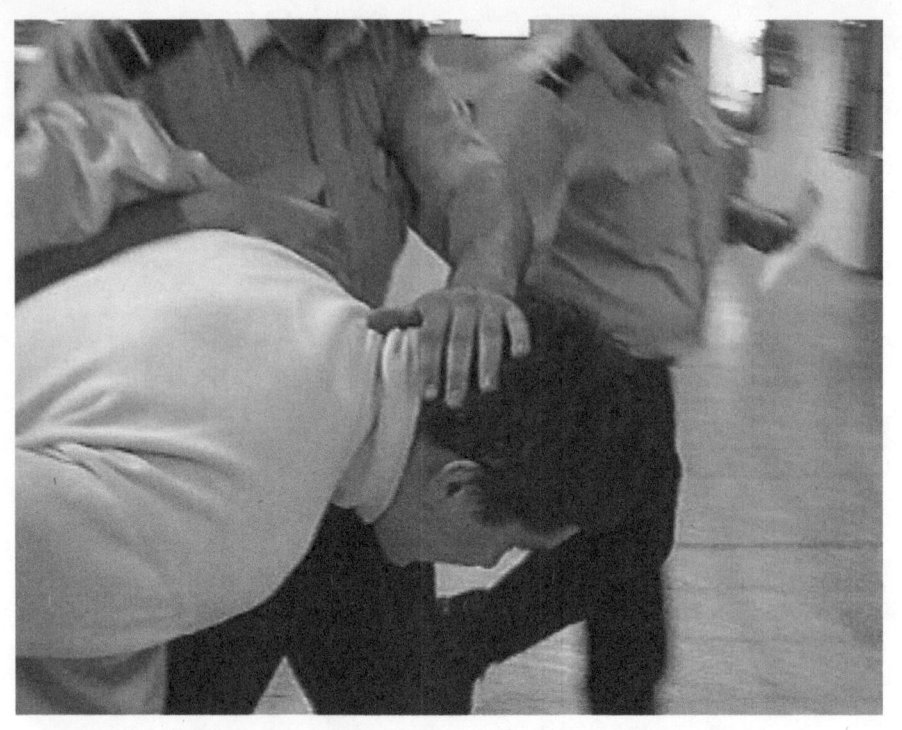

22. Chińczyk avoided the initial police raids on Pruszków by fleeing to Sweden, Serbia and then Mexico, but couldn't escape justice forever. *(© PAP SA)*

23. Jarosław Sokołowski, aka 'Masa', leveraged his time with the gang into a career as a Polish celebrity that earned him millions, but the law eventually came calling. *(© PAP SA)*

IV

THE POLISH GODFATHER, 1999–2000

14

Smuggling is Our Cultural Heritage

Jarosław Maringe liked to think of himself as an intelligentsia, but a genuinely smart man wouldn't have made so many mistakes. It might have been a clever move to stay in Gocław rather than alert the tax authorities by buying a huge new mansion, even if it meant having to tolerate the alcoholics drinking whatever offered the best money-to-booze ratio below his window every day. It was less clever to fill the apartment with expensive paintings that were visible from the street and park a caravan of sports cars outside. Soon, everyone knew that Poland's biggest drug dealer lived upstairs at ul. Biskupia. The new nickname of 'Chińczyk', thought up by dealers as a tangled in-joke about the supposed origins of the heroin they sold and perhaps also a reference to Maringe's jet-black hair, didn't help much either.

His biggest mistake was to assume that true love and organised crime could co-exist. Luiza was a delicate blonde from a respectable family who was introduced by friends at a party. Maringe fell hard for this smart, educated law student who possessed the rare gift of making him behave like a decent human being. She had a boyfriend and intended to stay faithful but was intrigued by her new acquaintance, who appeared to be 'on the one hand, a thug', as Maringe described himself, 'on the other, a boy who gives the impression of an intelligent, sensitive person'. They parted ways, but the attraction stayed fiery enough for Luiza to send a text at Christmas coyly announcing she'd be in Zakopane for

New Year's Eve. Maringe was on an Austrian skiing holiday with Żaba's family but immediately jumped in a car and raced to southern Poland.

He and Luiza welcomed in 1999 at a party, talking intensely through the night while her boyfriend, a well-known model, sat in the corner feeling ignored and abandoned. By the time fireworks were painting neon palm trees on the midnight sky, Maringe and Luiza were officially a couple. 'I felt that finally I'd found the right woman with whom I could build a normal home and family,' he said later.

Their young love lasted less than a month before police officers marched into Maringe's flat with an arrest warrant. He was charged with the relatively minor offence of supplying a packet of heroin to a junkie police informer. None of the officers bothered to pretend the accusation was anything more than an excuse to cage Maringe while they dug up more serious charges. Poland was finally cracking down on organised crime.

A coalition of conservative, liberal and Christian Democrat parties had taken power at the last election with promises to introduce much-needed reforms that would open the door to membership of NATO and the European Union. Some good work was done but the government had the sloppy habit of distributing important posts to former *Solidarność* activists who were known more for their loyalty than their professional competence. A school teacher badly out of his depth nearly bankrupted the social security system inside a few months and the economy promptly tanked, with unemployment rising for the first time in years. The government tried to regain public trust by launching a law-and-order offensive against the gangsters who'd turned the country into a battleground for so long.

Oczko's gang in Szczecin were locked up after an insider agreed to testify – a result that satisfied both Poland's legal eagles and more than a few crooks in Pruszków, who thought Medvesek had shown too much independence recently. He got thirteen years in prison.

Pruszków was less pleased to lose Maringe, who was an important part of their narcotics division. At first, he remained calm, convinced no breadcrumb trail of evidence connected him with the drug business, but his spirits drooped as weeks turned into months, his designer clothes shops went bankrupt, Luiza stopped visiting and a gangster called Krzysztof, aka 'Kozioł' (Goat), replaced him as Żaba's right-hand man. Maringe spent months in a cell with a group of street thieves who respected his Pruszków connections but offered nothing approaching intelligent conversation or a respite from the endless boredom. He pretended to understand why Luiza preferred not to come see him, but that didn't soften the loneliness when the lights went out.

A police officer arrived one day and offered to protect Żaba's operation in exchange for information on rival drug gangs. The Frog 'was pleased with such a strategic alliance. We gave the dog meat – he gave us peace of mind', but the deal wouldn't stop Maringe being transferred to a tougher prison and a cell shared with two toothless thugs who played cards from dawn to dusk and mocked his tales of supermodels and cocaine.

As summer turned into autumn, his fear that this world of piss-stinking concrete might become a permanent home intensified. The prison psychiatrist prescribed anti-depressants. They didn't work and Maringe tried to kill himself twice, not having the nerve to go through with it the first time and later being rescued before the noose cut off too much oxygen. Afterwards, he turned to religion and prayed every day, daydreaming about a new crime-free life with Luiza if the prison gates ever opened.

Religious devotion wasn't unusual in Pruszków. The management board and their wives wore ostentatious gold crosses and attended church every Sunday for a long, droning Mass in their most expensive outfits. Gangsters regularly donated money to the church and cried out to God when faced with danger or a long prison sentence. Kiełbacha had wrongly believed the Lord protected him and was known for making large donations after every successful score, as well as marching informants into church to swear on the cross that their tales were true. Słowik had even wanted to be a priest when younger and had friends in the church hierarchy who claimed not to understand what he did for a living. During Pruszków's Christmas parties in Zakopane, he put on a cassock and drunkenly blessed passersby with great solemn movements, looking like an alcoholic man of the cloth as he stumbled through the snow.

Maringe believed as intensely as the rest but sometimes felt the only thing keeping him sane was the more secular pleasure of dope smuggled into prison and smoked in discreet corners. Visiting gangster friends tried to cheer him up with reassurances that life was safer behind bars now that Pershing was back on the streets and causing trouble alongside Masa. He wasn't sure he believed them.

The prison authorities confiscated his dope and Maringe was on the verge of cracking up again when, miraculously, the heroin charge was dropped, and the police had nothing left with which to hold him. He walked out the prison gates and immediately forgot all about God, quitting the drug business or starting a family with Luiza.

Maringe was soon spending endless days in his apartment, snorting cocaine and stagnating 'like a donut in butter' while Luiza tried to ignore the strippers and casual hook-ups who were now back in his life. Her boyfriend had nothing to show for the last twelve months except slacker morals and worse table manners.

The crew went on holiday to Spain that summer and wondered if they should be concerned when Żaba was held by uniformed men at the Warsaw Okęcie Airport gates and released with only minutes to catch his flight. A few days around the hotel pool broiling in the sun was enough to calm their fears.

One morning, Maringe was watching a TVP Polonia news broadcast on satellite, feeling genuinely content for the first time in ages, when images of a familiar part of Warsaw appeared on screen. 'In the glow of the Spanish sun, even the Polish language sounded like singing poetry,' he remembered. 'The poetic mood passed when I saw police officers removing the paintings from my home on ul. Biskupia.'

The authorities were raiding properties connected to Pruszków across the country and making arrests. Most of the management board were already behind bars. A council of war was held in the hotel at which Żaba announced plans to stay abroad until the crackdown had passed. A new country was required, one that was corrupt and crime-ridden enough to welcome a clique of international drug smugglers. Maringe, for all his intellect, never even considered abandoning the criminal life.

Visitors to the Bulgarian capital Sofia back in the days before the Iron Curtain rusted away found fog-grey buildings, onion-domed churches, dirty yellow trams and miserable people. The economy was bad, and the secret police worse, as exiled dissident Georgi Markov discovered in 1978 when a *Darzhhavna Sigurnost* (DS) agent fatally jabbed him in the leg with a poisoned umbrella tip on a London bridge. Visitors to Sofia didn't tend to stay long and most locals wished they could leave too.

Peel back the Marxist Leninist orthodoxy and a very different side of the capital was revealed. Sofia was the heart of a smuggling network that reached out through neighbouring Greece and Turkey to stretch its tentacles across the world. Originally a Cold War operation that exported weapons of death to leftist guerrillas, the DS soon discovered an alternative, less socialist use for their ratlines in shipping heroin and other contraband to the West for a healthy profit.

The men who killed Markov looked like Bolshevik stormtroopers but acted more like Mafiosi in an organisation that rivalled Wall Street for its capitalism. 'Smuggling is our cultural heritage,' said political scientist Ivan Krastev. 'In the Balkans, we know how to make those boundaries disappear. We can cross the roughest sea and traverse the most forbidding mountain. We know every secret pass and, failing that, the price of every border guard.'

At least 14,000 employees of the DS lost their jobs when communism fell, and no one was surprised when many transferred their skills into the emerging world of organised crime. Mafia gangs were everywhere in Bulgaria as democracy arrived and former DS agents helped newly emerged gangsters, most of them fat-bellied former weightlifters with arms like sewer pipes, turn the country into a post-communist smuggler's paradise where corruption was baked into every transaction. Ordinary Bulgarians despaired. A survey at the end of the decade found a clear majority believed life had been better under communism, and the number of those who felt optimistic about the future had dropped by 10 per cent over the same period. It was the perfect place for Żaba's crew to begin a new life in exile.

A friend lent Maringe and his boss an apartment in Sofia, and the pair relieved the tension by working their way through the bars and brothels of the quarter. They acquired fake diplomatic passports and a car with matching plates to speed drunkenly through the city past herds of mangy wild dogs, men leading pet bears on leashes, kiosks selling spicy porn magazines and gaping holes in the road covered by what looked like sections of wooden fencing.

After a few weeks of alcoholic dissipation, Maringe sobered up enough to start rebuilding their narcotics empire. The Poles fitted neatly into an ethnic jigsaw of international criminals who had made Sofia their home in exchange for a tithe to the local Mafia. Ukrainians trafficked women, émigrés from former Yugoslavia exported weapons and Albanians monopolised the drug market. Maringe formed an alliance with a heroin-dealing Kosovan clan knitted tightly together by blood and Islam but happy to deal with outsiders if the money was right; the Kosovans hadn't even seen a problem in working with Serb gangsters while their countries were at war.

Maringe's earlier heroin trafficking had been limited to feeding Polish appetites, but now he had bigger plans to flood Western Europe with dope. He paid an army of innocent-looking travellers 1,000 euros a trip to smuggle kilos of brown powder hidden in false-bottomed suitcases back to Warsaw, where contacts divided the contraband up for transportation into Germany and beyond.

Money came pouring in and the gang lived like kings. Żaba opened a restaurant next door to the Polish Embassy, in a modernist interwar villa the colour of old margarine, not bothered that his photograph was on wanted posters in every post office from Sopot to Zakopane.

Luiza was now Maringe's fiancée, but her occasional visits didn't stop him tomcatting around with local prostitutes. He paid the price with a 'heart episode' while in bed with a Bulgarian call girl, which left him paralysed and wheezing, feeling the Grim Reaper's knuckle bones around his throat. The girl calmly got dressed and left without a word, but the cleaning lady called an ambulance.

That heart attack was the beginning of the end for his relationship with Żaba. In hospital the old paranoia returned and Maringe couldn't stop circling back to a moment before his arrest when the old drunk had unexpectedly offered him $10,000 a month 'royalties' in exchange for handing over the job stashing cocaine and heroin to Kozioł. At the time, Maringe was happy to take the deal ('I've never hidden the fact that my priority is making money,' he said, 'not gangsterism, which was just a tool'), but now it all seemed more significant. Was he being frozen out? Or set up? Lying in bed, wired up to beeping heart monitors, he thought obsessively about a recent incident when his contacts in Warsaw were wrongly blamed for robbing another dealer, and he became convinced that Żaba had orchestrated it to smear his reputation.

When Żaba unexpectedly came to visit, accompanied by a glowering Kozioł, the heart monitors pinged like church bells. What might have seemed to onlookers like an inconsequential, meandering chat between three friends felt to the sick and paranoid Maringe like the prelude to a savage beating. After a long, tense conversation about health, the pair made some awkward jokes and left. Maringe lay there convinced that Żaba had come to kill him but aborted the plan at the last moment. 'My life had become a fucking rollercoaster,' he said. 'I didn't know where it was going to stop.'

Perhaps it was just drug-induced paranoia that made Maringe think the worst of his boss, but others in the gang remembered Żaba's frustration at having to rely so much on a talented dilettante whose commitment to a life of crime wavered at every glimpse of the prison bars. True *Git-Ludzie* could take a stiff sentence without flinching, but Maringe had cracked up after only twelve months in prison and no one knew what he'd do if the handcuffs clicked again. A once-vital part of the gang was starting to look like its weakest link and, in Pruszków, that journey usually ended with an unmarked forest grave.

It suited everyone fine when Maringe got out of hospital and announced his intention to spend some time with friends in Sweden. He gifted the Balkan Route to Żaba in exchange for a down payment and regular 'royalties'. As he packed a suitcase, local gangsters were still asking questions about the earlier arrests in Poland, but Maringe didn't know what to tell them. He knew only that the gang had turned on each other after Pershing left Białołęka prison and the authorities had used the bloodletting as a pretext to launch a wave of arrests. One thing was certain, he told his Balkan friends: Masa must have played a role in all this trouble.

15

I'm the King Here

The main entrance to Białołęka prison was a brown gate wide enough to admit a boxy prison van or an elephant that liked swinging its hips. Anyone without wheels or tusks used a smaller door set into the lower right of the gate. Early in the morning of 10 August 1998, the door swung open and a big man emerged, wearing glasses and an expensive suit that had been very fashionable four years earlier. The group of young thugs in leather jackets waiting on the street outside respectfully shook his hand then ushered him into the back of a Mercedes headed to a party to celebrate his release. Andrzej Kolikowski was finally free.

Polish prisons are never fun places to spend time, but Pershing had received better treatment than most. Białołęka was Europe's largest detention centre, housing 1,500 men in a complex of four-storey brick barracks sealed off from the outside world by concentric rings of concrete wall and mesh fencing. Most prisoners lived in overcrowded cells, but Pershing's status as the nation's best-known gangster got him a rare single-occupancy room originally built for communist party big shots to do their time with more dignity than the ordinary proletariat. The authorities even installed a carpet and colour television.

He expected to be treated with respect, and when a young guard made the mistake of ending telephone privileges early one day, Pershing punched him in the head, shouting, 'I'm the king here and you're the prisoner!'

A squad of prison guards rushed in with truncheons to separate the pair. Afterwards, Pershing bribed a staff member to identify them and sent men to attack the guards at their homes. No one disturbed his telephone privileges again.

The Ożarów crew were good at targeting off-duty prison staff but otherwise struggled to stay relevant with their boss behind bars. Early during Pershing's incarceration they'd tried to take over some protection rackets controlled by the Wołomin gangster 'Uchal' during a confrontation behind Bar Paragraf, an old-style net-curtain café popular with retirees on a budget. A mass brawl broke out with a dozen street soldiers on each side. Florek was in the thick of it and someone got hit in the face so hard that an eyebrow on a flap of skin spun off into the air. The fight became big news in the media, with reporters exaggerating the numbers involved into the hundreds, but the real story was Pershing's mob being defeated and limping back home.

Now their leader was out and the boys from Ożarów were looking to regain the crown. Underworld rumours claimed the Pruszków management board had handed Pershing a bag stuffed with $60,000 compensation for all his rackets they'd absorbed over the last four years. If true, it was an insultingly small amount for a portfolio worth millions and explained why he announced plans to run Ożarów as an independent crew on his release rather than rejoin the gang. Both sides seemed relieved they wouldn't be working together.

Pershing settled back at home, hit a few casinos to scratch that gambling itch, then began the slow grind of rebuilding his criminal empire. The pace picked up when Masa arrived one day looking for shelter, having finally severed ties with the management board. After the fallout from the Nikoś murder, he'd been brought back into the gang by Kajtek, who was one of his mother's many boyfriends from decades ago and still felt protective towards the younger man, but the rest of the board remained suspicious. Parasol only tolerated his presence because Masa's several hundred-strong crew was an essential part of the Warsaw machine, and frequently slapped him around. 'He was never my friend,' Parasol told a journalist later. 'Well, I must admit that I beat the shit out of him a few times, to put it brutally. He was strong, he trained on steroids, but he had absolutely zero fighting heart.'

The breaking point came when members of the management board insisted on receiving a percentage of the income Masa was making from shrewd private investments in legitimate restaurants and nightclubs.

Guns were waved around when he proved reluctant. By the end of the year, an unhappy Masa had quit the gang which had been his life for over a decade and taken his crew over to Ożarów, seeking Pershing's protection. A cash payment of $15,000 was eventually made to Pruszków as a kind of underworld transfer fee, but the management board would never forgive the betrayal.

Masa brought with him the seed of an idea that would soon sprout into a money tree. In the last few years, slot machines had become popular in Poland by providing an easy introduction to gambling for the *Kowalskis* (i.e. typical Poles), who would never normally visit a casino or racetrack. The machines appeared everywhere, from pubs to restaurants, shops to reception areas, and the cash poured through them in a cupronickel waterfall. Organised crime took notice.

A few months back, a contact had asked Masa for help in expanding a fledgling racket shaking down the companies that rented out the slot machines. The man brought along a potato sack stuffed with cash to demonstrate the potential profits. Masa was sceptical but passed the offer to his new boss. Pershing liked the idea. 'We went looking through the National Court Register for companies that dealt with gaming machines,' said Masa:

> You wrote down the address and went to the president. The conversation was short: you pay us $100 a month [per machine], and we ensure that the equipment will not be damaged and will work for the benefit of all concerned. If the company had over a thousand machines, it paid only $50. Everyone was happy, after all, 100 or 50 greens was no problem for anyone.

Anyone who wasn't happy had their kneecaps beaten until their mood improved. Later, Pershing bought his own unlicensed machines, forced bar owners to pay $50 a month for the privilege of hosting them and took half the profits. The shakedown business expanded nationwide until the potato sacks were splitting at the seams with cash. Masa estimated that the gang had tens of thousands of machines operating across Poland, with profits of over a million dollars every month.

There was one drawback: Pruszków's tentacles had already probed their way into the business. In 1998, the management board had been approached by representatives from the *Sojusz Lewicy Demokratycznej* (Democratic Left Alliance – SLD), who were a collection of former communists who'd been in power until the last elections. The reps explained, in quiet voices over an expensive meal, that some slot machine companies were important donors to the party and it would be financially beneficial for all concerned if customers in Warsaw dealt only with SLD-approved vendors. Pruszków crews went to war against rival suppliers with baseball bats and the vendors paid $50,000 a month each to maintain their monopoly.

Few victims ever went to the police. Most were terrified by Pruszków's reputation and the few who did try to complain found themselves ignored by a broken system with closer connections to criminals than victims. 'I go to the police station once every ten years,' said a business owner. 'The cutthroats go once a week, so they know them.'

Pershing's rapidly expanding operation inevitably bumped into territory claimed by Pruszków and no one was surprised when the two rackets proved as compatible as sandpaper and skin. Both sides were reluctant to start a war, so Parasol and the others came up with a deal to divide territory between the two gangs and avoid conflict. It was a generous offer from men not known for their flexibility, but Pershing felt powerful enough to push his luck and demand half the monthly payments from SLD-connected vendors. The management board agreed, but couldn't hide their anger.

Pershing was too wrapped up in his growing empire to care. The slots had made him rich, but investments in legitimate businesses, initially for money-laundering purposes, were proving unexpectedly lucrative. A good income came from a Gdynia-based CD-pressing plant that stamped out Disco Polo albums – a genre heavy on cheap dance beats and cheeky titles like '*Majteczki w Kropeczki*' ('Polkadot Panties'). Caricatured as the music of taxi drivers and market-stall holders, Disco Polo was so ubiquitously catchy that even its fiercest haters would rush to the dance floor at weddings after a few vodkas to belt out a chorus. The hunger for CDs of the stuff was huge and Pershing began talking seriously about shifting more of his operation over to the straight world and perhaps one day becoming a law-abiding man of business.

But that was all for the future. In early 1999, he was still the top gangster in Poland. Crews across the country who were formerly loyal to

Pruszków began switching allegiance, including a several hundred-strong mob from Grodzisk Mazowiecki, while up north, a major Szczecin gangster was so happy to be acknowledged by Pershing in a hotel lobby that it 'felt like Christmas in summer'. Anyone who refused to do business received a focused blast of violence, like the Bydgoszcz underworld boss who lost both feet in a car bombing.

The Polish underworld gave Pershing a new nickname: 'Papież' (The Pope). Like all religious leaders, he would soon have to distinguish between true believers and heretics. A member of the management board wanted to defect.

The defining moment of Andrzej Banasiak's life came at 18 years old on a drunken night out with friends in his hometown of Stargard, a city of red-brick buildings and medieval churches in the north-west. The car he crashed into a ditch was stolen, but his friends came from important families, so Banasiak was the only one to end up in prison. 'I found myself among truly depraved people without any scruples,' he said, 'whose only goal in life was to become the best criminal.'

He was a religious man who'd once considered becoming a priest, but three years in prison changed all that. Back on the streets, bitter and ostracised by his family, he wanted only to spit in society's face as a professional crook. Banasiak picked up the nickname 'Słowik' after breaking into a grocery store of the same name, but he couldn't stay out of prison long and was soon back among the depraved. He insisted that prison made him into a criminal ('they rebuilt my value system'), but Słowik enthusiastically pursued the life, establishing himself as a tough *Git-Ludzie* behind bars then moving to Warsaw to rob warehouses as one half of an inseparable double act with Bolo. He'd spent less than a year of his adult life outside prison by the time communism fell in 1989 and a more lenient regime granted him Christmas leave, unaware that Słowik had no intention of coming back.

Bolo joined the emerging Pruszków mob and became an important figure. He opened the door to his friend, whose ruthless approach to debt collection impressed the troglodytes enough for a rapid rise up the hierarchy. Short and neat, Słowik hid his ruthlessness behind a deceptively charming façade. 'He was a genius at manipulating people,' Jarosław Maringe remembered:

> And he usually seemed like a nice person. But I remember an incident when his benevolent mask fell off [at a meeting]. And for the first time in Słowik I saw the look of a murderer. He had the eyes of someone who had murdered or will murder someone. That's how I perceived it, that's how I felt. It gave me shivers then. He wasn't so nice then, or as outgoing and witty as usual. Evil emanated from him.

A pardon from Lech Wałęsa solved the prison escape issue, but in May 1998, Słowik found himself back in a cell alongside Wańka for the illegal takeover of the Dekadent nightclub years earlier. A well-compensated doctor provided a medical certificate that was alarming enough to persuade the authorities that immediate bail was the only thing standing between Słowik and permanent crippling pain. Wheeled out of the prison gates the next year, his first move was to make a miraculous recovery and approach Pershing.

It seemed obvious to everyone that Słowik was a Trojan horse that had been left at the city gates by Pruszków, but Pershing thought differently. His sidekicks couldn't convince him, not even when they explained how Słowik was doubly dangerous because he told his wife everything. The Polish underworld was a patriarchal, often misogynist, place where women were expected to ask no questions, bring up the kids and spend their leisure time gossiping over a cigarette in beauty salons. '[Y]ou don't wake up a sleeping dog,' said a gangster's wife. 'Better not to ask questions you don't want answered.' Słowik's marriage was one of the rare exceptions, like Żaba and Baśka's double act or the time Masa's wife carefully washed a bloodstained baseball bat he'd dropped by the front door after a long night of brutality.

Słowik had married Monika Zielińska, in flashy mobster style, in Las Vegas and then again, in a quieter religious ceremony in Nazareth, Israel, to satisfy his spiritual side. Fond of tanning beds and cigarillos, Monika had ducked out on her artistically inclined family, left an unexciting fiancé at the altar and ended up as secretary for a Pruszków front business where Słowik was a regular visitor. They fell hard for each other and the marriage was a strange mix of sexual abandon, church-going and pampered mothering. Masa used to joke that Monika practically wiped Słowik's nose before her husband set off to accomplish some especially hardcore underworld task.

She was involved enough in the life to be briefly kidnapped by rival gangsters and then targeted in the November 1996 bombing attempt. She said:

> When we were a few steps from the building stairwell, boom! The charge was buried in the ground, so no one saw anything suspicious. Those who wanted to kill us detonated it from a distance. It was like an explosive geyser, the bang is unbelievable! The bomb crater was large enough you could hide in it.

The would-be assassins took off running as a bloody Słowik pulled a pistol from his jeans and staggered after them shouting, 'Don't run, you motherfuckers, look me in the eye, cowards!' Monika noted the back of his jeans was threadbare from carrying a gun every day, then fainted.

The pair spent more time abroad after the attack. In Miami, they draped themselves in Cartier jewellery while eating lobster and truffles. Monika bought designer clothes and Thierry Mugler's Angel perfume, and together they watched polo matches in Jamaica and played golf in Aruba. There were exclusive restaurants in Japan and luxury hotels in Monte Carlo.

Earlier foreign trips had been less relaxing. The pair spent time in Colombia as human collateral at an early stage of the *Jurata* cocaine deal and were lucky to be back in Poland when things went wrong and Wańka had to settle accounts with some angry Colombians. Then it was prison for Słowik, bail and a visit to Ożarów.

Pershing didn't care about Słowik's unconventional marriage or the suspicions of his underlings and welcomed the Pruszków man on board. The reasoning behind the decision was never clear, even to the inner circle, but a crony of Masa probably had it right when he said simply, 'Pershing was a very trusting man and Słowik easily convinced him of his friendship'. The new arrival became a permanent fixture at gang meetings, listening hard as details of their operations were discussed and making darkly funny asides about mutual contacts.

The gang had plenty to discuss. A former senator was fishing for investment to establish a tax-free zone on the border that would make smuggling easier and even technically legal; someone else important wanted Pershing to recover a $500,000 debt from the disgraced politician Sekuła; and the slot machine rackets were bringing in more money than anyone thought possible. The future looked bright, even if a few gangsters saw dark clouds boiling in the distant sky. 'The [Pruszków management board] weren't going to be content with the scraps when Pershing and Masa were drinking the financial cream,' warned an Ożarów member.

Masa viewed Słowik with even more suspicion than most but knew better than to contradict his boss. He preferred to concentrate on what was rapidly becoming Warsaw's biggest nightspot. Klub Planet was where celebrities came to be seen, the club kids came to dance and American basketball stars chased women. Masa owned a lucrative piece of the action and was getting dangerously close to becoming a legitimate businessman.

16

Planet Masa

The crowds outside the night club parted like the Red Sea whenever he lumbered towards the entrance. No waiting in queues for Masa and his bodyguards: just a short walk from the Mercedes to the main doors of Klub Planet, with perhaps a brief stop on the way to pick one of the pretty girls shivering in thin dresses to be his companion for the night. Most would happily abandon their boyfriends for a chance to party in the VIP room. Then Masa would swagger inside the cavernous three-storey nightspot in the western outskirts of the capital like he owned the place.

Under communism the building had been a factory producing tank parts but now its high ceilings and wide-open spaces housed a booming superclub that could fit 4,000 sweaty dancers on a good night. Clubbers entered through airport-style metal detectors where meaty bouncers scanned them for weapons and transgressions of the smart-casual dress code. No trainers, no tracksuits, no negotiation. Then Masa and his entourage plunged into the dark interior throbbing with bodies and noise and a soundsystem loud enough to drown out a war. 'Techno music pumps from speakers everywhere, even under the floor,' reported a British journalist from *The Independent*. 'Your sternum throbs in time. The walls vibrate. The only lighting is the strobes and lasers.'

The nightspot Masa jovially called a 'cave of debauchery' had been born from the closure of the old Colosseum Club on ul. Górczewska, a leaky blue and white circus tent with no air conditioning run by some expat Germanic DJs. A death trap from the start, the club had managed to fight off countless termination orders from the local authorities while still hosting performances by surprisingly top-shelf Western bands like the Beastie Boys and Black Sabbath. The owners finally gave up the fight in autumn 1997 and shuttered Colosseum with a farewell live broadcast of local boy Andrzej Gołota taking on Lennox Lewis for the WBA Heavyweight Boxing Championship in Atlantic City. Clubbers watched Pershing's old friend get knocked out in ninety-five seconds, then danced all night.

Planet was the bigger, better sequel to Colosseum that introduced Polish clubbers to the delights of a Western-style superclub. It took serious financing to put together, but the pain was softened by big money paid upfront for product placement by brewers and cigarette companies before the club opened. Everyone knew Planet was going to be a success, including the executives at MTV, who greenlit a series to showcase live performances by big-name bands when the club was little more than blueprints and hope.

On opening night, half of Warsaw fought its way inside and celebrities packed the VIP lounge overlooking the dance floor. International figures would soon be making regular stops at Planet, including the son of Libyan dictator Colonel Muammar Gaddafi and a famous American basketball star. A rare black visitor to a country still almost untouched by global migration, the American walked through the doors and immediately demanded a cigar, cocaine and a girl. Masa hustled over to oblige with such authority that everyone assumed he must be the club owner.

On paper, the official boss of Planet was former Colosseum man Andy Edlinger. The Austrian DJ and entrepreneur told reporters that Masa was simply an investor who'd provided some of the finance necessary to get the place up and running. Masa claimed to be a 'silent partner' in media interviews, although one who clearly had trouble keeping quiet, while other gangsters were under the impression he was the real owner. Whatever the truth, the big gangster was a frequent visitor who never seemed to pay for drinks. Sometimes, Edlinger wished his investor would find somewhere else to hang out, but Masa's presence proved useful whenever an eccentric basketball star with bleached-blond curls turned up demanding drugs and women.

Officially, the club had a zero-tolerance policy to drugs (even if Masa would later claim to have once smoked dope backstage with a member of a famous British all-girl group following a promotional performance), but a packet of white powder was quickly located for the American sports star. The search couldn't have taken long if Słowik was correct that 'in the restrooms, Masa peeped through a barely visible window in the ceiling, noting who was taking drugs and whether the drugs had been bought from him'. True or not, the American had a good night and one that got even better when a pretty barmaid shimmied over to entertain him.

Planet had seven bars staffed by twenty-one barmaids earning 50 złotys a night but often taking home as much as 1,000zł in tips. Polish clubber tastes were unsophisticated and the staff earned their money for doing little more than serving up vodka shots or mixing orange juice and spirit in a highball glass. Efforts by foreign drinks firms to introduce modern cocktails were greeted with astonishment by a clientele who regarded lemon wedges as the height of sophistication. 'The customers had never seen anything like this,' remembered *The Independent* journalist. 'One stared at a bottle of Angostura as if it had fallen from outer space.'

Masa sometimes boasted that the bar girls did more than just serve drinks and cosy up to celebrities – they were also sexually available to himself and his guests. Edlinger denied the claim but no one who knew Masa's Stone Age attitude towards women would have been shocked to find it true. He expected bar girls to provide oral sex on a rota basis, just as he expected the dancing girls in local go-go clubs to sexually service his gangster crew once a wad of dollar bills had been thrown on the floor.

One night, the go-go dancers fled when Masa's men arrived, so he went hunting for them in the basement storerooms by the flame of a cigarette lighter ('this brought to mind films about the wartime occupation and the SS men who fished out people hiding in dark cellars,' he said), then ordered the girls to line up, strip and give oral sex to the crew. Masa insisted this was simply a business transaction, even if most decent human beings would call it something else.

At least Masa kept the worst of his debauchery out of the family home. 'A wife is a wife; a piece of ass is a piece of ass,' he said. 'These are two very different things.'

His wife Ela was a quiet woman who'd been with Masa since both were young teens. Friends claimed she sometimes wore dark glasses to hide the black eyes when her husband's alcoholism tipped over into domestic violence. They begged her to start a new life with the kids far away, but Ela tolerated the abuse, perhaps because ending the marriage would mean saying goodbye to their new but much-loved $2 million three-storey house of marble and gold in Komorów: an area popular with celebrities known as the 'Polish Beverley Hills'.

Not many Poles got to live in a home with a fountain in the foyer and a 2,000-litre aquarium filled with piranha fish. Downstairs was a disco for friends and family, called 'Masalandia' by her egomaniac husband, full of chrome piping and grey walls, dominated by a full-scale bar shimmering with bottles of exotic liquor. The speakers alone cost $17,000 and the sound system in the nearby home cinema was powerful enough to shake the foundations when the volume was dialled up. 'No government office ever had such splendour!' said Masa, a man with limited cultural references.

Ela found it equally hard to walk away from other perks, like the day Masa spent 1.3 million złotys ($325,000) in cash to buy three top models at a Warsaw Mercedes dealership or the time the entire Legia football team from the capital came to her teenage son's birthday party with a signed shirt in his name. But a wife's craving for love and respect can only be sated by luxuries for so long, and eventually she would kick Masa out of the house when one of his binges turned more violent than usual. For a few weeks he drank himself half to death then begged her to reconsider with promises to see a doctor for Esperal implants to fight his alcoholism.

Ela gave the marriage another chance, to her friends' disgust, and Masa redirected his taste for domestic violence towards more willing victims at a brothel he owned. 'Some of the ladies also demanded that they be handcuffed and beaten with a leather whip; this was what I did with great skill, especially when I brought to mind the image of a debtor chained to a tree in the woods.'

Masa's reformed act extended to telling journalists he'd quit crime and was supporting himself purely from legitimate business. In reality, Planet was struggling and the 100,000zł previously earned in a week was now taking a month to arrive. The reason was simple: clubbers were getting poorer. Poland had finally achieved its dream of joining NATO and was on track to become part of the European Union by 2004, but the reforms required had sent inflation and unemployment soaring until even the party people of Warsaw couldn't afford regular nights out.

Masa's real wealth came from crime, as it always had done, and within the Ożarów gang he prided himself on running a crew so fanatically loyal that a drunken Bysio once had to be physically prevented from sawing off a finger during a party to prove his devotion. 'It's like a game,' said a gangster who worked for Masa:

> He keeps you on a leash and you remind him that the dog needs to be fed and petted occasionally. He counts on you, you can count on him. You earn money for him, he gives you such a good deal that you want to keep bringing him this money.

As the spring of 1999 warmed up, life was good. Masa had a string of front businesses, a place in Pershing's criminal empire, a marriage that might still work and more money than he knew how to spend. Within a year his life would be in ruins.

The first rumblings of the earthquake that would bring down the Polish underworld were heard on 31 March 1999 at the Gama restaurant, a *pierogi* and fried cutlet place on the ground floor of an apartment block in west Warsaw. An unglamorous combination of beige awning, pale yellow brickwork and the usual net curtains ensured the Gama never attracted much passing custom.

On a chilly spring day, the place was mostly empty as five men ate *pierogi* and discussed business over a cheap red tablecloth at one of the window tables. The two older, menacing figures were Wołomin bosses Maniek and Lutek, and the other three subordinates going by the names 'Piguła' (Pill), 'Kurczak' (Chicken) and 'Łysy' (Bald). The Gama's lack of clientele didn't bother men who preferred not to be overheard.

Just before 13:00 a potential customer walked through the front bar and into the restaurant, looked around and quickly left. Maniek and the others barely looked up from their lunch. Then three men in black balaclavas ran into the back room with shotguns and blasted the gangsters out of their chairs. When the police arrived, the floor was ankle deep in a soup of blood, mushy *pierogi* and water spurting from pellet holes in a radiator.

The Gama massacre was the climax of a fierce internal feud among Wołomin gangsters which had started with a slap. Over the last year, Maniek and Lutek had been expanding into territory once held by their former colleague Wariat and had big plans that involved serious talk with Pershing about joining forces. The merger would have changed the face of Polish crime, but hardman Maniek had a taste for pushing around junior members of his crew and made the mistake of smacking Karol Sarna, aka 'Karolek', across the face in a row over money. The insult would not be forgiven by his partisans.

In December 1998, a bomb was placed under Maniek's car outside the Géant hypermarket on Praga's ul. Jubilerska, which succeeded only in putting his chauffeur in hospital. On 6 January, some of Maniek's cronies were talking by the side of the road when a Dodge truck drove slowly past and someone inside sprayed automatic fire through the open window. One gangster was killed and two wounded. Two months later, another Maniek loyalist barely escaped death when attempts to lure him into the concrete plaza outside the TGI Fridays near Hala Mirowska in central Warsaw failed and gunmen shot dead an innocent man who strolled out the front door at the wrong moment.

Maniek was feeling more fragile than one of the porcelain cat figurines littering his house when he called an inner circle meeting at the Gama restaurant on the last day of March. He had been passing a photograph of Karolek around the table to prep his underlings for a hit when gunmen burst in and ended the conversation. Karolek immediately reached out to Pruszków, looking to get support for his new role as Wołomin leader and a meeting was arranged at a restaurant. Masa was present as part of some effort to keep the peace between his old bosses and Ożarów.

As the vodka slipped down easily, Karolek revealed more about the hit than he should have done. 'I remember that at one point Karol turned to [Bolo] and said that without your help it wouldn't have happened,' Masa remembered. 'It followed that the management board helped target Maniek.'

He hurried away to tell Pershing that the Gama massacre had been less about internal score settling and more an oblique warning for

Ożarów not to extend its territory east of the river. Pershing wasn't sure Karolek's words supported that interpretation but agreed that Pruszków had been in a dangerous mood since the contentious slot machine deal. The shooting had come less than a month after Pruszków man Zbigniew Szczepaniak, alias Simon, who ran the gang's operations down in Katowice, was enticed outside his restaurant Zielone Oczko (The Green Eye) by a phone call from a trusted source. He immediately regretted it.

Simon got his nickname from a local prostitute who thought him dark and good-looking enough to resemble Simon Templar, the hero of television programme *The Saint*. The real Simon was the opposite of his fictional crime-fighting namesake in every way, running a construction company as cover for his citywide protection rackets and drug networks. In 1996, he slipped up and spent two years in prison, then got out to discover Pruszków suspected him of skimming money. His improbably cheerful denials only made things worse.

On 5 March 1999, Simon walked out of the Zielone Oczko and climbed into his Audi A6. He was in the leather seat and plugging a key into the ignition when someone fired through the windscreen. One bullet hit his heart and Simon died in hospital three days later.

At the funeral, over 200 mourners listened as the priest lectured them about morality, 'I appeal to all people involved in the structures of evil: gang members, rapists, drug dealers. Stop doing evil. Be reconciled with God and your neighbours.' The congregation bowed their heads and ignored his words.

Shortly after, a member of Malizna's team called Ryszard Bogucki, a former associate of Nikoś who'd switched sides when his boss died, took over the Katowice operation.

Pershing understood that a gang which punished its own members like that would treat enemies even worse and tried to remain on good terms with Pruszków, at least outwardly and often to the surprise of his own people. Florek remembered partying at the Polonia hotel, a favourite hangout, when management board members settled at a nearby table. 'Did you invite them?' Florek asked, getting up to start trouble. But he was verbally slapped down by Pershing, 'Sit back on your arse. They're brothers, they can party with us.'

All that changed in early summer 1999 when Pershing got into a drunken fight with Malizna after a pointless argument in a Sopot nightclub. The Ożarów boss beat up the former taxi driver and rang Florek afterwards to spread the word: 'I gave Malizna a slap on the head in front of everyone and now he's finished. From now on, even you don't have to respect him.'

A coke-numbed Malizna boasted about the fight for a while as proof of his toughness, but then the drugs wore off and resentment took over. He began talking openly about revenge. Things escalated.

At 10:15 on the hot summer morning of 6 June, a T-shirt-wearing Parasol was strolling through the car park of his Pruszków apartment block when a gun barked behind him. Parasol was hit in the back, turned to see a hooded figure and ran as more shots slammed into his lungs and liver. He made it around a corner, hailed a taxi and went to hospital bleeding over the back seat.

For the next few weeks, gangster bodyguards crowded out the ward as the patient recovered and even Pershing made a visit, taking away a bloodstained T-shirt for Jackowski to soothsay over and discover who'd been responsible. Parasol gave a thin smile, already convinced someone connected to Ożarów had pulled the trigger. Warsaw braced itself for a war between the 1,000 core gangsters loyal to Pruszków and the 500 hardmen under Pershing.

Tension remained high as summer turned into autumn and the biting cold swept down from the north. One of Jarosław Maringe's dealers was stabbed and dumped outside a hospital to die, but the violence never boiled over into carbombs and shootouts, thanks to the unexpected appearance of a third force. Not long after the attack on Parasol, the *Urząd Ochrony Państwa* (Office of State Protection – UOP) secret service had been alerted about threats made by a drunken Pershing to kill Polish President Aleksander Kwaśniewski.

An election was due next year, and the government was trailing the SLD. In desperation, Kwaśniewski's allies were curbing the slot machine business to reduce their opponents' war chest and inadvertently damaged Pershing's income at the same time.

Under normal circumstances, no one would have cared about a boozy threat, but this was a crime boss talking not long after the murder of former police chief Marek Papała. The UOP initiated surveillance on Pershing that was obvious enough for the underworld to back off from total war. No one wanted to provoke the leviathan of the secret services.

That November, Pershing headed to Atlantic City in America to take care of some business far from the problems of rival gangs and law enforcement. He left Słowik in charge. The two were closer than ever after the former Pruszków man introduced him to a girl called Patrycja during a drunken evening out in the coastal town of Ustka. Pershing hoped to spend a weekend skiing with her in Zakopane on his return.

17

Who Killed Pershing?

Back in the bad old days of prohibition, this salty resort town had been a magnet for anyone who enjoyed beaches, boardwalks and gallons of illegal booze served up by scar-faced gangsters with the police in their pocket. Atlantic City prided itself on being a magnet for human weakness.

Hard times swept in when prohibition was repealed, until the locals spotted a different kind of vice to exploit and legalised gambling. Big sporting events brought in the crowds and the card sharks sent them home poor. By November 1999, the Jersey Shore hotspot was a circuit board of neon-lit casinos hosting overflow crowds for the big fight between Polish boxer Andrzej Gołota and talented black heavyweight Michael Grant at the Taj Mahal Hotel.

The cable television cameras caught Gołota clumsily crossing himself with gloved hands as his seconds stripped off a white and red satin robe, like a deconstructed Polish flag. He'd been living in America for nearly a decade now but had never forgotten his roots. Relaxed-looking opponent Michael Grant jogged down the aisle, wriggling his shoulders to a dance track and pumping a gloved fist into the air from the corner post as the capacity crowd cheered hard. Grant's manager had a title fight lined up for next April and no one, except the more optimistic members of Gołota's entourage, expected the American to lose tonight. '[Gołota] will beat him like a dog,' predicted the Pole's manager, Ziggy Rozalski, to smirks from the bookmakers.

Then the usual lecture from the referee, the excited talk in the commentary box and the bell for round one. Sitting in the audience three rows behind Taj Mahal owner Donald Trump was a large, bald man in a black suit and glasses, who watched intently as the boxers shuffled into the centre of the ring with their fists up. Pershing had $70,000 on his old friend to win.

As far as the immigration authorities were concerned, Andrzej Kolikowski was a Polish businessman who had flown in to attend the fight and get some long overdue dental work done. The UOP spies might have sketched a different narrative, but their surveillance had ended, so no one was watching when Pershing slipped away to discuss money-laundering opportunities with local gangsters.

His psychic friend Jackowski occasionally attended to predict potential double-crosses with his otherworldly powers, but mostly just gawped at the attendees. 'Pershing suggested, "Let's go meet the minister"', remembered Jackowski:

It was then, in an Italian restaurant, that I met the [Polish] sports minister, Jacek Dębski. His name meant nothing to me then. With him were two businessman-looking Poles and an Italian. Pershing claimed [the Italian] was a high-ranking Cosa Nostra mafioso. Another person in this respectable group was a young, slim guy. 'Krzych, take a good look at that skinny one,' Pershing whispered in my ear. 'He's Al Capone's grandson.'

Then it was back to swaggering down the boardwalk in flashy tracksuits pretending to be tourists, surrounded by a phalanx of bodyguards. Pershing looked confident as ever, but cracks were starting to appear in the façade. Every morning, he neurotically counted and recounted his thick rolls of dollar bills, seeking some significance in the parade of presidents and monuments flicking through his fingers. The bodyguards assumed the habit had some connection to Pershing's platinum credit card being constantly scrutinised by staff who didn't associate Polish names with a high credit score. Only Jackowski recognised it as a neurotic tic.

The end of UOP surveillance had unfrozen the conflict with Pruszków and phone calls from back home were full of bad news. Florek's car had been blown up in front of his apartment after a row with Malizna, but the chauffeur escaped unhurt. Słowik oversaw peace negotiations that supposedly eased the tension, but Florek remained wary, and another Pershing bodyguard would soon be murdered with his girlfriend in the Wola district.

It was clear to everyone that a full-scale gang war was coming ever closer, like a shark fin gliding towards a swimmer, and the stress was starting to show. Behind the closed doors of his hotel suite, Pershing spent hours in the bathroom, scrubbing his skin clean, then pink, then red raw. He had recurring nightmares about being attacked at home and running around unable to find a gun with which to defend himself.

Jackowski provided a sympathetic ear but didn't help much by sharing a psychic vision of Pershing being gunned down outside a Warsaw hotel. He managed to reassure the gang boss that avoiding that location would outfox the evil spirits on his tail. The advice calmed Pershing down and by 20 November he was closer to his old, confident self, as Gołota and Grant lumbered towards each other for round one.

The Pole knocked down his opponent at the two-minute, eleven-second mark and left Grant sitting on the canvas with his elbows on his knees looking sheepish. Out in the audience Pershing leapt to his feet cheering. Another punch from Gołota sent his opponent sprawling into the corner post as the round ended and had Pershing jumping up and down with excitement. It was 'like horses fighting', thought Jackowski, as heavyweight sweat and blood sprayed over the front rows.

Some right hooks by Gołota in round two sent Grant's legs wobbling but the American had recovered by the time the bell rang. In the third round, Gołota got a warning for a low blow – an intervention some thought unfair as Grant's shorts were pulled up so high that anything below the nostrils looked like a foul. Hopes of a quick ending faded as the American rediscovered his grit and began to fight back. Over the next seven rounds the bald man in the black suit jumped to his feet less often.

By round ten, the judges still had Gołota ahead on points but then Grant unleashed the firepower with a heavy right hook and a battery of targeted strikes that sent his opponent crashing around the ring and to the floor. Gołota staggered up groggily and was asked by the referee if he wanted to continue, but just shook his head and muttered, 'No'. The fight was over: technical knock-out.

Grant's supporters hooted and cheered around the arena while the Polish fans sank deflated into their seats and lowered the white and red flags that looked like snow settling on blood. Pershing gave a bunch of flowers to Gołota after every fight and dutifully got up to push through the crowds towards the ring. Then the reality of the loss hit him as he waited in line and the gangster threw the flowers to the floor and strode off.

In the following days, Pershing and his entourage moved on to Las Vegas, where the gang boss lost $180,000 at the tables in a miserable end to a disappointing trip. Back in Warsaw, their car convoy was stopped leaving Okęcie Airport by police and soldiers who held them at gunpoint by the roadside as identity cards were checked. Pershing was so sure of arrest that he handed an expensive gold watch to Jackowski for safekeeping, but after an hour of questioning the officers let them go.

Jackowski stayed in Ożarów that night. The next day, Pershing took him to a studio apartment that had been recently acquired to settle a debt and demonstrated how the suits hanging in a closet slid aside to reveal a secret door. Behind was an enclosed room with a bar, which Pershing admitted was the only place in the world he felt truly safe. As they sat and drank, Pershing reminded the psychic to copy a video he'd made of their Las Vegas trip, with its fountains, hotels and street bustle, on to a VHS tape for him to watch later. Despite the losses and stress, he'd enjoyed his time abroad. Then they hugged and parted ways.

In the opening days of December, Pershing avoided Warsaw and spent time on the Baltic coast, where Nikoś' successors were debating whether to join forces with his crew or Pruszków. Negotiations were interrupted by local police following Pershing around and constantly asking for identification – a targeted harassment that had never happened before.

He put the talks on hold, rented a Mercedes S500 and picked up Patrycja for a weekend skiing down south. En route to Zakopane, he stopped off at a McDonald's for a last bit of business, where Masa saw him moving from plastic tabletop to plastic tabletop, shaking hands with members of a Łódz gang who'd agreed to transfer their loyalty away from Malizna. The gang boss seemed self-conscious of the new teeth he'd got in America, so white and Hollywood they shone from his mouth like a searchlight. Then he drove off with Patrycja in the passenger seat and no bodyguard in sight.

Florek had been supposed to accompany the pair but had trouble locating a new car and set off late. He ran into a sudden snowstorm that had him sliding all over the road and abandoned the trip to Zakopane.

His boss didn't seem to mind when they spoke on the phone, explaining that a local fixer called Wiesław would be providing security for him and his little 'mouse' this weekend.

Pershing and Patrycja ate a meal in a highlander restaurant that evening and looked forward to skiing away the weekend. The snow lay like whipped cream across the slopes. It was Friday, 3 December.

On Sunday afternoon, Masa's phone buzzed by his plate and then Bedzio was on the line saying the boss had been shot and was on his way to hospital. Local man Wiesław had rung from the Kasprowy car park as the ambulance peeled away. The friends and family Masa was treating to an old-school Polish lunch at the Kredens restaurant in central Warsaw watched in astonishment as he lumbered to his feet in panic and rushed out, convinced the killers would come for him next. 'After Bedzio's phone call,' he said, 'I immediately went home to Komorów, called [my bodyguard] Bysiu and told him that there would be security guards at my house twenty-four hours a day.'

The surgeons did their best in the Zakopane trauma room, but Pershing's skull had cracked like an egg and soon Bedzio was ringing back to say the boss had died on the operating table. News spread fast. Florek got a call at the Alamo steak house in Warsaw from Pershing's long-time girlfriend. The fork fell out of his mouth and clattered to the tabletop as Agnieszka sobbed down the phone.

Of all Pershing's lieutenants, Florek felt the loss the hardest. He'd grown up in an orphanage: a vicious, deprived world that turned him into a muscular adult with a bottomless reservoir of rage. He drifted into Pershing's orbit through petty crime at the Bazar Różyckiego ('personally I was a supporter of the educational use of objects such as a stick or a chair leg,' he recalled. 'Not too much, but enough for a successful result.') then a stay in prison.

He officially joined the gang in 1991 after some business involving a stolen car and went on to discover his true purpose in life by serving Pershing as a chauffeur, bodyguard and factotum. The big man had been a substitute father after an upbringing without one, but the phone call turned Florek into a devastated 35-year-old orphan.

He was part of the Ożarów team led by Bedzio that drove down to Zakopane later that day to interrogate Wiesław; the fixer had been sitting in the Mercedes at the time of the murder and remembered a figure in ski goggles wagging a finger at him through the window to warn against any heroics. Afterwards, the team just missed grabbing Patrycja before the police took her into custody, then stood miserably around the Kasprowy car park as the crime scene tarpaulins came down to reveal Pershing's Mercedes and a dark red stain on the snow.

Bedzio locked his own grief deep inside that solemn, pudgy face on the endless drives back and forth between Warsaw and Zakopane to locate anyone who could identify the killers. A car thief claimed to have seen them and talked about distinctive tattoos. Someone else suggested the hit had been revenge by the karate enthusiasts who had been tortured with an electric drill all those years ago; others, that Wariat loyalists had revenged their dead boss or the Colombian cartel involved in the *Jurata* had reappeared to settle accounts.

Bedzio discounted most rumours but established that Patrycja had been a sidepiece girlfriend of Słowik until recently and was rumoured to still be infatuated with him. From that point on, the Mafia murder mystery didn't seem hard to solve, especially when Ożarów affiliates around the country reported visits by tough strangers announcing a change of leadership. 'I started receiving calls from various people that the management board were coming in and taking over Andrzej's business,' remembered Masa. 'I also met with Bedzio, who told me that the board killed Andrzej and had taken over all his interests. He was with me when Parasol called and insulted Bedzio and told him that he would soon be lying next to Pershing.'

The final tile in the game flipped over when Bedzio heard about a trio who'd arrived in a stolen car the day before the shooting and registered under false names at a Zakopane hotel. One was identified as Malizna acolyte Ryszard Bogucki, who'd fled for Mexico within days of the murder. Afterwards, Ożarów street soldiers gathered in a chilly cemetery where Masa handed out weapons from the boot of a car and ordered them to find Słowik.

In the middle of this chaos, they said goodbye to the boss at a quiet, intimate ceremony in a freezing church, followed by cremation. Bedzio and Pershing's daughter Magda could finally be open about the relationship they'd been keeping secret for months and he showed his love with a promise that no photographs of her father's funeral or corpse would find their way to the media. The promise was kept, although no one knew how he'd managed it with Pershing's death being on the front page of every Polish newspaper and reported in foreign publications as distant as Britain's *The Independent* and *The Gazette* of Montreal, Canada. The only pictures to escape into the wild showed the Mercedes in the snowy Kasprowy car park. Magda was grateful for Bedzio's efforts but couldn't stop thinking about her father in the mortuary: 'He looked like he was sleeping [...] just that trickle of blood from his ear.'

Plans for revenge derailed on 8 December when the police issued an arrest warrant for Masa on an extortion charge, and he fled to Silesia in the south-west. While in hiding and worried for his family, he reached out to the management board and received an earful of persuasion and threats. 'I think it was two or three days before Christmas Eve,' he said:

> I called Pawlik [i.e Krzyś] from my mobile [...] It turned out that Pawlik was eating herring at that time in a restaurant in Saska Kępa on ul. Paryska. At some point, Pawlik gave the receiver to Szwarc [i.e. Kajtek], who said to me 'Jarek what are you doing, don't hide from us, we need to sit down at the table and talk'. He also said that if I didn't agree to their terms, and I quote, 'they'll take you away like Pershing'.

Other Ożarów members and affiliates had already accepted the new order and transferred their allegiance to Pruszków. Masa might have swallowed his distrust and followed them, but then the police swooped in to lead the big gangster away in handcuffs while the rest of Poland geared up to celebrate the New Year. His crew found themselves surrounded by enemies in Pruszków and, accepting the inevitable, rejoined the gang under the command of Parasol. The following month, Ryszard Bogucki was arrested in Mexico but fought extradition hard, apparently more afraid of assassination than jail.

Bedzio tried to keep the gang's territory intact around Warsaw but couldn't stop Malizna muscling in on the $500,000 debt owed by former politician and one-time PRL deputy prime minister Ireneusz Sekuła. He muscled too hard and on 23 March 2000 Sekuła, who had serious drug and alcohol problems along with other debts, died by suicide in his Warsaw office. Conspiratorially minded Poles got suspicious when they heard Sekuła had shot himself twice in the stomach and once in the heart, but the police dismissed accusations of murder.

Not long after, Bolo invited Bedzio to bring the remains of his crew into the welcoming arms of Pruszków or be exiled forever from the capital. During the conversation, Bolo admitted that members of the management board had ordered Pershing's murder. In response, an Ożarów team blew up his car that May and put the Pruszków leader in hospital with serious leg injuries.

More conflict seemed unavoidable, but Bedzio understood a war with Pruszków was unwinnable and stepped back to reorganise, eventually concluding that the time for revenge had passed. Not all Pershing loyalists agreed. Florek criss-crossed Warsaw trying to put together a coalition to fight the management board, but soon discovered it wasn't going to work: 'I was too weak – let's say – politically. Besides, I was not the type for wet jobs [i.e. murder].'

Another Ożarów clique, many of them former policemen turned gangsters, blew up the Spartakus restaurant and killed a bystander as part of a plot to trigger a gang war across Warsaw that would blow back on the management board. The plan faltered and faded away.

Krzysztof Jackowski seemed the only one of Pershing's friends not calling down vengeance on his killers and instead quietly mourned the dead man from a hiding place in the south of Poland. The police had advised him to take a long holiday to avoid any potential score settling. Jackowski preferred to remember the Ożarów leader not as a Mafia boss, but as a more romantic figure, far removed from all the broken bones and car bombs. 'He was a really nice guy!' said Jackowski. 'Just a little lost [...] well, about women. He was surrounded by crowds of beautiful girls, but he was looking for true love.'

By the summer of 2000, the Pruszków Mafia were running Poland again, bigger and more powerful than ever. The management board could congratulate themselves on having taken out their chief rival, absorbed his territory and humbled his loyalists. The new millennium lay there for the taking.

Victory tasted sweet but evaporated quickly. On 24 August, police raids rounded up Parasol, Wańka and Bolo, along with twenty other leading members of the gang. Malizna and Kajtek escaped but were arrested soon after, while Słowik went on the run in Spain after leaving his wife behind to stonewall the authorities. Few were surprised when Malizna, the coke-snorting former taxi driver and 'Don Corleone of Mazowieckie', as Masa mockingly called him, was charged with ordering Pershing's death. Bedzio was in no position to take revenge after being arrested with other Ożarów members in a separate raid.

By November of the next year, Jarosław Maringe was the last man standing. After fleeing Bulgaria, he'd become a drug baron at the head of a global smuggling empire and was flying back into Stockholm to finalise the biggest deal of his life. He didn't realise the tall, blond men who'd been sitting near him ever since the plane left the Dominican Republic were undercover police and everything he'd created was about to come crashing down.

V

POLSKA STRIKES BACK, 2001–03

18

Interpol Red Notice

The Serbian visitor found him sitting at a desk inside an airfield hangar somewhere in northern Norway. Jarosław Maringe was wrapped in a fur coat, smoking a cigar and saying his goodbyes to two beautiful blonde girls. Behind him sat a stack of Louis Vuitton luggage packed with almost $1 million in cash. It was the autumn of 2001 and the Serb was the only person with the political connections and private jet necessary to get Maringe out of Scandinavia before the police arrived.

Maringe had touched down in Stockholm earlier that year, glad to leave Bulgaria and the heroin trade behind. Żaba's promises to buy out his share of the business had vanished the moment they parted company, but there was no point making threats when the police had rounded up the Sofia operation not long after. Maringe's old crew had annoyed some powerful people and it wasn't a coincidence that the Bulgarian authorities suddenly remembered about those Interpol Red Notices for anyone connected to Pruszków. He'd got out just in time.

The Swedish capital offered a fresh, chilly start for a man on the run and Maringe spent his first days after landing at Arlanda Airport drifting through the streets marvelling at the clean roads, beautiful buildings and well-stocked shops. Swedes claimed to be an honest people and official figures proved them right. In the five years since 1995, crime had increased by only 2 per cent and convictions for both drug trafficking and homicide were down. Maringe had found an affluent, placid social democrat paradise just begging for a crook like him to take advantage.

At first he kept a low profile, living in the spare room of a Polish friend's apartment and limiting his hellraising to a brief holiday at the small ski resort of Salen, where road signs warned motorists not to brake for reindeer. He sliced down the pillowy snow of the slopes, chatted up local girls and watched amazed as a jug of hot water emptied outside turned to ice before it hit the ground.

Life was peaceful and relaxed, but then Maringe came back to Stockholm and the old gangster itch soon returned after a few weeks of sitting around the apartment like 'a vegetable in a gilded cage'. 'I never wanted to be a grey person,' said Maringe, looking to justify his return to criminality. 'I did many things in my life to rise above the boring, grey masses.'

His friend had a sideline smuggling in spirits from Eastern Europe to undercut the overpriced, overtaxed local products. Maringe saw an opportunity to apply a similar methodology to the more profitable contraband of narcotics. He built a crew around a core of Balkan Route veterans and consulted with a veteran crook who went by the name 'Kartofel' (Potato) and had been a player in the 1970s Warsaw underworld.

Kartofel advised him to forget about harder drugs for the time being and concentrate on amphetamine. Its bitter chemical tang was popular with Swedish clubbers, who liked to stay wide awake and paranoid until the early hours.

The operation made good money at first, but Maringe managed to offend local decorum by speeding around in an expensive car, flashing a knife at anyone who crossed him and holding indiscreet phone calls with contacts back home. Neighbours began wondering what he did for a living.

Before the police could take an interest, a bout of petty, drug-fuelled resentment ripped the crew apart and resulted in Maringe being abandoned near Salen with a broken leg from a snowboarding accident while supposed comrades ignored his frantic phone calls. He drove back with one foot on the dashboard and the other operating the pedals. Kartofel advised him to calm down and move the operation to a quieter part of the country. He recommended Gävle.

Maringe's new home was a frosty harbour town known to outsiders mainly for a straw goat mascot that locals regularly set on fire. Maringe found an apartment, rebuilt the crew and marked his territory by bashing any local dealers who objected to having their customers poached. The Swedes looked tough but had never dealt with anyone from Poland, where notions of a fair fight rarely extended past agreeing not to call an airstrike. 'The pattern of each confrontation was more or less the same,' remembered Maringe. 'We approach a guy who can help us, we talk, we look around and see guys staring at us, sending clear non-verbal signals to each other [...] They didn't realise who they were dealing with.' Gävle's dealers quickly discovered their Polish opponents were ruthless professionals and exited the battlefield, leaving Maringe with a monopoly on drug sales in local clubs.

He felt secure enough to meet Luiza and her parents in Gran Canaria for a holiday and flew there using the passport of a friend with similar facial features. Everything was going well until pale, badly dressed men trying to look like tourists began congregating outside the hotel and Maringe realised the Polish police had followed his fiancée overseas. He went on the run, spent the night in a youth hostel and headed to the airport the next morning after dyeing his hair. The guard at Swedish passport control casually waved him through, despite Maringe's nervous grin and the Interpol wanted poster with his name and photograph pinned at the back of the booth.

No more foreign holidays after that. He concentrated on expanding the drug network and sold meth to the local Hell's Angels, who looked like Norse gods on motorcycles and always paid on time. Increased demand led to new methods for duping customs officials. Many Polish cars ran on a hybrid gas/petrol system, and it wasn't difficult to seal amphetamine tablets into the X-ray-proof gas cylinders welded into the chassis.

Off the clock, Maringe slept his way through the local blondes, both amateur and professional, until he'd drifted too far from his fiancée to reconnect. He coped with the break-up by partying on a friend's boat stocked with drink, drugs and girls, where the hedonistic days passed in a haze of dope smoke. Reality became a second-class citizen.

'I remember watching the attack on the World Trade Center on television,' Maringe said. 'At first I thought it was a strange movie, but I only realised what was happening when the second plane hit.' Security tightened after 9/11 and shipments started getting intercepted at the border. Swedish police eventually traced the drugs to Maringe, so he fled into Norway and contacted an old friend to help him escape the tightening noose.

One of his comrades from the Warsaw clubbing days was the hedonistic son of a Serbian diplomat who enjoyed hanging around anyone involved in drugs and crime. 'Dragomir' had returned to private life in Belgrade a few years back but still had the kind of connections that could rustle up a government plane and a flight plan into a remote Norwegian airport. The Pole flew out with few regrets, cheerfully waving goodbye to the 'fucking weather [and] the omnipresent greyness, one big nothing – humidity, clouds, no sun' and hello to the war-scarred Balkans.

Over the last decade, Serbia had been at the heart of a rolling series of ethnic conflicts that ripped the region apart until NATO intervened to bomb the country into submission. Peace returned but the economy spiralled, corruption grew and soon the only people getting rich were warlords and gangsters. Ordinary Serbs struggled to put food on the table, but Maringe had found an ideal refuge free from the fear of extradition or any meaningful law enforcement.

Dragomir owned an expansive home in an elite neighbourhood, distinguished from the rest of Belgrade by mildly more pleasant brutalist architecture, and gifted him a bedroom. Maringe quickly returned to the smuggling game by importing gas cylinders filled with liquid ecstasy, ready for conversion into pills, with the help of a corrupt UN peacekeeper. The drugs were sold to the Zemun clan: one of Belgrade's biggest organised-crime families. Soon Maringe's drugs were helping the rich and connected party away, bug-eyed, to trance beats in their bomb-damaged capital.

He took a holiday with some Zemun friends to nearby Montenegro, where the Serb elite spent their summers broiling on the beaches. Maringe preferred to count cards at the blackjack table and was winning big when the casino management pulled a few tricks and he found himself down by $200,000. A contact drove down from Belgrade with a suitcase of cash that kept Maringe in the game until his losses had been reduced to a tenth of the original amount and he was allowed to stumble drunkenly outside into streets jammed with Porsches and Lamborghinis. He thanked his contact by hiring him a prostitute, but the woman who knocked at the hotel door was so cross-eyed that the man fell off the bed laughing when she faked an orgasm, and broke his ankle.

Maringe had to pay his medical bill. With all the drugs and alcohol, this kind of craziness seemed almost normal.

Maringe earned his own bruises by sleeping with the sister of a local gang boss and being kicked half to death by a squad of thugs in a car park. Some Zemun friends saved him, but it was time to leave the Old Continent for somewhere new. He bought a plane ticket for the Caribbean, a tropical paradise where a drug baron could corner the cocaine market and live like a king.

The cockroaches were 3in long with abdomens the colour of burnt caramel. Welcome to the Dominican Republic, a beautiful and underdeveloped half-shell of an island, home to hurricanes, jungle and sugar cane, where the elites lived in luxury at one end of the racial hierarchy and everyone else struggled in the dirt. 'The darker, the poorer,' observed Maringe cynically, as he moved into a bug-infested house on the outskirts of the capital Santo Domingo. His new home had security guards but no running water.

After fighting off the cockroaches, he got in touch with a former Pruszków man who'd fled abroad when the arrests began and was wallowing in vice under the Caribbean sun. The expat introduced him to the honorary consul for Poland – a broken-down degenerate who was addicted to amphetamines and underage girls, but who had some useful links to Colombian cocaine cartels. Maringe squeezed him for an introduction then headed to Mexico, where the narcotraficantes preferred to work and party. He wasn't sad to be leaving behind the insect life.

Things got better in Mexico City – a throbbing, technicolour carnival where he could satisfy a sex drive that was rapidly turning into an addiction with less chance of catching HIV. After touring the brothels, Maringe made contacts with a Colombian cartel who agreed to sell bricks of cocaine at $3,000 a kilo. He arranged for the goods to be smuggled into Sweden in false-bottomed suitcases, wrapped with aluminium foil to bounce away X-rays, then sold for ten times the original price. Together with a Polish sidekick nicknamed 'Pchła' (Flea), he used the profits to finance a more ambitious scheme that would ship 12kg at a time in bags of Dominican coffee, all certified by the honorary consul.

The plan required some fine-tuning in Scandinavia before the first shipment. In November 2001, Maringe boarded a plane at Mexico City for the flight back to Europe and immediately realised something had gone badly wrong when the airport security staff discreetly recovered a glass he'd just emptied. The authorities wanted to check his fingerprints. Suspiciously blond fellow travellers spent the flight observing the back of his neck. Maringe washed down a sleeping pill with a few drinks, resigned himself to his fate and slept through the journey.

They took him off the plane for questioning during a stopover at Gothenburg. Once the Swedish police had officially established his identity, another short flight took him to Stockholm where travellers looked on curiously at the glossy-haired drug baron being escorted through airport crowds wearing handcuffs.

Maringe found himself in a detention centre desperately fighting extradition back to Poland. All inmates, even rapists and murderers, were allowed such lenient access to phones and computers that Maringe had a political epiphany and became convinced Swedish-style leftism was 'pure evil, pure hatred, and pure destruction', destined to eventually destroy Europe. The revelation didn't stop him using the phones to organise his own drug deals on the outside.

The main charge against Maringe – 'membership of an armed criminal group' – carried only a maximum five-year penalty and the Swedish judges should have granted bail. Some fast and barely legal moves by the authorities in Warsaw saw him extradited before his lawyer could protest. By June the next year, he was once again inside a Polish prison, surrounded by people he'd always despised as inferiors. 'You won't meet a smart person in the criminal world,' he said contemptuously. 'You won't have an intelligent conversation, because your partners are almost always for better or worse (usually worse) pretentious troglodytes.'

It would be several years and a court case before Maringe got a suitably intelligent companion in the form of a shared cell with Słowik. The Pruszków man had hidden in Spain since the original wave of arrests, with occasional excursions to the USA and Israel. He'd spent most of the time in a fruitless effort to persuade the Polish public of his innocence. In August 2001, the ever-faithful Monika took time out from raising their 3-year-old son to be interviewed on live television news programme *Pod Napięciem* about the government's supposed vendetta against Słowik. He made a surprise appearance as a voice on the phone, ranting for three minutes about being a thrusting but honest entrepreneur who'd annoyed powerful people.

Later, contacts passed Monika a floppy disk containing the manuscript of Słowik's autobiography. She found a publisher but wasn't sure the book would help her husband's case. 'I didn't like the book,' said Monika. 'Its style is, let's say, moderately good, not to say bad.' Her husband wasn't the literary type and whoever helped Słowik write *Skarżyłem się Grobowi (I Complained to the Grave)* had filled the pages with protestations of innocence, statements of religious faith, some bile spat at unfriendly fellow gangsters like Masa and several photographs of the author with Pershing to prove their friendship. 'Do not expect to read a crime story about a contemporary Polish gangster,' Słowik announced in the introduction. 'I am more interested in debunking the myth of a ruthless bandit that the police and the media portray me as than gaining even more publicity.'

Crooks had talked with journalists ever since *Życie Warszawy* set up its telephone hotline, but an entire book written by a notorious crook was unprecedented. News of the forthcoming publication caused a sensation, until the police stepped in and confiscated most of the print run, to Słowik's disappointment.

Even worse, a self-published book by rival gangster Dziad somehow avoided the fate of his own work and made it to market not long after. *Świat Według Dziada (The World According to Dziad)* had an inaccurate cover blurb proclaiming it 'The Sensation of the XXI Century' and pleaded the gangster's innocence from behind bars, where he was doing time for running a crime family and attempted kidnapping. Distributed through an amateurish website, the book achieved less publicity than Słowik's banned effort and few readers believed Dziad's claim to be a 'political prisoner of the Third Republic'.

Słowik didn't have much time to fume about his abortive literary career. The authorities had already traced the *Pod Napięciem* call to Spain but couldn't isolate a specific area until the young son of a senior police officer returned from a working holiday near Valencia. The proud father pinned a handful of holiday snaps to his office corkboard and an astonished colleague pointed out that Słowik was clearly visible in the background of one photograph. Spanish police were alerted, but the actual arrest only occurred by accident when officers raided the house of another fugitive Pole and thought they'd better check the fingerprints of his wary, rat-faced guest.

'If a dish for receiving Polish television had not been installed in the house where they were detained, [the police] might not have been able to locate them,' said an increasingly exasperated Monika. 'It's like hanging out a Polish white and red flag with the inscription "Here we are".'

The Spanish authorities extradited Słowik back home in February 2003 and, like Maringe, he found himself observing from a cell as the trial of his management board friends came to a climax. The star witness was a figure from the heart of the gang who'd turned traitor and was helping the authorities prove their case against Pruszków. He'd been working with the police for nearly a decade.

19

A Moveable Beast

The informing had started back in May 1994 when the top men from Pruszków gathered at a restaurant in Warsaw to celebrate Bolo's birthday. It was the usual vodka-soaked debauchery until armed figures in black flooded through the door and the partygoers dived for cover, convinced that Wołomin gangsters were about to spray the place with bullets. The relief was palpable when lead gatecrasher Piotr Wróbel flashed his police ID and informed everyone they were under arrest.

Wróbel knew the gangster mindset well. He'd grown up in a rough part of town where many of his schoolfriends would eventually end up behind bars, but a stern father working for the *Milicja* had persuaded him that law and order offered a more rewarding future. In the last years of the PRL, Wróbel proved himself in the ZOMO riot police before moving on to officer training school and graduating just as the communist system crumbled to dust. He remembered a serious row in the last days of the PRL, when the school's diehard instructors discovered every student had voted for *Solidarność*, but then the old order vanished and Wróbel was policing the increasingly violent streets of a new democracy.

Back then, the battle against organised crime was in its infancy, but a small unit, marked on the payroll as 'Anti-Mafia', welcomed him into its lonely crusade against the country's gangsters. The unit launched a series of 'combat reconnaissance' by interrupting parties, invading homes and appearing unexpectedly wherever criminals felt safe. Their raids rarely did much lasting damage, but occasionally a nugget of gold would shine among the riverbed trash in the form of an illegal weapon, a broken alibi or perhaps a new informer.

The war between Pruszków and Wariat was at its height at the time of the restaurant raid. Wróbel and his friends intended their combat reconnaissance to remind the gangsters that not every cop in the city could be bribed to look the other way. Partygoers were rounded up and taken to the police station, where Parasol glowered silently through his interrogations while the more easygoing types passed the time bantering without revealing much.

Wróbel had a decent grasp of hardman psychology and sensed something promising in the more cooperative attitude shown by one of the detainees. He tugged at the loose thread until it unravelled. 'We talked and I kept letting him know that we just needed someone who could help the police work in the right way,' said Wróbel. 'We needed a police consultant.'

The gangsters were eventually released without any charges and Wróbel's man quietly agreed to become an informer. It was Masa.

The big thug hadn't magically transformed into a solid citizen. He was scared. The terrorist tactics initiated by Wariat and his brother had almost wiped out Pruszków at the Multipub in Saska Kępa and they didn't look like stopping any time soon. Masa was capable of extreme violence, as any debtor knew, but hadn't signed up to risk his life in a gang war. Passing on information about Wariat's psychotic crew would make the streets safer for Pruszków's criminal thugs and whatever conscience Masa possessed could be salved by his new policeman friend being realistic enough not to expect much information about anyone else. The two men shook hands and agreed to work together.

Informer and handler met every month or so at Warsaw Zoo or in a private apartment. On one occasion, Masa arranged to see Wróbel at his own police canteen, having persuaded fellow gangsters that the officer was giving him information and not the other way around. Wróbel wasn't happy about being labelled corrupt, but his bosses told him to 'keep going [and] be very careful', as he remembered later, 'because this is a big crook, and a top shelf one at that'.

The relationship between the two men rolled on through the decade and survived Masa's arrest for rape, although the gangster remained bitter that no effort was made by Wróbel to get the charges dropped.

It took one of the management board bribing the alleged victim with a new car for the case to go away.

After Pershing's murder in December 1999, Wróbel tried to persuade his informer to join the recently introduced 'crown witness' programme that offered immunity in exchange for useful testimony. The legislation had been borrowed wholesale from the British tradition of 'turning King's evidence', hence the inappropriately royal-sounding terminology that had linguistic purists protesting that Poland's last sovereign had been kicked off the throne 200 years ago. Wróbel believed the programme would help take down Pruszków's bosses, but Masa disagreed and refused to sign up, preferring the protection of his own crew to that of the authorities.

The gangster's options abruptly narrowed when police raided his $2 million Komorów house and sent him fleeing into Silesia. He was sitting despondently in a prison cell 350km from his family when agents from the newly formed *Centralne Biuro Śledcze* (Central Investigation Bureau – CBŚ), a specialised organised crime unit, begged him to reconsider the crown witness proposal.

The CBŚ was the first Polish law enforcement agency with the manpower and resources to stand a chance against the country's top gangsters and its agents were eager for Masa's cooperation. They got him to agree the underworld was a hellscape 'lined with dick where long term involvement results in various unpleasant occupational diseases', in the gangster's own words, '[where] the cake looked very nice, but when we licked it, it turned out to be inedible', but they couldn't close the deal.

That all changed in the summer when Masa's terrified wife brought news that Pruszków gangsters were threatening the family in an effort to get their hands on the slot machine money. A full-sized coffin had apparently been tossed over the fence of his Komorów property and thugs cornered Masa's teenage son in a boxing gym. 'Soon you'll be fucking lying next to your father,' one snarled.

Whatever *Git-Ludzie* tough-guy credentials Masa possessed melted away when his family was in danger, and he agreed to collaborate with the CBŚ in exchange for armed protection before any trial and a new identity afterwards. Wróbel was jubilant, until his informer stabbed him firmly in the back.

Masa remained deeply unhappy about the circumstances that had put him behind bars and was convinced the policeman had organised the original arrest to force him into testifying against Pruszków. Strange rumours began circulating around the CBŚ alleging Wróbel was corrupt, with one story claiming he'd taken a bribe to organise Masa's earlier escape from Komorów. The big gangster alternately denied or hinted at being the source. An official inquiry eventually cleared Wróbel, but senior officers made it clear that the stain on his character would never wash off and suggested an early retirement to avoid any more unpleasantness. Wróbel was left bitterly wishing he'd never got involved with the new crown witness.

By the summer of 1999, Masa had other things to worry about than disillusioned ex-policemen. His protection detail had received a phone call from someone important ordering Masa immediately be driven out to Nadarzyn, on the highway to Katowice, and left there. The caller had the right codewords and authorisation, but the transfer order was so obviously a prelude to assassination that the guards refused to obey, and the matter was escalated to Lech Kaczyński, Minister of Justice. An investigation failed to identify who made the call.

Kaczyński doubled the guards around Masa and ordered him brought to Warsaw by armoured car so the interrogation could take place in a more secure location. In a tiny office, as cramped as a confessional, the gangster answered question after question while a stenographer recorded the answers in pencil on a legal pad. Masa was finally unburdening his soul.

> I have understood the allegation made today. I admit to them all. I would like to provide explanations on this matter as a crown witness. I declare that I have been instructed on the procedure and conditions for acting as such. I declare that I've never committed a murder, I've never solicited a murder, nor have I founded a criminal group, nor did I lead such a group.

With these words, spoken on 4 June 2000, Masa began a testimony that his interrogators hoped would lay bare the secret history of the

Pruszków Mafia. The last sentence of the opening statement was more than just legal boilerplate. Crown witnesses were not expected to be saints, but the system had to draw the line somewhere and refused to grant protection to gang bosses or anyone involved in a murder, no matter how compelling their evidence.

Unfortunately for Masa, too many people claimed to remember him lumbering around town in 1996 boasting about the death of his friend Kiełbacha. The CBŚ had been forced to spend the preceding weeks digging for information that would definitively prove or disprove any link to the death. Investigators found nothing. '[A]fter so many years there would have been someone, I mean some Pruszków gangster, who had real knowledge of it,' said a prosecutor. 'I mean evidence, not allegations. No such person appeared.'

Masa had long insisted any talk of murder had been a lie to boost his underworld reputation, but some cynics wondered how deep the agents went in an inquiry whose success would have disqualified their best chance at bringing down Poland's leading crime family. Lawyers insisted all due diligence had been done.

Declaration over, the interviewers turned to the crimes Masa did admit to carrying out. For the first week, he ploughed steadily through them in flat, granular detail:

> We agreed that we would protect this store for $1,000 a month but then after a few months [the owner] told us that this amount was too much for him and he paid us $500 each month. In this case, it so happened that he called the next day after the first meeting to say that he was having a row in the store. [We] found five hobos in the shop taking alcohol from the window. We beat them and then the store was quiet. I don't think they reported the beating anywhere, they looked like criminals.

Whatever Masa thought a criminal looked like went unrecorded. The interview went on, littered with gangster pseudonyms, pointless specificities ('I received alcohol in the form of two cases of vodka containing bottles of 0.33 liters, one carton containing lemon cream bottles, one carton containing orange cream bottles'), and boastful talk of getting rich from 'extortion, robbery, fraud, trading in psychotropic and narcotic drugs and other crimes'. He had earned $650,000 from the sale of stolen cars alone.

The authorities wanted to know about the contacts on Masa's mobile phone, so he flipped it open, tapped in an unimaginative 9999 pincode and laid out the Polish underworld in alphabetical order: '601 940 XXX: Bedzio, Pershing's deputy. I think I contacted him on this number on the day of Pershing's murder, on that day Bedzio called me, then I called him, we spoke 5–6 times [...] 604 292 XXX: Kenys, Pawlik's adjutant, former plumber.'

He identified suspects from photographs and gave capsule descriptions of those the police had failed to catch on film. The stenographer recording his answers didn't bother to note down any questions and the resulting transcript presented Masa as an obsessive monologist circling back endlessly to key moments in his past without any concern for chronology, context or appropriate levels of detail. The prosecutors decided to untangle it all later and ploughed ahead.

On 10 June, a lawyer arrived to represent Masa as the crown witness officially pleaded guilty to all the crimes confessed over the previous week. At the last moment, Masa tried to sweeten the endless thuggery by recalling charitable efforts to help children at his daughter's school and the funding of a summer school for special needs kids. 'I also financially supported nuns,' he told the interviewer, and the scepticism in the room was could almost be felt through the transcript.

With the confession wrapped up, the interview moved on to the red meat of the gangster's knowledge: the Pruszków structure. The prosecutors desperately needed a pyramid-shaped organisational chart of dons, underbosses and consiglieres, like that of the American Mafia, if they wanted to cripple the gang with a few well-aimed arrest warrants. Masa knew the structure was far messier in reality, but gave his interrogators what they wanted.

The resulting oversimplification presented tidily segregated subgroups connected to the management board through a layer of middle-management gangsters like Masa. It looked neat but obscured a savage dog-eat-dog reality in which crews fought each other for territory, forcibly overlapped their business interests, sometimes got strong enough to drift away into independence and did deals with sworn enemies if the money was good enough. To confuse things further, the management board was less united than it liked to appear, with plenty of feuds, backstabbing and private armies that rampaged across the organisational chart, sniffing out opportunities and ignoring prior claims. The interviewers disregarded the contradictions, at least for now, and moved on.

Subsequent questions focused on guns held by the group, the relationship between Pershing and the management board, events like the Klub Park attack (with Masa casually noting the bouncer Czaja had later been murdered for burgling the apartment of a Pruszków man), endless lists of pseudonyms and subgroups, rumours about those responsible for high-profile murders and different accounts of Kiełbacha's death. The information poured forth like a ruptured sewer line alongside unprompted details on a hundred other topics, like the team of lawyers on permanent call for the gang, arms dealers who supplied weapons, doctors bribed to diagnose fictitious conditions to beat prison sentences, money invested in businesses and real estate, how Parasol would say, 'We're going hard' to signal that guns should be brought on a mission, Masa claiming to dislike firearms so much he only carried a harmless airsoft pistol in his glove compartment and the Pruszków version of compulsory redundancy. 'If someone did not fulfil his obligations to the group,' said Masa, 'he was beaten, fined, and after taking everything, he was driven out of the city, which meant that such a person could no longer earn money illegally.'

Then there was just time to incriminate Słowik in a number of major crimes, while insisting the information had nothing to do with revenge for Pershing's death and pointing the finger at other old adversaries. Masa seemed to take particular pleasure in outlining Jarosław Maringe's role in the drug business, his skill with a knife, alleged fondness for beating girlfriends and even darker crimes.

Throughout the interview, Pruszków remained the heart of the discussion, but Masa had no problem ratting out the Ożarów gang or members of his own crew who'd risked their lives to protect him after Pershing's death. Bedzio, Florek, Szlachet, Bysiu and others received thumbnail sketches and a casual stab in the back.

The talking stopped on 7 September and arrest warrants were rushed out later that month for the management board and others lower down the food chain. The government was trailing the SLD opposition in the polls and hoped that rounding up the country's biggest organised crime gang would attract voters.

Masa and his family were moved to an isolated house on the Baltic coast with police protection to await the coming trials. They tried to live normally but gangster habits are hard to break, and Masa couldn't stop himself buying an ostentatious BMW Series 7 that stood out in the small town like a rat scampering up a wedding dress.

One day, he slipped out the house and got blackout drunk in a nearby hotel and had to be dragged home to his sobbing wife by a squad of officers. They would soon get used to regularly escorting him home, a sodden mess, from the local brothel. Reports of his behaviour were sent back to Warsaw and further lowered the spirits of those going through the interview transcript line by line.

The meandering nature of the interview – 'something between gibberish and a stream of consciousness,' as Masa later admitted – had initially obscured the limits of the crown witness's knowledge. Put under the legal microscope, the evidence looked worryingly thin. Masa was prominent enough in Pruszków to have heard about crimes that could put the gang leaders away for decades, but he rarely witnessed anything directly and his most damning information came second or third hand.

Lawyers tried to spin the material into something more substantial but couldn't silence unhappy murmurings in the corridors of power. 'When we started dismantling Pruszków, I looked through the materials provided by "Masa",' said Adam Rapacki, Deputy Chief of Police. 'His first testimony disappointed me. It was vague and chaotic, full of: "I heard", "supposedly", "they say in the city". We had to talk with him further on various matters, to clarify, to obtain specifics, to draw details.'

A lot would depend on his performance in the court room – something his enemies were aware of, judging by rumours of a $2 million bounty on Masa's head. He was lucky the underworld had different priorities than hunting down a penitent gangster.

With the big names from Pruszków now under arrest, the capital and all its riches were ripe for a takeover and new gangs were emerging every day to fight for dominance. The bloodiest and most brutal were the Mutants: a barely literate crew of crazies who came crawling out of the Piastów housing estates, thirsty for blood.

20

Here Come the Mutants

No one had told the armed police kicking in the door that one of the men inside was a former Belarusian Special Forces soldier with a passion for homemade explosives and two dozen murders on his conscience. A lovingly constructed bomb in the entranceway of the house exploded and took out two leading officers as they charged forward. Then the Belarusian's friend – a gang boss with a Kalashnikov and a death wish – opened fire from an upstairs window. It was late at night on 5 March 2003 and the gangsters, Igor Pikus, alias 'Aleksander', and Robert Cieślak, aka 'Cieluś', had no intention of being taken alive.

The house in Magdalenka, a small town to the south-west of Warsaw, had looked easy enough to storm when police units were moving forward through the stark expanse of tall, branchless trees that passed for a garden. A smallish two-storey construction in white, its narrow attic was barely tall enough for a man to stand upright and the downstairs had never progressed past a rough mess of bare stone-block walls smeared with mortar. The two gangsters had rented the place hoping police would never suspect them of hiding out in a property whose only notable feature was an unusually steep black roof to keep the snow off in winter.

'I didn't know they were wanted murderers,' the owner said defensively later:

> They looked completely different from the criminals in the newspaper photos. One had dyed hair and looked more like a playboy than a bandit, the other had a Spanish beard [a kind of goatee], hair tied in a

ponytail, wore gold-rimmed glasses, and gave the impression of being a businessman.

The man with the dyed hair was Cieluś, a non-smoking, non-drinking psychopath from Piastów, who cared about nothing in this world except dogs and his girlfriend. He'd made a name in the underworld during the early 1990s by decapitating a man to whom he owed money rather than paying it back. Not long after, he met Jerzy Brodowski, aka 'Mutant', a steroid-abusing beefcake gangster with cropped hair and a neck bigger than most tree trunks. The pair went into business together, with Mutant providing the muscle and Cieluś the brains. Together, they formed a crew which spent most of the decade as the Praetorian guard of a Wołomin smuggler called 'Malarz' (Painter), until persons unknown shot him dead in December 1997 outside his home.

Cut adrift in the Polish underworld with nothing except an intimidating name borrowed from their most visible member, the Mutants soon clashed with Pruszków and came out covered in bruises. They needed protection from someone big and found it by bending the knee to Kikir, leader of Wołomin's Marków gang and the last man standing after the Gama restaurant massacre. He needed violent thugs for his protection rackets and the Mutants had the right skill set.

A ruthless hardman, Kikir's authority over the new arrivals diminished when police threw him in jail for dousing an elderly couple with acid during a savage burglary. Without his oversight, the Mutants made the mistake of kidnapping the son of an important man close to Wołomin and refused to listen to Kikir's reprimands afterwards. The relationship broke down. On the night of 23 September 2000, the gang boss was driving with his wife and bodyguards towards Warsaw on a five-day leave from prison when a dark off-road vehicle drew level and someone fired an automatic rifle into the car.

A wounded Kikir was planning his revenge from hospital when a Mutant walked into the ward dressed as a priest, pulled out a pistol and shot him dead. The gang boss's pyjama-clad body thumped on to the floor next to his bed and bled out. The priest strolled calmly away, casually telling a horrified nurse to 'fuck off' as he passed, before leaving the building and climbing into a waiting car. 'The Mutants were motherfuckers who weren't afraid of anything or anyone,' said a police officer who attended the scene.

After Kikir's death, no one even tried to control them. They blasted off Kalashnikovs during kidnappings, truck hijackings and robberies; Cieluś carried around a bag of hand grenades and wasn't shy about using them; Belarusian member and former soldier Aleksander had an obsession with homemade explosives and plenty of experience in turf wars back home; and Mutant strutted through the underworld intimidating lowlifes, with a tattoo collection that included general's epaulettes on his shoulders and one that read '*VIDE CUI FIDE*' (Latin for 'be careful who you trust') on his arm.

The gang soon felt powerful enough to challenge Pruszków again, leading to another cycle of violence that saw Macro shoot-out veteran Matyś dragged off the street and held for ransom. His friends turned to the occult rather than pay. 'We hired a seer,' said one Pruszków gangster:

> He began to mutter something, that he saw some old cottage, some well, a road to Płońsk. As far as possible, we checked these visions, but found nothing. Then we got another seer, and he was blabbering about a dark forest, so there was no point in pursuing the subject at all. You have plenty of forests here, don't you?

Matyś was never seen again. A full-scale war between the gangs only failed to erupt because Masa's statement led to the arrest of the Pruszków management board, leaving the Mutants free to rampage through Warsaw's power vacuum for the next two years.

Life got a lot cheaper. In 2001, Poland saw 1,325 murders (compared to 717 that year in the UK, excluding Northern Ireland): an all-time high. The price of a contract killing dropped from 10,000zł to around 3,000zł as the bodies hit the floor.

Michał Pawłowski, briefly arrested as a suspect in death of Wariat, was shot dead leaving a disco late at night. Two young members from what remained of Pruszków were murdered in the Sport pub, allegedly as part of an internal feud. In early 2001, the newspaper headlines were full of Jacek Dębski, the Minister of Sport, losing his job and life in quick succession.

The balding Dębski had long used his political position and friendships with high-level gangsters as leverage to borrow large sums of money from underworld lenders who rarely got repaid. A political scandal in February saw him kicked out of the government and gave his creditors an opening for revenge. Two months later, Dębski was dining with a younger woman, allegedly an expensive call girl, at a Saska Kępa restaurant with the heavily ironic name of La Cosa Nostra. He'd managed to forget his money troubles for the night and was looking cheerful when a man approached on the street outside. The former minister didn't even see the gun come out.

The killer and an expat gangster who'd ordered the murder would both be arrested only to die by suicide in prison, while Dębski's female friend got eight years for setting him up. Motives and the extent of the conspiracy were never entirely clear. 'We were just pieces in the puzzle,' said the woman. 'I didn't know the full plan.'

With all the blood being spilled, something special was required to still horrify Poland. The Mutants managed to oblige. On 23 March 2002, a team of police officers was staking out a truck loaded with stolen plasma-screen televisions hidden in a barn just outside the capital. They expected a routine arrest when the crooks returned to collect their booty, but instead found themselves in a vicious firefight with a dozen or so Mutants carrying automatic weapons. Deputy Commissioner Mirosław Żak was sitting in his vehicle when the bullets hit. He tried to crawl out but collapsed after being shot again by a gangster firing in short, controlled bursts. Police blasted back and Cieluś was hit but got dragged away by sidekick Aleksander.

The police radio crackled with pleas for an ambulance and reinforcements, but the minutes ticked past before anyone answered. Heavily armed officers eventually arrived to find Żak dead, the barn empty and the Mutants escaped.

A senior police officer had been killed and his colleagues wanted retribution. A noticeboard went up at Piastów police headquarters with photographs of all known Mutants pinned in a triangular collage of shaven heads and vacant stares. Cieluś and Mutant were at the apex. Officers crossed through each photograph with a thick marker pen as gang members were jailed or killed resisting arrest.

As the Mutants disappeared one by one, other gangs both old and new began hacking away chunks of the capital for themselves. In the feeding frenzy of a post-Pruszków world, most wouldn't last long.

Poles loved to dump their rubbish but preferred not to pay for the privilege. Local authorities regularly begged residents not to litter the forests with rubbish bags, old sofas and unwanted pets, but no one listened when the alternative was paying a little extra for a council collection. In the morning of 13 November, an unemployed man bicycled up to an unofficial dump site near Nadarzyn to do some scavenging and noticed a black Audi A6 half-hidden behind the bushes of an adjacent clearing. He took a closer look and discovered the car was peppered with bullet holes and had two corpses sat slumped in the front seats. Ożarów had just lost another leader.

After Pershing's death, the gang had been taken over by the 52-year-old 'Klajniak' (Child), who'd missed most of the action due to a long stay in a German prison. He got back to find Pershing assassinated and Bedzio under arrest, so he took over what remained of the crew to focus on drug dealing and extortion.

Klajniak kept a lower profile than most gang bosses and his death was suitably mysterious. He was accompanying his son-in-law to a meeting about a relatively unimportant underworld deal when someone raked the car windscreen with automatic fire as it came to a halt. No one was sure if Klajniak had been the target or was collateral damage in some low-level score settling. The Mutants were accused of involvement but nothing was ever proved. A bruised Ożarów went to ground as the gang tried to find someone new who was prepared to take a throne that sat permanently beneath a sword suspended overhead by a fraying human hair.

Klajniak's death came three months after Wołomin had already exited the game. Maniek's son Jacek, known to all as 'Klepak', had been in prison when the Gama restaurant massacre and assassination of Kikir killed off the gang's original leaders and scattered their successors. He got back on the street determined to rebuild the gang and hunt down those who'd killed his father.

In March 2002, a man called Leszek was shot dead in his car outside a pub, the victim managing to start the engine but smashing into a fence before bleeding out. Another suspected Gama shooter was chased through back gardens and over fences in Sulejówek before the killer shot him in the back.

In the aftermath, Klepak hid out from law enforcement in the countryside with a crew of bodyguards. On 17 August, they were drinking in a small bar called Okoń (The Perch) when three young men ran in and opened fire. Klepak died on the floor and a police officer who chased the killers was shot dead in the street outside. The authorities came down hard on what was left of Wołomin and destroyed the gang with a wave of arrests.

Less well-known figures trying to muscle their way in that year suffered similar fates. A crew led by Tomasz Suga, aka 'Komandos' (Commando), eliminated rival drug dealers by clamping their heads in a vice and sawing off their hands. Bodies were wrapped up in wire fencing weighed down with paving stones and thrown in the Wisła.

Komandos' reign didn't last long. That May, he was sitting with three colleagues outside a restaurant at the Klif shopping centre: a fashionable location that had been one of the earliest Western-style malls when it opened five years earlier. The group were so deep in conversation that no one noticed the man strolling confidently in their direction with a pistol. Two died, one was injured, but Komandos got away.

Not long after, a killer in a baseball cap shot him ten times in the back as he vacuumed out his car at a petrol station. The gunman came from a gang led by drug dealer and talented amateur footballer Rafał Skatulski, alias 'Szkatuła' (Casket), who took over Komandos' territory for his own brief moment in the sun.

A gang from Mokotów were the ones who really worried the authorities. Born in the early 1990s from the decrepit housing estates of south-west Warsaw, the gang was run by 'Korek' (Cork), an intelligent, methodical family man who had set himself the goal of earning $30 million and retiring. For most of the decade, Korek's gang was somewhere between a subgroup and competitor of Pruszków, specialising in drug distribution and kidnapping until the management board's arrests cleared the space for independence. Mokotów soon expanded to several hundred strong, with many new members being young men caught up in the pop-culture glamorisation of gangster life.

'While in the early 1990s the average age in the bandit profession was over 30, today it is 22–25 years old,' noted journalist Piotr Pytlakowski:

> The new mafiosi are getting younger, more predatory and more dangerous. They grew up with media images in which the life of a gangster had more advantages than disadvantages. They saw a criminal driving the latest model of Mercedes or BMW, with a gold signet ring, surrounded by beautiful girls.

Recruits would soon discover the reality of gangster life meant acting as poorly paid low-level thugs helping their boss Korek make his millions. Korek dreamed of getting rich through cocaine smuggling and put together the financing by having Mokotów men in fake police uniforms kidnap high-profile targets off the street. The victims had a grim time in a remote farmhouse, where drugged, bored gangsters passed the hours by burning obscene words into captive flesh or painting eyelids with hydrochloric acid. If a prisoner's family couldn't get the money then a few fingers would be pruned off and posted with the warning, 'If the ransom is in pieces, then the victim is in pieces'. Some were released; others disappeared.

Mokotów took it as a special insult when the Mutants flipped the script and kidnapped one of its members. The two gangs had been in conflict ever since Kikir's death, when negotiations over territory broke down and senior Mutants had unwisely threatened Korek. 'From now on, you're living on credit,' one shouted down the phone. 'Enjoy every new day, because it won't last long.'

A fortnight later, the gangster who made the threat was walking his dog when two men wobbled past on bicycles, pulled out pistols and shot him dead. The Mutants seethed and, looking for revenge, kidnapped a Mokotów accountant known as 'Bolek'. They demanded $200,000 for his release. Korek refused to pay and sent out his 'Death Commando', as a *Życie Warszawy* journalist had christened the gang leader's personal strong-arm squad, to settle matters. Two Mutants were kidnapped, tortured and murdered. A half-dead Bolek was eventually released, but the conflict rolled on and a dozen more gangsters died.

The war might have continued except for the police crackdown that followed the death of Deputy Commissioner Żak. By the spring of 2003, the Mutants had been all but dismantled in a series of raids and their leaders were on the run. That March, a police patrol car was cruising slowly through the streets of Magdalenka, the cold so intense that everything had been reduced to shades of black, white and grey, when one officer recognised a pedestrian in a thick winter coat. It was Aleksander.

They tracked the Belarusian to a house in the neighbourhood shared with Cieluś and two guard dogs. Just after midnight, an anti-terrorist unit rode an armoured Land Rover through the garden gates and sped towards the house, unaware that the two men inside had an arsenal of weapons and had seen them approaching. Officers who got to the front door were knocked back by a fiery booby-trap that killed two before a hail of automatic fire opened up from the attic.

'People were getting hit like ducks,' remembered an officer who took part. 'We hid wherever we could, but you can't hide from a grenade behind a tree. It was like in a movie, a grenade flew from the building, a bright flash, and three of our men immediately fell to the ground.'

The firefight lasted several hours. Seventeen police officers were wounded, some as they tried to drag injured friends to safety, and the house caught fire when a huge explosion in the front room sent flames boiling up the walls. The two gangsters ran from window to window in the attic, firing at anything that moved, while fire and smoke slowly consumed the building.

Cieluś had time to call his girlfriend, say he loved her and mourn the fate of two dogs trapped on the ground floor before the phone cut off. When firefighters eventually extinguished the blaze, the two gangsters were found dead from smoke inhalation in the attic. Aleksander was clutching a rifle bullet in his fist – an old Special Forces tradition for those who preferred to die in battle rather than be taken alive.

A year later, the man called Mutant was discovered hiding out on a housing estate in Mszczonów, a thirty-minute drive from Magdalenka. The newspapers had been carrying detailed descriptions of the fugitive for months ('Distinguishing marks: left forearm – incision scars, tattooed skull; right forearm – tattooed tiger's head; a dot tattooed under his left eye', etc.), but Mutant was only caught after getting lonely and visiting family for Christmas. Police followed him home and dragged the gang leader half-asleep out of bed in the early hours of the morning.

The collapse of the Mutants left their rivals in Mokotów as the biggest gang in Warsaw, but everyone knew the situation depended on the Pruszków leadership remaining behind bars. As Cieluś and Aleksander's charred bodies were removed from Magdalenka, the biggest criminal trial Poland had ever seen was coming to a close in the capital. Masa was testifying for the prosecution, and the gang were doing their best to prove him a murdering, lying alcoholic whose evidence couldn't be taken seriously.

21

The Eagle Versus the Octopus

The court room cost 40 million złotys and the designers seemed to have spent most of the budget in Ikea. Everywhere to sit or stand was wooden, pale, smooth-cornered and Scandinavian-styled. A showcase trial required a suitable stage and the authorities had spent time and money transforming this disused army barracks in Bemowo on the outskirts of the capital into a clean-lined modernist forum for justice.

Beneath the Swedish design choices lay some serious security measures. A well-polished wall of armoured glass sealed off the defendants from the rest of the room and a labyrinth of corridors funnelled them smoothly from prison van to court with little sight of the outside world. Armed guards with itchy trigger fingers stood ready in case anyone got suicidal enough to lunge at a judge.

The precautions turned out to be unnecessary. Pruszków's management board spent most of their trial lounging on the defence benches with crossed arms and sceptical looks. Bolo, Wańka, Malizna, Kajtek and Parasol were accused of establishing and leading an armed criminal gang (Article 258 of the Polish Criminal Code) – a crime punishable by up to eight years in prison. Prosecutors alleged the accused ran the Pruszków Mafia, a crime family that earned huge sums of money through alcohol and cigarette smuggling, importing and distributing drugs, protection rackets and fraud. Its business methods were threats, bribery, corruption, intimidation, arson, beatings and murder.

News reports crowed that the management board were finally facing collective justice, but some big names were missing from the court-room action. Słowik had been fighting extradition from Spain for most of the proceedings, and Krzyś was released from custody after doctors diagnosed terminal cancer and sent him home to waste away in his wife's arms. Neither man would be present when the panel of judges prepared to deliver its verdict after seven months of evidence and cross-examination.

Jail or freedom all depended on the success of the accused men's legal strategy, as laid out on the first day of the trial in the autumn of 2002, when Parasol leaned over the wooden lectern and growled a prepared response into the microphone:

> As for the charge of leading a criminal group, I wish to declare that I have never led such a group. This is another slander of me by a well-known thug who wants to avoid criminal liability, the ruthless hustler Jarosław Sokołowski, commonly known as 'Masa', and hidden by [the authorities] behind the curtain of the institution of crown witness.

Things got spicier when he accused Masa of murdering Kiełbacha six years previously and claimed the whole case had been dreamed up by the former conservative government to rebrand itself as a party of law and order ahead of the 2001 election. The government had lost to the SLD anyway, but the case lumbered on like a legal zombie. Parasol was no great public speaker but the line of attack was clear: Masa's testimony should be discarded on the grounds that his own crimes disqualified him as a crown witness – a status he'd only achieved as the result of an ill-defined political conspiracy.

More than a few people shifted uneasily in their seats at the mention of the current government. Everyone knew SLD donors had been intimately entwined with Pruszków during the slot machine scandal, but few of the legal attack dogs on court-room duty could see any career advantage in bringing up the subject. Even Masa's original interrogators had avoided diving too deeply into links between organised crime and politics for fear of making powerful enemies. Parasol's statement threatened to turn a straightforward criminal case into something with the potential to threaten the careers of some important people. Questions were already being asked after former Pershing adjutant turned Pruszków man Małolat was arrested while serving as founder and head of the SLD's Bemowo branch – the same district now housing the courtroom.

After Parasol's speech, the other prisoners stayed silent or kept it short and unconvincing.

'I am a victim', insisted Wańka.

'Nobody ever called me "Bolo"', said Bolo. 'This is an invention of the press, commissioned by the government.'

All claimed to be gainfully employed individuals working for printing firms, garages, small businesses; they denied transferring houses and cars to the names of wives and children, but couldn't explain why their only current possessions were a few sets of clothing and the ubiquitous luxury wristwatch.

Journalists covered the case's early scenes under excited titles like 'A Historical Trial' and 'Pruszków to Prison!', but interest died away as the days descended into dull cross-examinations of police officers, experts and victims interweaved with minute analysis of the miles of documents and photographs. The political angle threatened by Parasol failed to materialise for reasons that were never clear, although it may have been connected to an obliquely threatening letter written by Bolo to a senior SLD politician that hadn't achieved the desired effect. 'There are no political threads in the Pruszków case,' a senior prosecutor told journalists firmly, trying to refocus their attention on the kind of criminals who didn't need votes.

The case was tricky enough to follow even without a political angle. Prosecutors had fired off a shotgun blast of additional charges against management board members and spun them into separate trials: Malizna had to fight a parallel case for ordering the murder of Pershing; his brother Wańka had other ongoing trials for amphetamine sales and the *Jurata* cocaine-smuggling affair; Kajtek was accused of running an amphetamine factory, Parasol of extortion, and Bolo of assault and illegal possession of weapons. All the hearings took place on the same Swedish-style benches in Bemowo and turned the court room into a buzzing hive of overworked lawyers and overlapping jurisdictions.

Whatever trial was under way, the gangsters did their best to look like the legitimate businessmen they claimed to be, alternately shocked and unimpressed by the drama unfolding on the other side of the armoured glass. Not even the appearance of three crown witnesses – all gangsters who'd fallen out with Pruszków and turned informer – got a response. Only the testimony of the fourth sparked a reaction.

Most Pruszków members couldn't understand how Masa had ended up working for the authorities while they sat behind bars. 'We didn't even think that someone who took over such important business after the mysterious murder of Kiełbiński could testify against others while remaining completely unpunished,' said Jarosław Maringe, following the trial from his cell. 'After all, the Crown Witness Act excludes this status for persons in the leadership of criminal groups. As you can see, in the "rule of law" there are equal and then there are more equal.'

Masa appeared in court wearing a black balaclava, although there can't have been many present who were unfamiliar with his face. He seemed unconcerned by the scorching waves of hatred radiating across the court room from the defendants and served it right back at them in his opening statement. He disingenuously claimed to admire his old enemy Parasol for enduring everything the Polish prison system had thrown at him during the PRL years, including being slapped in the face by a prison guard's penis. It was the ultimate insult to a veteran *Git-Ludzie* for whom any hint of homosexuality was taboo and sent the prisoners leaping out of their seats ('inarticulate screams', noted the stenographer) to hammer on the armoured glass. Parasol charged the microphone and bellowed, 'It was Sokołowski who was the biggest fag and sucked off everyone.'

The judges eventually restored order and Masa's testimony continued. A bulky figure leaning over the microphone, he calmly described the murders, extortion and theft that had made the gang into the most powerful crime family in Poland. Masa gave names, dates and locations to back up his accusations and earned some sympathy from the judges' bench by relating the safe houses and armed guards required to keep his family safe.

Hostile questioning uncovered only that he was undergoing treatment for alcoholism using medical implants. He denied abusing drugs, running a gang or involvement in Kiełbacha's murder. Defence lawyers protested that no one with Masa's criminal history could be trusted as a witness, but the panel of judges appeared spellbound by his recollections of extensive conversations with every important gang member.

'The funniest thing is that everyone went to Masa as to a bishop,' Parasol sarcastically told a journalist afterwards. 'Insignificant Captain Masa, and everyone confesses to him.'

Masa's testimony shovelled more dirt on the gang's coffin with every sentence. Only one other trial in Bemowo had more at stake. Malizna was looking at additional decades in jail if found guilty of masterminding the murder of Pershing. The prosecuting lawyers claimed he'd had help from a dead alcoholic and a former Young Businessman of the Year.

Back in January 2000, Mexican police arrested a short-haired, round-faced Pole strolling along a street in Cancún. A photograph taken at the station caught the suntan and sportswear of a typical expat but the 1,000-yard stare of a man facing a difficult future. The official reason behind Ryszard Bogucki's arrest was an expired visa, but the noise from the Mexican authorities made it clear he was much more dangerous than that. 'Mexico should not, cannot, nor will allow the country to become a sanctuary for criminals,' said a government official.

Bogucki fought the deportation order with a panicky desperation, but a year later, he was being escorted through Warsaw Airport in handcuffs. By the time of the management board trial, he was in the Bemowo court room alongside Malizna, protesting his innocence of murdering Pershing down in Zakopane.

The police had cracked the case without much sweat. Not long after the shooting, underworld rumours had led them to an alcoholic bank robber called Adam, who broke under questioning and confessed to driving Bogucki and a man called Ryszard Niemczyk, aka 'Rzeźnik' (Butcher), to the southern ski resort. Adam claimed Malizna had ordered them to prove their loyalty by killing his hated opponent; when Bogucki suggested hiring a foreign shooter from the Soviet diaspora to do the job, Malizna snapped back, 'Don't do it with the Russians, do it yourself!' The hit team had stayed in a local hotel the night before the shooting, then Adam had driven them to the car park of the Kasprowy hotel as the afternoon light faded. Rzeźnik fired a burst from an automatic weapon to scare off any heroes and Bogucki put two bullets in Pershing's brain.

Adam's confession led police to 26-year-old Rzeźnik in Kraków the next year, but he escaped the detention centre in late October by clambering over the roof to a waiting car and went on the run. That left only Bogucki and Malizna to face the judges, both claiming to be the victims of mistaken identity.

Bogucki leaned heavily into his respectable background as a young entrepreneur. Originally from Silesia, a chunk of land in the south-west that had been fought over by Poles and Germans for centuries, he'd barely got out of school when communism fell but showed an instinctive understanding of the new capitalist reality by making a quick fortune selling used cars and cheap video recorders. Aged only 21 years old, he opened a Ferrari dealership at a glittering event attended by many Polish celebrities. Bogucki went on to marry a Miss Poland and was awarded the Silver Ace of Polish Business award. Life looked good. Why, he asked, would a man like himself be involved in the murder of a Polish crime boss?

Prosecutors had the answer. Beneath the shiny surface of his business empire were problems with bank loans, missing vehicles, financial irregularities and missed alimony payments to an ex-wife. By 1993, Bogucki was fighting charges of extortion and fraud convincing enough that he spent time in prison, where a friendship with Rzeźnik drew him into the underworld. Out on bail in 1997, he failed to reappear in court and hid out on the Baltic coast with the help of Nikoś, sinking deeper into the gangster life. After the gang boss's death, Bogucki transferred his loyalties to Pruszków and the cult-like crew of Malizna.

The defence managed to throw a few nails under the tyres of the prosecution. Adam had died of complications from alcoholism before the trial started and couldn't be questioned without the help of a Ouija board. Conspiracy theories already surrounded the murder – not unusual in a country that had learned to distrust official narratives during decades of communist rule and never lost the habit. Some thought it suspicious that Pershing's girlfriend snapping his sim card in half had been accepted as the act of a shell-shocked innocent observer, rather than anything more sinister. A journalist claimed, based on 'inside information', that Pershing was being monitored by the UOP at the time of his death and a video recording of the murder existed which would demolish the narrative being pitched by the prosecution.

The tape never appeared and probably didn't exist. No one with real knowledge of the security services believed surveillance had been taking place at the time of Pershing's death or that the UOP was even capable of mounting a sustained operation. 'It's normal that the secret services only carry out so-called periodic observations,' said a former secret policeman. 'So, for example, there is figurehead X and he's followed for a month. Then he is left alone for six months, then followed again for a month or a week depending on what the person running the operation wants.'

None of that stopped the defence bombarding judges with confusing counter-narratives and missing gunmen, all of it presented with the same desperation as the gang's lawyers in the main trial trying to have Masa's evidence excluded. The judges in both cases remained sceptical.

The joint management board trial eventually came to a close in April 2003, with Masa still on board as a trustworthy witness and the prosecution doing everything possible to make it easy for the judges to convict. 'The gang's bosses did not have to order specific crimes, just as those committing these acts had no need to contact their bosses,' said the prosecutor. 'What was important was whether they shared profits with the management and whether individual subgroups did not get in each other's way.'

A month later, the judgement arrived. All members of the management board were found guilty. Bolo, Parasol and Kajtek got seven years each. Wańka received six and a half years as he'd been in and out of custody since 1998, but his sentence would be lengthened in the coming months by additional penalties for cocaine importation and the Dekadent nightclub takeover. His brother, Malizna, got seven and a half, thanks to an additional penalty for a charge involving forged documents. The only bright spots were Parasol dodging his extortion charge and Bolo being found not guilty of illegally possessing weapons.

As the prisoners digested the verdicts, the authorities began making moves to seize Pruszków's earnings from crime. 'The tax police will leave the gangsters standing in only their socks, confiscating their assets, even if they were transferred to wives or partners,' announced Krzysztof Janik, Minister of the Interior and Administration.

More bad news came two months later, when the Pershing murder trial concluded. Bogucki got twenty-five years for the shooting, while

Malizna received ten years for ordering the hit. The public absorbed the news but reserved any genuine surprise for a political scandal when *Wprost* magazine published details of the SLD's relationship with Pruszków, apparently sourced through Masa. In response, a senior party official 'admitted that the number of reports about the scandalous behaviour of party members exceeded an acceptable level. Therefore the party has decided to take decisive measures.' Despite the strong words, the only decisive measure the SLD took was threatening to sue *Wprost* for printing the allegations, before deciding it would cost too much.

The success of the management board trial led to a wave of further arrests against Pruszków. Masa's former crew had scattered across the country after the August raids, but some made the mistake of returning to Pruszków to oversee their rackets and ended up in handcuffs. Szlachet was hauled off to Białołęka prison to receive 'the standard equipment: two blankets, two sheets, a small pillow, toothbrush, razor, a bar of grey soap, washing powder in a foil packet, and a plastic set for meals i.e. a soup bowl, a plate, and some cutlery' and await his own day in court.

By 2002, over 2,200 people across Poland had been charged with belonging to an armed criminal gang. Szlachet barely stood out from all the other young gangster clones with shaved heads, baggy jumpers and expensive watches.

Agents from the *Centralne Biuro Śledcze* could congratulate themselves on their first three years of fighting crime. The CBŚ logo now seemed justified, with its eagle representing justice swooping down through a map of Poland towards the wriggling black octopus of organised criminality. After the long, losing battle of the 1990s, the eagle had finally won, even if some cynics thought the victory only temporary. 'We locked them up, that's true, but so what?' said one officer. 'In a few years' time they'll get out and be able to spend more on one dinner than most people earn in a year.'

One tentacle was still twitching under the fluorescent lighting of a jail cell. Jarosław Maringe's court date was approaching and he had some serious decisions to make about the future. Should he keep his mouth shut like a good *Git-Ludzie* or become an informer to take revenge on those who'd wronged him?

VI

AFTER THE DELUGE, 2004–PRESENT

22

Ashes and Diamonds

Poland is a blood altar that has seen much human sacrifice. Nearly 3,000 people were executed after the war at a grey complex of buildings on ul. Rakowieckiej 37 for opposing the new communist regime. Many who spent their last days behind its dank walls were *Żołnierze Wyklęci* (cursed soldiers), members of guerrilla bands who fought the Germans then stayed in the forests to wage war on the next wave of tyrants from Moscow. They saw themselves as martyrs but Poland's communist flunkies barely noticed the freshly dug graves around the city.

In 2005, the cells held only ordinary inmates on remand, but the detention centre remained as grim as ever, with its stone walls casting an oppressive shadow on any pedestrian brave enough to wander through the Mokotów district. Among the inmates was Jarosław Maringe, worrying about his upcoming trial and troubled by dreams of those who had been executed at Rakowieckiej generations before, which family lore insisted included at least one relative. Maringe was self-aware enough to understand the cursed soldiers had died for their country, while his own fight had been purely for personal gain, but that didn't make it any easier to sleep at night.

He'd been charged with membership of the Pruszków Mafia and breaking every narcotic law on the statutes, but another even more serious accusation was looming over him. During a recent chat about his case with defence lawyers, Maringe had been allowed to read the transcript of Masa's witness statement. He dismissed most of it as 'nonsense [and] mistaken facts', until the big thug accused him of murder.

A few years previously, Żaba's crew had spent the day at an Olsztyn lake drinking, swimming and messing around on jet-skis. One gangster called 'Rakiet' (Rocket) couldn't swim but was drunkenly bullied into joining Maringe for a jet-ski ride which went wrong somewhere near the heart of the lake. Rescuers pulled Maringe from the water but his friend drowned and lifeguards took six hours to find the body. In the aftermath, Maringe was convicted of causing a fatal accident but didn't serve any time. It was a grim day and not one he liked to remember, but buried in Masa's statement was a brief recap of that day, all second-hand, warped to claim that Rakiet had been deliberately drowned to prevent him revealing gang secrets.

If the prosecution believed the story and pursued a murder charge then Maringe was looking at decades in prison. He shook hands with his lawyers, returned to his cell and tried to hang himself with the electric cord from a heater. Maringe woke up on the floor with his head spinning, back badly bruised and the cord snapped. He was becoming a veteran of failed prison suicides. Afterwards, he convinced himself to live and prayed prosecutors would dismiss Masa's accusation.

No one doubted that Polish justice showed little mercy to murderers these days. In April, Ryszard Niemczyk had been arrested in Germany and extradited back to Poland to stand trial for the assassination of Pershing. At a press conference, Niemczyk insisted to anyone who would listen that he would clear his name at trial. He got twenty-five years.

Veteran criminals understood that fighting the legal system head-on wasn't always the smart move. Later that year, Żaba, Słowik and Bedzio tried a different approach at their trial for establishing and leading an armed criminal gang. Some observers expected a fierce legal battle: the charge didn't seem applicable to either Żaba or Bedzio, both being subordinates within larger structures, although the evidence against Słowik was a little firmer.

The court never got a chance to debate the issue. All three men submitted to 'voluntary punishment': the Polish version of pleading guilty to avoid a trial with the twist that they weren't required to accept responsibility for the crime. Whoever recommended the tactic had a fine legal brain. Żaba got only three years and eight months and was released almost immediately for time served; Bedzio got two years and was out in eight months after paying a security; while Słowik received a six-year sentence, but that included a separate penalty for extorting the Dekadent night club years earlier.

At his own trial, Maringe somehow beat the charge of gang membership and was intensely relieved when the prosecution decided not to pursue a murder indictment, but the narcotics charges were extensive enough to get him twelve years. He ended up sharing a cell with Słowik in the maximum-security section. Wearing the red jumpsuits reserved for dangerous prisoners, they passed the days talking about their lives, working out and listening to Słowik sing sad Spanish Gypsy songs. 'We almost became friends,' said Maringe.

Słowik had more trouble heading his way. On top of the six-year sentence, he was also charged with the murder of General Marek Papała, the former policeman who was mysteriously shot dead in 1998. A car thief-turned-crown witness had named the Pruszków man as the brains behind the killing, with Ryszard Bogucki as the shooter. Słowik maintained a stoic *Git-Ludzie* façade as the trial approached, which only cracked when his wife Monika began an affair with another gangster, and he began to cry softly at night with his face turned towards the wall. Maringe pretended not to hear.

They had been sharing a cell for close to eight months when lawyers from Żaba approached Maringe with a proposal. His old boss was back behind bars after forming a new drug-smuggling gang that had been quickly dismantled by police; this time, the charges were heavier and Żaba was looking at fifteen years. Sick from years of alcoholism, the veteran gangster couldn't face doing the time, especially after being beaten up behind bars by a furious Szlachet and friends, who thought him accepting voluntary punishment the first time round had destroyed their, not especially unconvincing, defence that Pruszków was a figment of Masa's imagination. The lawyers suggested Maringe join their client in taking advantage of the Criminal Code, Section 60.

Known as the 'small crown witness', Section 60 promised reduced sentences in exchange for useful information and Żaba wanted to team up in spilling the names of every street dealer and mid-level distributor from the pair's past and present. Maringe was unimpressed by the proposal.

'Żaba, you fucking prick, you smuggled so many drugs using my methods, you haven't settled up with me and you still want me to deal with you?' Maringe thought, still bitter at not getting his share of the Balkan Route:

> Out of 2–3 million złotys, he did not give me even one złoty, and he still had expectations of me. And for what! Żaba wanted me to fuck up the boys who worked for us. I was no angel, I often broke ethical rules, but this proposal was simply immoral to me.

After many sleepless nights, he decided to follow the advice of Żaba's lawyers, but on his own terms. He would apply for Section 60, independently of his former boss, and rat only on the Balkan Route's senior figures. This would make his jail time shorter and his conscience a little less tarnished.

Other gang members were already doing the same in a new set of Pruszków trials that targeted younger members of the gang. They'd become disillusioned after the financial and legal help promised for times of trouble had failed to materialise following the implosion of the gang's fiscal infrastructure. The final stake through the heart had been the arrest of Wańka's son, 'Młody' (Young) Wańka, as he was desperately trying to hold together the remnants of Pruszków, and the murder of gang money man 'Balbin', who took five bullets in the head and chest climbing into his Mercedes outside a grocery shop.

Maringe was accepted as a Section 60 witness. Słowik soon discovered this breach of the *Git-Ludzie* code, and the pair fought viciously in their cell until guards separated them. A battered Maringe told prosecutors all he knew about Pruszków and the Balkan Route, resulting in a new cell and a release from prison in 2008, six years early.

He was cynical enough about the Polish legal system not to be surprised when Żaba was also granted freedom, although only as a temporary measure for the duration of his trial after providing information of his own to the prosecution, along with a diagnosis of cancer. He died in 2009 before the verdict was returned and never discovered how much compassion his illness and cooperation would have brought him. The dead man was officially recorded as a pensioner who'd been getting by on 460zł a month. No one mentioned the villas, real estate and gold stashed in various safety deposit boxes.

'You could say I liked Żaba,' said Maringe, years later, with either a large dose of hypocrisy or the mellowing of age. 'He was a terrible smartarse, but the first impression was positive – a warm, good man.' Ultimately, the death of the gangster who'd brought him into the higher echelons of the Pruszków Mafia and changed his life forever didn't bother Maringe much. He was starting a new life on the right side of the bars and wasn't the kind to look back.

By 2012, globalisation had settled on Warsaw like snow, soft as a blanket and cold as knives. British coffee shops with Italian names were everywhere, allowing businesspeople and students to feel sophisticated for pronouncing 'cappuccino' correctly. Huge advertising hoardings for German cars hung storeys high across buildings, blocking out the light for tenants but filling the bank accounts of their landlords. The French supermarket Carrefour was selling an 800ml jar of mayonnaise for more than the price of two 400ml jars, confident that local shoppers still didn't understand economies of scale.

Poland had joined the European Union eight years earlier. Around €50 billion was pumped into the country by Brussels bureaucrats to fund roads, shopping centres, education, urban renewal, investment and the lifestyles of various corrupt politicians. The wheels on the economy finally began to turn at something closer to Western speed. Despite some grumbling about the loss of sovereignty over the years, not even the most Eurosceptic patriot ever considered leaving the EU. When it's raining money, no one puts up an umbrella.

It was a whole new world, but some gangsters hadn't lived to see it. Old-school crook Dzikus' kidney problems had finally carried him off a few years earlier, while Dziad died of a cerebral haemorrhage in a Radom prison on 30 October 2007, while playing table tennis. He'd been due to get out soon but his son had recently been killed in a gangster feud and the pain unique to a grieving father had destroyed Dziad's health.

Other old-timers struggled to make their mark on the new EU Poland. When Kajtek got out of prison and decided to visit a fashionable club in central Warsaw to show off his freedom, the bouncers decided he was too old for admittance and refused to lift the velvet rope. He shouted about Pruszków and retaliation, but the bouncers neither knew nor cared what he meant.

Later, Bolo summoned the current leader of Mokotów to a bar for a meeting about dividing up the city. The Finger Cutters had been severely diminished after Korek got twelve years for cocaine smuggling and arrests took out other senior members, but the gang still remained the biggest crime family in Warsaw. Its new leader showed his contempt for the old guard by rolling up to the bar at the last possible moment with a crowd of bodyguards and barely exiting his car before telling Bolo to 'stay out of Warsaw' and driving off.

'They don't even have people,' said a CBŚ officer about the Pruszków management board. 'Their soldiers are gone. New spheres of influence have emerged [and] there have been no wars lately. Looks like everything has been sorted out. And no one wants to give up their income or share anything with the "old ones". New times, new people.'

Kajtek and Bolo struggled on. They gathered some street soldiers and teamed up with their one-time enemy, Rympałek, who'd finally left prison in 2007 after the authorities ran out of charges to keep him inside. The trio dived nose-deep into the cocaine trade, but found the business tougher than expected. Rising police wages made bribery less acceptable, politicians were slightly less corrupt and the musclebound poor had more law-abiding ways to afford a good car and a designer T-shirt. By 2011, this Pruszków splinter had been rounded up and the three men were back in prison. It was a different world.

Someone who did understand the new Poland was Maringe, busy making a legitimate life for himself on the outside. He cleansed the palate with a marriage of convenience to a prostitute that changed his name to 'Jarosław Wilimberg', then studied for an MBA and put the qualification to good use by opening a construction company, a law firm, a record label, a restaurant and a tennis management company.

He spent his evenings in brothels wallowing in flesh then tried to make amends by helping working girls find new lives. 'You know, first I became addicted to prostitutes,' he said, 'and later, after listening to the stories of these women, I became addicted to getting them out of this circle of evil.'

Occasionally, he thought about rejoining the underworld but always quashed the impulse. Kajtek, Bolo and Rympałek had found out the hard way that the golden years of the 1990s were gone forever but not everyone got the message, especially after an unexpected victory for organised crime in the Polish courts.

The trial against the younger Pruszków footsoldiers, ongoing for the last seven years, finally ended in 2012 and the result shocked the prosecution. The fifty-seven accused had already been narrowed down after a score of them turned informer, took voluntary punishment or saw their charges dropped. In September, the remainder were in court to hear the judges deliver the ruling and could barely keep the smiles off their faces when over half the charges resulted in not guilty verdicts. Those convicted rarely got more than two years in prison. Most had been locked up on remand for longer than that and immediately walked free, muttering self-righteously about applying for financial compensation.

Subsequent appeals and retrials would even the score a little, but for the moment, it looked like the state had suffered a significant defeat. During the summing up, the lead judge was harshly critical of the prosecution's reliance on Masa and his testimony, while praising the prisoners for their tolerance of the situation. 'Thus, at the end of a long trial, prosecutors and gangsters changed places,' said journalist Piotr Pytlakowski. 'It seemed that the latter could even put on [lawyers'] gowns and make accusations themselves.'

Słowik got his own lucky break the next year. The judicial disparaging of Masa's testimony provided an opening to appeal his previous conviction and be retrospectively acquitted, although the judges refused to wipe away the stain of Słowik's extortion charge. He remained a prisoner as the Papała trial reached its bizarre climax.

The case hinged on a Łodz car thief nicknamed 'Patyk' (Stick), who took time out from putting former friends and corrupt police officers behind bars to mention seeing a criminal colleague of Ryszard Bogucki close to the murder scene on the night of the killing. Patyk lived nearby and had what seemed a good excuse for being in the vicinity, although rumours of the car thief's links to Masa, through gangsters from the Ochota district of Warsaw, seemed important to conspiracy theorists, if no one else.

Police sensed a Baltic coast connection via Bogucki's friendship with Nikoś, which fitted in neatly with their suspicions about expat businessman Edward Mazur, who was one of the last to see Papała alive and a frequent visitor to Gdańsk. Another gangster facing life in prison for a grisly kidnapping conveniently remembered seeing Bogucki meet with Słowik and Mazur up north to plot the policeman's death. The informer received a lenient fifteen-year sentence in exchange, which wouldn't stop him from dying of a drug overdose in his cell a few years later. About the only good news for Słowik's lawyers was that their client had been in prison when the shooting occurred, so he was only accused of directing the murder, while Bogucki was charged with being the actual assassin.

Over in America, the Chicago District Attorney refused to extradite Mazur on what looked like very flimsy evidence, so the trial began in 2009 with only Słowik and Bogucki in the dock. Things were bleak for the two until prosecutors from Łodz unexpectedly announced that further investigations had proved Patyk's testimony so unreliable that men he'd put in prison were already being freed. Then a legal bombshell was dropped that demolished the Papała case: one of Patyk's imprisoned colleagues was now claiming the car thief had killed the General himself and used his crown witness status to incriminate others. The resulting legal chaos saw Słowik and Bogucki found not guilty. Patyk would never be charged with anything.

Bogucki stayed in prison, still proclaiming his innocence of the Pershing murder, but Słowik walked free with his sentence more than served. His first act was to take revenge on Monika by selling their flat, putting her belongings in storage and taking custody of their son. He then joined what remained of the management board for a meeting at Warsaw's Hilton Hotel that allegedly discussed reactivating Pruszków, but no one seemed sure how to proceed in the changed criminal climate.

Maringe was also spending time with old contacts, although his motives were very different. Looking to get revenge for the story about his drowned friend, he'd contacted Masa and turned on the charm, resulting in a lake cruise where his old nemesis behaved like a 'village idiot' and no protection officers bothered to attend. It looked to outsiders like two fellow informers sharing memories, but Maringe was hoping to record something incriminating that would prove Masa didn't deserve his crown witness status. He mostly got footage of Masa snorting cocaine, complaining about money and discussing his brutal daily weight-lifting programme.

Eventually, Maringe compiled enough of what appeared to be evidence to contact prosecutors. Nothing happened – except the judges unexpectedly recalculated his prison sentence until it no longer included time spent on remand and ordered him back to jail. His lawyers successfully fought the request, but not until Maringe had spent a lengthy period abroad as an economic advisor in the Democratic Republic of the Congo, safe from Polish justice but conveniently close to conflict diamonds. He came home with a Congolese passport and driving licence, both of which would irritate officials for years to come.

Maringe blamed the mess on a corrupt system, but the truth had more to do with Masa's new public status. The crown witness had unexpectedly become a celebrity who made a lot of money, and that provided immunity from all kinds of evil.

23

Triumph of the Swill

The people from the television station wanted him to appear on the Polish version of *Strictly Come Dancing* (known as *Dancing with the Stars* internationally), but insisted his balaclava would have to be removed for the cameras. Masa turned them down. He knew enough about murder to understand that showing his face on national television was just making life easier for any hitmen still after him. The media people accepted his decision and dreamed up some new ideas. Masa didn't like any of them:

> I received an offer to appear in several other programs. For example, in a cooking one where I was supposed to wear an apron and balaclava and beat the participants. Totally sick idea, but violence and profanity sell the best. However, this would have been a disgrace for me and the institution of the crown witness.

He'd been less concerned about profiting from violence and profanity a decade earlier, when a pair of journalists approached with a business proposition. The management board trial had just wrapped up and the public were hungry to find out more about the arcane world of Polish gangsters. Piotr Pytlakowski and Ewa Ornacka had been reporting on organised crime for years and were obvious choices to front a groundbreaking TVN television network programme on the subject. They reached out to Poland's best-known crown witness for help. In exchange for an alleged $40,000, he agreed to act as both advisor and interviewee on *Alfabet Mafii* (*The Mafia Alphabet*), a ten-part series heavy on moody dance music, with a sombre voiceover, shaky camera footage and a lot of men in red prison jumpsuits claiming to be innocent.

The programme was a hit. An all-star cast of imprisoned gangsters from Parasol to Dziad had been convinced to take part, most of them hoping to use the programme as a platform for future appeals. Their complaints of wrongful imprisonment were intercut with a well-curated selection of informers and police officers who had very different views about the savage realities of life in the underworld. Masa made the biggest impact of all with vivid, sweary anecdotes in a distorted voice from under the black balaclava, now always worn when cameras were around.

A slimmed down ninety-minute film version was produced alongside a book of interview transcripts overseen by Pytlakowski and Ornacka. The Polish public was now better informed about the underworld than ever before but remained hungry for more. TVN gave them the fictional crime drama series *Odwróconych* (*Inverted*), based on the criminals of Pruszków, and the thriller film *Świadek Koronny* (*Crown Witness*) about a Masa-like character.

Viewers tuned in, but the film's inspiration was less pleased. 'I've been used,' said Masa:

> There are too many similarities to my life in the movie. I was guaranteed in writing that the recorded materials [from *Alfabet Mafii*] would never be used for other purposes. Meanwhile, my honest confessions, including those that are not on the tapes because we also talked privately, over dinner for example, became – without my knowledge or approval – the basis for a feature film.

Despite the outraged tone, Masa's main concern was TVN's refusal to pay for using his life story. Money was on his mind a lot these days. He'd been allowed to keep some of his wealth after turning crown witness, but a recent divorce, high living and an unquenchable thirst for steroids had thinned out his resources. In 2012, he managed to monetise his minor celebrity with a column in *Focus – Sledczy* (*Focus – Investigators*), which was a popular monthly magazine devoted to crime. A journalist transcribed his recollections of Pruszków and other gangs then moulded the flow of consciousness into a more reader-friendly format. Masa had many unexpected talents, like cooking a very respectable chicken in blue cheese sauce, but styling prose wasn't one of them.

His insights into the underworld became popular enough for a publisher to suggest putting together a full-length book. Masa reached out to Piotr Pytlakowski, but the veteran journalist was busy working with Ornacka on a new, updated edition of the *Alfabet Mafii* book. Fellow *Focus* writer Artur Górski was enlisted instead, following a meeting in a crowded restaurant where members of Masa's police protection detail sat at a nearby table eavesdropping on the conversation and looking increasingly gloomy as they realised the public exposure involved.

Books by gangsters weren't new, but previous efforts by Słowik and Dziad had been aimed at whitewashing reputations and influencing judges. As a crown witness, Masa could tell the truth without worrying about any legal consequences and the timing was right for some titillating revelations.

Poland's crime rate had dropped from a high of 2.39 per 100,000 in 1994 to 0.79 twenty years later, thanks to generous EU funding and police crackdowns. Warsaw had reverted into a placid backwater where locals enjoyed being able to stop at a red light without automatically locking their doors, and the *Kolorowe Lata 90* was a distant memory ripe for repackaging to a new generation whose understanding of organised crime was limited to imported pop culture like *Goodfellas* and *The Sopranos*. Foul-mouthed, incorrect and sometimes brutally funny, Masa would be Poland's guide to a decade when the height of glamour was a BMW with a model in the passenger seat and a Kalashnikov in the boot.

The creative process was simple. Masa, apparently now drinking again, was fed vodka while Górski recorded their conversations, sometimes augmented by old friends dropping by to join the chat. Florek even made an appearance, having quit the gangster business after tattooing Pershing's date of death across his knuckles and apologising to those he'd hurt over the years. Few had seemed very forgiving, but perhaps that wasn't the point.

The subsequent taped sessions kept circling back to the subject of women, so Górski edited the final interview transcript around that theme and added in enough connective tissue to orientate readers. A neat Who's Who of gangsters supplemented by Masa's pithy opinions was prepared for the back of the book.

In 2014, *Masa o Kobietach Polskiej Mafii* (*Masa on the Women of the Polish Mafia*) appeared in bookshops across the country. The cover traded on Masa's crown witness image by showing only the back of his shaved head and muscular neck. Inside were tales of groupies, wives, abuse, rape, violence and the everyday life of Poland's most feared gangsters, all told by a 52-year-old former crook with a colourful vocabulary and a talent for vivid stories. Sometimes he entertained, sometimes horrified, but there was no doubt readers were getting an unprecedented insight into what life had been like inside Pruszków at its height. The book became the most purchased title of the year at the huge Empik bookshop chain and a national bestseller, even if reviewers damned it as exploitative trash fit only for landfill.

Górski was a talented journalist who'd written some well-regarded novels and couldn't hide how much the criticism of his peers hurt. 'I know that if you write this, a bucket of swill will be poured over me,' he told one hostile interviewer. 'I'm begging you: please give it a rest.'

His co-writer wasn't the kind for such fine feelings, especially when the money was rolling in. Attempts by media to trap Masa into expressing regret or shame floundered in the face of his obliviousness to conventional morality. 'I don't consider myself a bad person because I've never hurt anyone *that much*,' he told a journalist. 'Yes, people fought for their lives in intensive care because of my orders, but no one "turned over" [i.e. died].'

Eleven more books would pour out under Masa's name in a literary avalanche over the next four years. Górski bundled up his co-author's transcribed conversations into themed *Masa on ...* books about killers, money, feuds, trials, bosses and more. 'I must have missed the book "Masa on the Suffering of Innocent Victims of the Pruszków Group",' noted a sarcastic reader. Others complained that later books brazenly recycled stories from earlier work, but sales remained healthy. In 2016, the Górski/Sokołowski partnership was the third-biggest earner among Polish writers; Andrzej Sapkowski, author of *The Witcher* saga, came fifth.

Masa married a model, sold the wedding photographs to the press and became enough of a celebrity to be offered parts on various reality shows. He rejected them in favour of a Facebook page where the public were treated to old photographs of gangsters in tracksuits posing with expensive cars in the 1990s, brief anecdotes of the period and praise for anyone smart enough to buy his books. Critics got some ALL CAPS abuse and a refresher course in underworld intimidation; he even threatened libel action against a commenter for posting a disobliging story about Masa that, it was quickly pointed out, had been taken directly from one of his own books.

Some of the more vicious exchanges on social media involved former gangsters who'd followed Masa's path through the media jungle to sell their own stories in ink or pixel form. In the true crime days, they'd sniped at each other with rifles, but now it was Facebook posts and YouTube videos. Things occasionally got heated enough for the old ways to make a comeback.

Jarosław Maringe decided the feud had gone too far when someone planted an artillery shell in the furnace of his restaurant. An Italian eaterie with a French twist, Boretti was an informal space of bare brick walls and stripped wood furniture in Praga that did a solid line in pizzas and crêpes. Reviews were never outstanding but the place made money. Then, one day, the police were ushering staff outside and explaining that, if the furnace had ignited, the whole building would have been levelled. No one knew who was responsible, but Maringe had his suspicions, mostly about Masa.

The crown witness's success had inspired a wagon train of fellow gangsters and the occasional police officer to saddle up for the promised land of celebrity. Słowik appeared in the video for a terrible rap song called 'Big Poppa' by Malik Montana, alongside the usual clichés of sports cars, night clubs and American sportswear. Others started Facebook pages, Twitter accounts and YouTube channels, gave interviews and talks, and published memoirs. Masa loomed over all their efforts like a harvest moon, inescapable.

Szlachet was out of prison after nearly seven years and working on a pair of self-published books about life as a Pruszków footsoldier that focused obsessively on his time working for Masa. Former police officer Piotr Wróbel wrote *Mój Agent Masa* (*My Agent Masa*) with the help of

Piotr Pytlakowski, whose *Nowy Alfabet Mafii* had lost sales to Masa's early books. Wróbel had only just finally cleared his name of corruption allegations – something he blamed on the crown witness – and the tone was more than a little bitter.

Other books came out about Nikoś, Mokotów and other gangs written by informers, members, victims and wives, with help from whatever journalist remembered the 1990s enough to sound convincing. Masa somehow managed to be mentioned in all of them. Off the page, he was the loudest voice among authors raging about old scores, fresh accusations and performative threats in the social media soap opera that publishers thought necessary to sell books.

Raging with the best of them was Jarosław Maringe, who'd abandoned his low-profile life as a Warsaw entrepreneur with a classy apartment and a girlfriend half his age to re-emerge into the spotlight. It would have made sense to stay quiet and keep making money, but Maringe couldn't bear to see his old enemy become a celebrity with the power to shape the narrative of the gangster years. He joined the media scrum to tell his own story and stick a few banderillas into Masa at the same time. 'He wrote one thing in his books, something else on social networks, and something else again when he testified to the authorities,' Maringe claimed.

This started a vicious back and forth across social media, with threats of legal action and wild accusations. Then the shell appeared in the Boretti furnace after a series of anonymous, hostile phone calls. The entrepreneur's past gave police a deep bench of suspects and no one was ever arrested, but Maringe was smart enough to dial down the social media grudge match. It had already generated enough publicity to launch his own book, the 2017 ghost-written *Chińczyk: Król Polskiego Narkobiznesu* (*The Chinese: King of the Polish Drug Trade*), telling the story of his journey from PRL tearaway to Bulgarian exile. Its cover showed a plump but well-dressed Maringe holding a pair of cute, tiny dogs and looking more like a fancy businessman than a thug.

The book earned him some television appearances and various interviews in the print press. For a while, he was first call for a press quote about drugs or prostitution, and usually took the opportunity to attack Masa at the same time. Sales figures were kept confidential but don't seem to have dazzled because the sequel hinted at being privately published. *Chińczyk: Przemytnicza Odyseja* (*The Chinese: A Smuggler's*

Odyssey) came out the next year with no sign of a co-writer and did a pretty good impression of a man in love with the sound of his own voice. Anyone desperate to hear Maringe lecture on Serbian architecture, Swedish women and the history of the Dominican Republic was in for a treat.

By the following year, Maringe had hit the pause button on autobiography and was living in Spain enjoying his wealth and telling journalists about his new obsessions:

> I am a creator of MMO games for mobile devices, this is my latest passion. Besides, there is a lot going on in my life. It is true that I got bored with writing books, but in their place I started creating a script for a director. Most of my time, however, is games and algorithms.

The management board might be expected to have strong views on the spilling of all these Pruszków secrets but found themselves otherwise occupied. Parasol, Wańka and Słowik hadn't been able to stay away from organised crime and in 2017 they were arrested for leading a gang involved in VAT fraud and various other offences. Kajtek was still fighting the system hard to delay his own trial, but co-defendant Bolo died of pancreatic cancer behind bars in September 2021 at 69 years old.

Rympałek got twenty-five years in prison for crimes that included the murder of a fellow gang member during his drug years. Meanwhile, Bedzio had beaten them all back to prison after getting arrested in 2014 for drug offences, and Żaba's widow Baśka got six and a half years for involvement in the activities of an armed criminal group.

With so many former gangsters back behind bars, Masa felt safe revealing some of Pruszków's links with the SLD and other politicians in a new book, produced with a fresh co-writer after ending his partnership with Artur Górski. He probably shouldn't have waited so long to tell the story. What would once have been scandalous was now ancient history, thanks to the SLD's plunge into insignificance after savage losses in the 2005 election.

Polish politics had become a battle between the two new conservative parties, *Prawo i Sprawiedliwość* (Law and Justice) and *Platforma Obywatelska* (Civic Platform), both run by ex-*Solidarność* activists who initially differed only in whether they went to church often or daily, although the ideological gap would widen over time. By 2018's *Bandyci i Celebryci* (*Bandits and Celebrities*), written with journalist Janusz Szostak, the gangster lemon was being squeezed dry as Masa made a book from memories of meeting anyone even vaguely famous.

His own celebrity was slipping away by the day, but would unexpectedly be revived by an event no one saw coming. 'Shortly after writing this book, Jarosław Sokołowski was detained and arrested,' wrote a bemused Szostak in the introduction. 'It was a complete surprise and not only for him. I have to admit that I didn't expect such a turn of events at all.'

The crimes involved bribing customs officials to reduce excise on an imported car, failing to repay bank loans, lying about traffic offences and not paying builders for work done on a new house. For the man who boasted of his role in the Pruszków Mafia, this was embarrassingly small-scale stuff, but it still carried a stiff legal penalty of ten years in prison. Five other people were arrested at the same time, including a senior policeman in Łódź who had previously served as one of Masa's protection officers.

The crown witness's disgrace was complete the next year, when boxer Andrzej Gołota won a libel suit over accusations that the Michael Grant fight had been fixed. Masa was forced to make a public apology and hand over 10,000zł to charity.

Maringe reappeared with a third book, gloating over his old enemy's misfortunes, in which he tried to take credit for the arrest. It received some attention, but a fourth volume about brothels and the sex trade made little impact. He returned to Spain, his MMO business and a more anonymous existence, having fitted more into one lifetime than most people could manage in ten.

Masa's response to the book or the charges remains unknown because lawyers seem to have advised him to tone down his public profile ahead of any trial. The crown witness's social media went dark and the apparently unstoppable flow of books abruptly ceased. Judging by rumours about declining sales, the decision wasn't difficult.

The genre of gangster true confessions barely outlived its creator. In 2020 came the last gasp, when Słowik collaborated with Szostak for *Słowik: Skazany na Bycie Gangsterem* (*Słowik: Condemned to be a Gangster*), a book the former Pruszków man seemed to have planned as another coat of whitewash for his reputation. Szostak eventually delivered something more caustic, but it seemed symbolic that the final book involving a senior gangster returned the genre to the motives behind that original volume written while Słowik was on the run in Spain.

After the Słowik book, any widespread public interest in the *Kolorowe Lata 90* ebbed away. For six years, the market had been flooded with content of varying quality by sometimes unreliable narrators who were more interested in a quick payday than settling the historical record. Gangster obsessives at sites like online-mafia.pl and pruszkownews.pl would keep the flame burning, but the Polish public had moved on to fresh topics for its national conversation. Fascination had, in many cases, been replaced by revulsion.

The MMA-VIP League was a recently formed Polish martial arts federation whose 'freak fights' pitted rappers against boxers, former criminals against reality show stars, and men against women. In January 2022, the league introduced its new boss at a press conference. As the theme from *The Godfather* played, a smallish man in a tuxedo sat on a gaudy red and gold throne and removed his mask to reveal the hollow-eyed, vulpine features of Słowik. He was out on bail and convinced this venture into the world of sport would help improve his reputation.

The league had hoped for a provocative publicity stunt but instead suffered a backlash that saw sponsors pull out and cities across the country ban scheduled events. People seemed genuinely disgusted by Słowik's involvement. That short window of glamorising violent crime in post-communist Poland had slammed shut and severed the fingers of anyone unlucky enough to be late climbing through. It will undoubtedly open again at some point in the future. Human beings have an unending fascination with anyone prepared to tear down society's rules and live by the law of the jungle.

24

Might is Right

By 1896, a tenth of Chicago's population identified as Polish-American. The community had been founded six decades earlier by émigrés, who fled the old country in search of a better life only to end up in a lakeside city with winters as bitterly cold as back home. They built churches, boiled *pierogi* and turned Division Street into a strip of imported culture soon nicknamed the 'Polish Broadway'.

Chicago's Poles were conservative, patriotic types who saluted the stars and stripes but reached for a revolver whenever they heard anything too radical. Polish-language newspapers preached daily that anarchists and free-thinkers were the real enemy, and their subversion just as dangerous as any Cossack horde back home. It wasn't surprising that the book review columns chose not to mention the publication that year of a new volume called *Might is Right or The Survival of the Fittest* by a small Chicago firm. Author 'Ragnar Redbeard' didn't sound Polish and, even if he had been, the message in his book was so profoundly insulting to Catholic Slavs and all notions of moral decency that the publisher's stock would probably have been publicly burned on Division Street had more people known about it.

Redbeard squashed together Nietzschean Nihilism and Social Darwinism into a tract that proclaimed the strong ruled the weak, men ruled women and physical force was the only arbiter of life's struggle. His philosophy tossed Christianity into the garbage can and pointed readers towards a world more in tune with nature's amoral barbarism, all red in tooth and claw. 'The strong must ever rule the weak / is grim Primordial

Law,' ran a poem that served as the book's conclusion. 'On earth's broad racial threshing floor / the meek are beaten straw; / Then ride to power o'er foemen's necks / let nothing bar your way / If you are fit you'll rule and reign / is the Logic of Today.'

Over the coming decades, many readers, and even a few Polish-Americans, would fall under the spell of Redbeard's philosophy and dream of a world where pitiless Nietzschean *übermenschen* ruled the sheep-like masses from towers dripping blood where the women probably wore chainmail bikinis. Unfortunately for all concerned, whenever anything close to the vision of 'Might is Right' has ever been inflicted on the world, it always looks a lot like Pruszków. A society without law, order or compassion will only ever benefit gangs of thick-necked, barely literate bodybuilders from the wrong end of town, all of them ugly as 8 miles of bad road. It is tracksuits and baseball bats, not natural aristocrats lit by lightning flash, that makes might right. That holds true in Chicago, in Warsaw and everywhere else in the world.

'These people go around pretending to be some kind of Robin Hood,' said Jimmy Holmes about former friends from a tough British gangster crew that ran Soho and east London, 'but the truth is that they're scumbags, and I should know because I used to be a scumbag too.'

The fittest got to survive in 1990s Poland because the tectonic plates of society had shifted to reveal new opportunities in the rupture point between communism and democracy. Gangsters made money from what could be called 'parasite activities' (preying on other people's honest work through extortion and theft) and 'contraband capitalism' (running businesses that supplied desirable but illegal products like drugs or gambling). As Pablo Escobar and Alvin Chau have discovered, the real wealth lies in contraband, but Pruszków was snuffed out in an early stage of development before that arm of the gang could fully mature. Perhaps if it had survived longer, business brains like Jarosław Maringe or shrewd operators like Masa could have risen to the top. Instead, the leg-breakers got to write Pruszków's legacy in blood across the face of a shocked Polish public.

In the gang's final days, Masa lieutenant Grzegorz Łubkowski, aka 'Mięśniak' (Muscle Man), experienced a well-overdue epiphany when a crowd of onlookers gathered to applaud the police arresting him. 'That was when we really learned for the first time,' he wrote later, 'that no one liked us.' Other critics showed their feelings in more direct ways. When Parasol's sidekick Krzyś died of cancer in 2004 at 51 years old, his grave was repeatedly vandalised by those he'd brutalised over the years.

Today, the tectonic plates have settled again, and Poland is a safer place. Membership of the European Union has provided successive governments with the cash and motivation to crack down on organised crime, mopping up the remnants of Pruszków and crippling gangs like Mokotów. Police are now paid enough to make bribe-taking the exception rather than the rule, and cash robberies have become impractical in a world where online transactions dominate. Crime and violence are never going to vanish completely, but Warsaw has become a more peaceful city, with safe streets an everyday reality and widespread extortion rackets a thing of the past.

Organised crime still exists but on a smaller, less-public scale. White-collar offences involving VAT or tax evasion have become popular because profits are high and the penalties relatively low. A smaller but tougher crowd who are less afraid of prison make their money through illegal narcotics. In 2015, record seizures of cannabis resin (843kg), cocaine (219kg) and methamphetamine (51kg) were reported. Despite this, native drug consumption is low by EU standards: in 2017 only 9.8 per cent of 15–34-year-olds admitted trying cannabis, as compared to 22.1 per cent in France, and only 0.4 per cent had tried cocaine, compared to the 4 per cent in the UK who'd shoved it up their noses. The lack of a lucrative local market means Poland is more transit point than destination, and smugglers will never achieve anything close to Pablo Escobar's society-distorting levels of wealth.

Crime gangs have faded back into the shadows and taken their bombastic public profiles with them. Journalists now mention once-famous thugs like Parasol, Wańka, Słowik and Kajtek in almost pitying tones, sketching them with a few lines and a pithy quote as ageing men spending their last precious years waiting for trials that never seem to arrive. Only Malizna gets some reluctant sympathy for having apparently taken a more law-abiding path into the restaurant business after leaving prison. Reporters seem sure his former colleagues will eventually die behind bars.

Other Pruszków veterans occasionally make the news. In 2016, a photograph appeared in the media of 40-something football hooligan Tomasz Czerwiński confronting a Spanish riot policeman with blood flowing down his face during a match between Real Madrid and Legia Warszawa. Under the nickname 'Czerwus', he'd been linked with Masa's crew in the last years of Pruszków. '[He] said after his arrest that he spent 17 years in a Polish prison and didn't care much about having to spend two days in a cell,' said a journalist covering the violence. 'During the fighting, Czerwiński punched up to 12 policemen.'

A bigger story arrived in 2022, when journalists discovered the head of Ukraine's International Legion was Piotr Kapuściński, aka 'Broda' (Beard), a former Pruszków gangster-turned-crown witness. Well connected enough that an interview with him appeared in Słowik's *Skazany na Bycie Gangsterem* book, Broda's testimony had put nine of his fellow crooks in prison before he vanished into Ukraine when prosecutors suspected him of remaining active in the underworld. Over the border, he was investigated by local police for rape, robbery and other crimes. None of the more serious charges seemed to stick and Broda was out on bail for possession of a firearm when Russian forces invaded. He joined the Ukrainian army, changed his first name to Sasha and ended up leading a group of foreign volunteers who'd come to help Kyiv.

It can't have surprised many people when Broda was accused of looting, robbing his own men, sexually assaulting a nurse, military incompetence and kidnapping. So far, no charges have been brought. Poles with long memories know Pruszków has provided soldiers for foreign wars in the past. During the mid-1990s, the gang made money smuggling Poles looking for adventure or escape into wartorn Yugoslavia. 'We were cannon fodder so that the Pruszków bosses could make money,' said one volunteer who joined up to flee trouble in Poland. 'Over there I realized that my problems at home were a paradise compared to what I saw in Bosnia.'

Squeezing money out of civil war was just another business opportunity for gangsters. Their charitable acts can be counted on the fingers of a blind sawmill worker, but apologists occasionally like to claim that Pruszków looked after its friends; that Parasol once bought the entire stock of a grocery shop to distribute to the poor; that Szlachet beat up a paedophile; that a hit on a rival gangster was aborted because his wife was in the car; that Masa was polite and considerate to anyone outside the world of organised crime. Perhaps, but their victims suffered out of all proportion.

Business owners were driven to bankruptcy and suicide, women traumatised by rape, the political sphere corrupted, law enforcement compromised and the economy so badly crippled that it only limped into developed status a few years ago. Former gangsters have their own sob stories, like the 17-year-old schoolboy who joined Pruszków as muscle in the protection rackets, but got stomped so hard during a gang fight outside a pub that his spine snapped. He will spend the rest of his life in a wheelchair. At least he lived.

'If you dig well,' said Masa about the forests of Poland, 'you will find several hundred more bodies, which no one remembers today.' Before you grab a spade and go mining for the past, trace a finger past the light-green patches that signify wooded areas on the map and locate the pale grey line of a road connecting Pruszków with the neighbouring town of Reguły. Out in the real world, anyone driving west between the two points will pass a pair of road signs attached to a metal pole where the town borders meet. Above, a red line slashes through the 'Reguły' plate to mark the end of its territory; below, 'Pruszków' remains untouched, so drivers know where they're heading. In Polish, the word *reguły* also means 'rules'.

'Where Rules end,' say the locals, with a knowing smile, 'Pruszków begins.'

Appendix

Gangsters of the Polish Mafia

Pruszków

Adrian aka Adrian Kołodziejek
Ali aka Zbigniew Kujawsk
Barabasz aka Ireneusz Piszczałkowski
Bedzio aka Robert Bednarczyk
  (Pruszków/Ożarów)
Bolo aka Zygmunt Raźniak
Broda aka Piotr Kapuściński
Budzik aka Wojciech Budziszewski
Bysiu aka Dariusz Bytniewski
  (Pruszków/Ożarów)
Carrington aka Zbigniew Mikołajewski
  (Pruszków/Lower Silesia)
Chińczyk aka Jarosław Maringe
Dreszcz aka Jacek Dresz
Dzikus aka Czesław Borowski
Florek aka Andrzej Florowski
  (Pruszków/Ożarów)
Jąkaty *see* Chińczyk
Kaban *see* Bolo
Kajtek aka Ryszard Szwarc
Kazik aka Kazimierz Klimas
Kiełbacha aka Wojciech Kiełbiński
Kiełbasa *see* Kiełbacha
Kojber *see* Masa
Kozioł aka Krzysztof
'Kręciłapka'
Krzyś aka Krzysztof Ryszard Pawlik
'Kuba Gwałciciel'
'Lulek'
Malizna aka Mirosław Danielak
Małolat aka Paweł Miller (Ożarów/
  Pruszków)
Mariusz, aka Szlachet
Masa aka Jarosław Sokołowski
  (Pruszków/Ożarów)
'Matyś'
Mięśniak aka Grzegorz Łubkowski
Oczko aka Marek Medvesek
  (Pruszków/Szczecin)
Papież *see* Pershing
Parasol aka Janusz Prasol
Pershing aka Andrzej Kolikowski
  (Pruszków/Ożarów)
'Pinokio' (Pruszków/Warszawa)
'Rakiet'
'Remek' (Pruszków/Warszawa)
Rympałek aka Marek Janusz Czarnecki
  (Pruszków/Warszawa)
Ryszard Bogucki (Gdańsk/
  Pruszków)
Rzeźnik aka Ryszard Niemczyk
  (Gdańsk/Pruszków)

Simon aka Zbigniew Szczepaniak
    (Pruszków/Katowice)
'Słoń'
Słowik aka Andrzej Banasiak

Szarak aka Andrzej Ciężczyk
Wańka aka Leszek Danielak
Żaba aka Jerzy Wieczorek

Wołomin

Ceber aka Czesław Kamiński
Cezary Dresz (Wołomin/Ząbki)
Dziad aka Henryk Niewiadomski
    (Wołomin/Ząbki)
'Golden' (Wołomin/Ząbki)
Karolek aka Karol Sarna
Kikir aka Andrzej Czetyrko

Klepak aka Jacek Klepacki
Lutek aka Ludwik Adamski
Maniek aka Marian Klepacki
Poldek aka Apoloniusz Dąbrowski
    (Wołomin/Ząbki)
Wariat aka Wiesław Niewiadomski
    (Wołomin/Ząbki)

Other

Aleksander aka Igor Pikus (Mutants)
Andrei Isaev (Moscow)
'Bogdan' (Warszawa)
'Bolek' (Mokotów)
Cieluś aka Robert Cieślak (Mutants)
'Czaja' (Warszawa)
Komandos aka Tomasz Suga (Warszawa)
'Korek' (Mokotów)
'Kura' (Gdansk)

Mutant aka Jerzy Brodowski (Mutants)
Nikoś aka Nikodem Skotarczak
    (Gdańsk)
'Patyk' (Łodz)
Szkatuła aka Rafał Skatulski (Warszawa)
Wiktor Fiszman (Minsk/Szczecin)
Zachar aka Daniel Zacharzewski
    (Gdańsk)
Zbigniew Nawrot (Hamburg)

Notes

1. Death of a Polish Gangster

'Baldy, you should take …' – Maringe & Majewski, *Chińczyk: Król Polskiego Narkobiznesu* (Zona Zero, 2017), p. 50.
'You will leave a …' – Szostak, *Kto Naprawdę Zabił Pershinga*, 25 May 2019 (newsbook.pl/2019/05/25/kto-naprawde-zabil-pershinga/).
'The alleged boss of …' – 'Pershing', *Nie Żyje*, 6 December 1999 (www.rmf24.pl/fakty/news-pershing-nie-zyje,nId,126059).
'We went on the …' – Górski & Sokołowski, *Masa o Porachunkach Polskiej Mafii* (Prószyński Media, 2015).
'Ninety percent of all …' – Teresa & Renner, *My Life in the Mafia* (Facwett, 1973), p. 126.

2. The 15:10 to *Juma*

'They have allowed themselves …' – Schom, *Napoleon Bonaparte* (Sharpe, 2018).
'Chelba? Nie ma …' – Roberts, *Napoleon* (Penguin, 2016).
'One of his tasks …' – Maringe & Majewski, *Chińczyk: Król Polskiego Narkobiznesu*, p. 16.
'Being taught etiquette, told …' – Swoboda, *Był Szefem Polskiego Narkobiznesu: 'Nie Wiem, Ile Zarobiłem. Dziesięć, Dwadzieścia Milionów?'*, 21 July 2018 (weekend.gazeta.pl/weekend/7,152121,22537800,byl-szefem-polskiego-narkobiznesu-nie-wiem-ile-zarobilem.html).
'In order not to …' – Maringe & Majewski, *Chińczyk: Król Polskiego Narkobiznesu*, p. 19.
'It was something my …' – *ibid.*, p. 20.
'A stocky worker in …' – Wren, 'Travel in Soviet Bloc is a Journey to Linked but Disparate Worlds', *New York Times*, 28 December 1976.

'It was very important …' – Maringe & Majewski, *Chińczyk: Król Polskiego Narkobiznesu*, p. 21.
'The biggest mistake of …' – Swoboda, *Był Szefem Polskiego Narkobiznesu: 'Nie Wiem, Ile Zarobiłem. Dziesięć, Dwadzieścia Milionów?'*, 21 July 2018 (weekend.gazeta.pl/weekend/7,152121,22537800,byl-szefem-polskiego-narkobiznesu-nie-wiem-ile-zarobilem.html).
'I was small, skinny …' – Maringe & Majewski, *Chińczyk: Król Polskiego Narkobiznesu*, p. 25.
'You attack or you …' – *ibid*.
Foreign cars could be … – Nawrocki, '"Autogangs": Car Smuggle [sic] to Communist Poland in the 1980s', *Studia Historiae Oeconomicae*, Vol. 34, 2016.
'Come to Poland …' – Banck, *DuMont Reise-Taschenbuch Usedom* (Dumont Reiseverlag, 2020), p. 268.
'As two drops of …' – Maringe & Majewski, *Chińczyk: Król Polskiego Narkobiznesu*, p. 85.

3. Enter the Goon Squad

'Like a Mongol warrior …' – Ornacka & Pytlakowski, *Nowy Alfabet Mafii* (Rebis, 2013), p. 158.
'Git-Ludzie …' – Also sometimes known as '*Grypsujący*'.
'Troglodytes …' – Górski & Sokołowski, *Masa o Bossach Polskiej Mafii* (Prószyński Media, 2015), p. 240.
'Milicja's notorious ZOMO riot police …' – ZOMO = *Zmotoryzowane Odwody Milicji Obywatelskiej* (Motorised Citizens' Militia Reserves).
'Grab whoever you can …' – Międzybrodzki, '"Mission Accomplished: Crowds Dispersed": Clashes Between Polish Citizens and ZOMO on the Streets of Polish Cities as Seen through the Eyes of Participants', 13 December 1981–31 December 1982, *The Polish Review*, Vol. 55, No. 2, 2010.
'Why aren't you chasing …' – Podracki, 'Początek Potęgi "Grupy Pruszkówskiej": Co Wydarzyło sie na Trasie Katowickiej?', 29 May 2022 (Pruszkównews.pl/poczatek-potegi-grupy-Pruszkówskiej-co-wydarzylo-sie-na-trasie-katowickiej/).
Crime figures that year … – Bełdzikowski, 'Ethics and Pathology in the Polish Police – Professional and Political Aspects', *Scientific Journal WSFiP*, No. 2, 2016.
'I felt a muffled …' – Ornacka & Pytlakowski, *Nowy Alfabet Mafii*, p. 170.
'They just set everything …' – Ornacka & Pytlakowski, *Nowy Alfabet Mafii*, p. 12.
'Who said you can't …' – Górski & Sokołowski, *Masa o Bossach Polskiej Mafii*, pp. 40 & 38.
'I saw with my …' – Ornacka & Pytlakowski, *Nowy Alfabet Mafii*, p. 13.
'No one liked her …' – Górski & Sokołowski, *Masa o Bossach Polskiej Mafii*, p. 73.
'Pruszków was not a …' – *ibid*., p. 44.

4. Savage Youth from the PRL

'A live sex show ...' – Latkowski & Pytlakowski, *Koronny nr 1: Pseudonim Masa* (Rebis, 2017).

'As a boy, I ...' – Czop, 'Pruszków oczami Jarosława "Masy" Sokołowskiego cz. II', 10 July 2014 (www.Pruszkówmowi.pl/2014/07/Pruszków-oczami-jaroslawa-masy-Sokołowskiego-cz-ii/).

'In those years, it ...' – Latkowski & Pytlakowski, *Koronny nr 1: Pseudonim Masa*.

'When he saw that ...' – Pytlakowski, 'Jak Jarek rósł w Masę', 27 March 2019 (www.polityka.pl/tygodnikpolityka/klasykipolityki/1786214,1,jak-jarek-rosl-w-mase.read).

'[Kiełbacha] was my best ...' – 'Wojtek K. "Kiełbasa". Chłopak z Dobrego Domu, Który Usiadł na Złej Ławce i Został Gangsterem', 21 October 2021 (wiadomosci.onet.pl/kraj/wojtek-k-kielbasa-chlopak-z-dobrego-domu-ktory-zostal-gangsterem/mkdcj2t).

'The girl shouted that ...' – Sokołowski, *Protokół Przesłuchania Podejrzanego* (2000).

'The 30 złotys (zł) needed ... – Pichaske, 'Poland in Transition 1989–91: Street Markets' (politicalcritique.org/cee/poland/2018/poland-in-transition-1989-1991-street-markets/).

'A margarine sandwich ...' – 'Skinheads in People's Poland and After', Part 3: 'Tough Times, Tougher Skins' (creaseslikeknives.wordpress.com/skinheads-in-peoples-poland-and-after-part-3-tough-times-tougher-skins).

'I travelled to Germany ...' – Ornacka & Pytlakowski, *Nowy Alfabet Mafii*, p. 422.

'Nothing has ever lasted ...' – Pichaske, *Poland in Transition: 1989–91* (Ellis Press, 2017).

One smuggler was able ... – 'Materials Produced during the 93rd International Seminar Course: "Policy Perspective for Organized Crime Suppression"', United Nations Asia and Far East Institute for the Prevention of Crime and Treatment of Offenders, 1993.

Poles were a thirsty ... – Gorsky et al., 'Anti-alcohol Posters in Poland, 1945–1989: Diverse Meanings, Uncertain Effects', *American Journal of Public Health*, Vol. 100, No. 11, November 2010.

'Their method was not ...' – Górski & Sokołowski, *Masa o Bossach Polskiej Mafii*, p. 21.

5. Day of the Troglodytes

'It must be said that ...' – Szostak & Sokołoski, *Bandyci i Celebryci* (Wydawnictwo Harde, 2018).

'Listen to how stupid ...' – *ibid*.

In the aftermath, Soviet ... – Chivers, 'In Ukraine, Spent Cartridges Offer Clues to Violence Fueled by Soviet Surplus', *New York Times*, 24 July 2014 (archive.nytimes.com/atwar.blogs.nytimes.com/2014/07/24/in-ukraine-spent-cartridges-offer-clues-to-violence-fueled-by-soviet-surplus/).

'Polish regulators acknowledge they …' – Engelberg, 'Poland's New Climate Yields Bumper Crop of Corruption', *New York Times*, 12 November 1991.
'Just some shabby Polish …' – Górski & Sokołowski, *Masa o Bossach Polskiej Mafii*, p. 46.
'Hitting was the only …' – *ibid.*, p. 47.
'Ali and Dzikus told …' – Ornacka & Pytlakowski, *Nowy Alfabet Mafii*, p. 15.
'Give me a cigarette …' – 'Zbigniew K. ps. "Ali", FC', 4 Janaury 2021 (online-mafia.pl/zbigniew-k-ps-ali/).
'Fuck, how they fucked …' – *ibid.*
'A few slaps and …' – Ornacka & Pytlakowski, *Nowy Alfabet Mafii*, p. 38.
'The boss didn't have …' – Górski & Sokołowski, *Masa o Bossach Polskiej Mafii*, p. 21.

6. Seks and Drugs

'Back then it was …' – Maringe & Majewski, *Chińczyk: Król Polskiego Narkobiznesu*, p. 63.
'I did not fit …' – *ibid.*, p. 57.
'Everything went white, then …' – 'Marek C. ps. Rympałek: Postrach Pruszków', 7 January 2021 (online-mafia.pl/marek-c-Rympałek/).
'Get up, they've already …' – *ibid.*
'I met a girl …' – Mieśnik, 'Król alfonsów o seksbiznesie w Polsce', 4 August 2017 (www.logo24.pl/Logo24/7,125389,22191266,krol-alfonsow-o-seksbiznesie-w-polsce.html).
'Don't think, however, that …' – Maringe & Majewski, *Chińczyk: Król Polskiego Narkobiznesu*, p. 67.
'Someone sold to celebrities …' – *ibid.*, p. 61.
'If the authorities allow …' – 'Warsaw Tourist Shops Close in Protest against Crime', *New York Times*, 7 August 1994.
'There were crowds of …' – Szulecka, 'Obecność Cudzoziemców na Targowisku Zlokalizowanym wokół Stadionu Dziesięciolecia z Perspektywy Kryminologicznej', *CMR Working Papers*, No. 24/82, 2007.
'They were from a …' – Górski & 'Nazar', *Ruska Mafia* (Prószyński Media, 2019).
'Slim guy with …' – Maringe & Majewski, *Chińczyk: Król Polskiego Narkobiznesu*, p. 57.
'Beat his girls in …' – Sumlinkski, *Czego Nie Powie Masa o Polskiej Mafii* (WSR, 2015), p. 53.
'[He was] an extremely …' – Sokołowski, 'Jak Żaba na Prochach', 11 July 2013 (www.focus.pl/artykul/jak-Żaba-na-prochach).
'The gates of paradise …' – Maringe & Majewski, *Chińczyk: Król Polskiego Narkobiznesu*, p. 34.

7. Rocket Man

'At first glance you …' – 'Tropem Mafii, Tropem Zbrodni', 13 October 2007 (wiadomosci.dziennik.pl/opinie/artykuly/206938,tropem-mafii-tropem-zbrodni.html).
'I thought I would …' – Górski & Sokołowski, *Masa o Porachunkach Polskiej Mafii* (2015).
The official police clear-up … – Haberfeld et al., 'Community Policing in Poland: Final Report', US Department of Justice Document No. 199360, 2003.
'We didn't think …' – Maringe & Majewski, *Chińczyk: Król Polskiego Narkobiznesu*, p. 49.
'There is enough honey …' – Latkowski, *Polska Mafia* (Świat Książki, 2011).
'Parasol and Krzyś would …' – Czerwiński & Szatkowski, *Pershing: Król Życia* (Mafia.pl, 2020), p. 40.
'If the gas had …' – Czerwiński, *Śladami Polskich Gangsterów: Miejsca Mafijnej Warszawy lat 90* (Mafia.pl, 2020), p. 195.
'As the driver hit …' – Górski & 'Nazar', *Ruska Mafia*.
As late as 1985 … – Jarusz, 'Old Age and Poverty in Poland, 1945–1989: The Status Regarding Knowledge and Research Problems', *Studia Historiae o Economicae*, UAM, Vol. 32, Poznań, 2014.
An investigation at the … – Kojder, 'Corruption in Poland Today', *The Polish Sociological Bulletin*, No. 99/100, 1992.
'The State robs me …' – Ledeneva (ed.), *The Global Encyclopaedia of Informality*, Vol. 2: *Understanding Social and Cultural Complexity* (UCL Press, 2018), p. 224.
'Dziad did not want …' – Sokołowski, *Protokół Przesłuchania Podejrzanego*.

8. 'Get in the Van, You Whore!'

'We spoke on the …' – 'Wojtek K. "Kiełbasa": Chlopak z Dobrego Domu, Ktory Zostal Gangsterem', 21 October 2021 (wiadomosci.onet.pl/kraj/wojtek-k-kielbasa-chlopak-z-dobrego-domu-ktory-zostal-gangsterem/mkdcj2t).
'Journalists helped us a …' – Ornacka & Pytlakowski, *Nowy Alfabet Mafii*, p. 35.
'Get in, you whore …' – Górski & Sokołowski, *Masa o Porachunkach Polskiej Mafii*.
'Long time no see …' – Latkowski, *Polska Mafia*.
'Tap the inner resources …' – Bennetts, 'Sixth Sense: Why Business is Booming for Russia's Psychics', 9 December 2014 (www.calvertjournal.com/articles/show/3439/why-business-is-booming-for-russias-psychics).
'I'm a believer …' – Czerwiński & Szatkowski, *Pershing: Król Życia*, p. 12.
'I know that Polish …' – Górski & 'Nazar', *Ruska Mafia*.
'Pershing was simple-minded …' – 'Jasnowidz i Gangster: Co Naprawdę Łączyło Krzysztofa Jackowskiego z Pershingiem', 20 January 2019 (newsbook.pl/2019/01/20/jasnowidz-i-gangster-co-naprawde-laczylo-krzysztofa-jackowskiego-z-pershingiem/).

'Tacky ...' – 'Tropem Mafii, Tropem Zbrodni', 13 October 2007 (wiadomosci.dziennik.pl/opinie/artykuly/206938, tropem-mafii-tropem-zbrodni.html).
'Get the fuck out ...' – Czerwiński, *Śladami Polskich Gangsterów: Miejsca Mafijnej Warszawy lat 90*, p. 197.
'Almost no pain ...' – 'Jasnowidz i Gangster: Co Naprawdę Łączyło Krzysztofa Jackowskiego z Pershingiem', 20 January 2019 (newsbook.pl/2019/01/20/jasnowidz-i-gangster-co-naprawde-laczylo-krzysztofa-jackowskiego-z-pershingiem/).
'Out with friends for ...' – Ornacka & Pytlakowski, *Nowy Alfabet Mafii*, p. 60.
'The police used to ...' – Borger, 'After the Wall: The Godfather – "Most Businesses in Warsaw Pay Protection Money"', *The Guardian*, 3 November 1994.
'If you don't know ...' – Pytlakowski & Wróbel, *Mój Agent Masa* (Rebis, 2015).

9. A Miniature Vietnam

'The bile ...' – Górski & Sokołowski, *Masa o Bossach Polskiej Mafii*.
'I practised karate for ...' – Czerwiński & Szatkowski, *Pershing: Król Życia*, p. 97.
95 per cent of adult Poles ... – Kojder, 'Corruption in Poland: Symptoms, Causes, Scope and Attempted Counter-Measures', *Polish Sociological Review*, No. 146, 2004.
'I remember press conferences ...' – Roszkowska, 'Mafia po Polsku: "Nie Jestem Bossem Żadnej Mafii. Ja tylko Bronię swoich Sąsiadów"', 18 Ocgtober 2021 (weekend.gazeta.pl/weekend/7,177333,27693195,mafia-po-polsku-nie-jestem-bossem-zadnej-mafii-ja-tylko-bronie.html).
'He was like a ...' – Górski & Sokołowski, *Masa o Porachunkach Polskiej Mafii*.
'A cow in the ...' – 'Wojciech B. ps. "Budzik"', *FC* (online-mafia.pl/2018/09/03/wojciech-b-budzik/).
'A miniature Vietnam ...' – Ornacka & Pytlakowski, *Nowy Alfabet Mafii*, p. 29.
Inflation was down 8 per cent ... – Galata, 'The Transformation of Poland's Economic System: 1985–1995', *Canadian Slavonic Papers / Revue Canadienne des Slavistes*, Vol. 39, No. 1/2, March–June 1997.
'You're safe with us ...' – Ornacka & Pytlakowski, *Nowy Alfabet Mafii*, p. 44.
'My company just collects ...' – 'Tropem Mafii, Tropem Zbrodni', 13 October 2007 (wiadomosci.dziennik.pl/opinie/artykuly/206938,tropem-mafii-tropem-zbrodni.html).
'The war was always ...' – Latkowski, *Polska Mafia*.
'I want to make ...' – Górski & Sokołowski, *Masa o Żołnierzach Polskiej Mafii* (Prószyński i S-ka, 2016).
'He snorted coke like ...' – Szostak, *Gangsterskie Egzekucje* (Harde Wydawnictwo, 2019).
'My eyes went dark ...' – Czerwiński, *Śladami Polskich Gangsterów: Miejsca Mafijnej Warszawy lat 90*, p. 213.

10. Making Friends with the Frog

'Probably the first such ...' – Maringe & Majewski, *Chińczyk: Król Polskiego Narkobiznesu*, p. 72.
'I had become very ...' – *ibid.*, p. 70.
'Żaba would drink himself ...' – Pytalkowska, 'Umarł król', 30 April 2009 (wiadomosci.gazeta.pl/wiadomosci/7,114873,6560272,umarl-krol.html).
'Żaba had charisma and ...' – *ibid.*
'Me, a boy from ...' – *ibid.*
'It turned [Kuba] on ...' – Maringe & Majewski, *Chińczyk: Król Polskiego Narkobiznesu*, p. 128.
'Finally, the scythe hit ...' – Górski & Sokołowski, *Masa o Kobietach Polskiej Mafii* (Prószyński Media, 2014).
20,000 heroin addicts and ... – Krajewski, 'Przestępczość Narkotykowa w Polsce w Latach 1985–1996 w Świetle Danych Statystyki Policyjnej i Sądowej', *Archiwum Kryminologii*, T. XXV, 1999–2000.
'I witnessed ripped stomachs ...' – '"Chińczyk", czyli Spowiedź Króla Polskiego Narkobiznesu', 10 October 2017 (Czytaj więcej na geekweek.interia.pl/styl-zycia/po-godzinach/news-Chinczyk-czyli-spowiedz-krola-polskiego-narkobiznesu,nId,2450597#).
Arrests for drug dealing ... – Krajewski, 'Przestępczość Narkotykowa w Polsce w Latach 1985–1996 w Świetle Danych Statystyki Policyjnej i Sądowej', *Archiwum Kryminologii*, T. XXV, 1999–2000.
'A lot of people ...' – Maringe & Majewski, *Chińczyk: Król Polskiego Narkobiznesu*, p. 121.

11. The Sausage Butchers

'At first I thought ...' – Górski & Sokołowski, *Masa o Kobietach Polskiej Mafii*.
'Masa was 100 per cent convinced ...' – Szostak, *Gangsterskie Egzekucje*.
'Rympałek commanded his boys ...' – Górski & Sokołowski, *Masa o Bossach Polskiej Mafii*, p. 173.
'I admit it surprised ...' – '3 Rzeczy, Których Nie Wiedziałeś o Polskiej Mafii', 3 November 2011 (www.pigout.pl/popkultura/mafia-polska/).
'Jarek, I know that ...' – Górski & Sokołowski, *Masa o Kobietach Polskiej Mafii*.
'[He] was surprised when ...' – Sokołowski, *Protokół Przesłuchania Podejrzanego*.
'At the time, I ...' – Szostak, *Gangsterskie Egzekucje*.
'You don't mean anything ...' – *ibid.*
'Like a lightly beaten ...' – Górski & Sokołowski, *Masa o Bossach Polskiej Mafii*, p. 188.
'It was not a ...' – 'Wojtek K. "Kiełbasa": Chłopak z Dobrego Domu, Który Usiadł na Złej Ławce i Został Gangsterem', 21 October 2021 (wiadomosci.onet.pl/kraj/wojtek-k-kielbasa-chlopak-z-dobrego-domu-ktory-zostal-gangsterem/mkdcj2t).
'The sheep of Pruszków ...' – Szostak, *Gangsterskie Egzekucje*.

12. We Are the Management Board

'In front of the …' – Górski & Sokołowski, *Masa o Bossach Polskiej Mafii*, p. 72.
Others stuck with their … – For an example of a gangster who preferred to go his own way rather than join Pruszków, see Gureczny, *Jak Zostałem Gangsterem: Historia Prawdziwa* (Wydawnictwo Agora, 2019).
'Although he didn't offer …' – Górski & Sokołowski, *Masa o Bossach Polskiej Mafii*, p. 87.
'He became unpredictable …' – *ibid.*, p. 91.
'Show everyone her ass …' – Szostak, 'To "Bolo" Stworzył "Słowika"', 21 November 2020 (crime.com.pl/25577/to-bolo-stworzyl-Słowika/).
'In a democratic country …' – Murphy, 'Call for Arms Resonates across Poland', *Los Angeles Times*, 11 May 1997.
778 homicides in Britain … – 'Homicide Statistics', House of Commons Research Paper 99/56, 1999.
'All right …' – Pasztelański et al., *Mafia Focus Historia Poleca* (Słowne, 2012).
Law enforcement numbers rose … – Haberfeld et al., 'Community Policing in Poland: Final Report', US Department of Justice Document No. 199360, 2003.
62,276 *Milicja* members … – Los & Zybertowicz, *Privatizing the Police State: The Case of Poland* (Macmillan, 2000), p. 132.
Average starting salary was … – Haberfeld et al., 'Community Policing in Poland: Final Report', US Department of Justice No. 199360, 2003.
In 1997, it was estimated … – *ibid.*
By the late 1990s … – *ibid.*
'It was a summer camp …' – Górski & Sokołowski, *Masa o Kilerach Polskiej Mafii* (Prószyński i S-ka, 2016).
'One minister asked the …' – Dudek, 'Mafia nie jest Kobietą. Masa Opowiada o Kobietach w Polskiej Mafii', 20 March 2014 (natemat.pl/95669,mafia-nie-jest-kobieta-masa-opowiada-o-kobietach-w-polskiej-mafii).
By the end of … – Górka & Tokarz (eds), *Teoretyczne i Praktyczneaspekty Polityki Bezpieczeństwa Publicznego* (Politechnika Koszalińska, 2015), p. 125.

13. Unholy Trinity

'There were stories circulating …' – Murphy, 'Hungarians Light up the Phones' (www.latimes.com/archives/la-xpm-1997-aug-28-mn-26587-story.html).
'Remember, we've been here …' – Sokołowski, *Protokół Przesłuchania Podejrzanego*.
'Żaba also told me …' – Szostak, *Gangsterskie Egzekucje*.
'It's better to live …' – *ibid.*
'Good morning …' – *ibid.*
'It's like weeds …' – Batyr, *Spowiedź Nikosia zza Grobu* (Zona Zero, 2018), p. 15.

'This whore from Gdańsk ...' – Latkowski, *Polska Mafia*.
'In 1998 only twenty-five ...' – Haberfeld et al., 'Community Policing in Poland: Final Report', US Department of Justice No. 199360, 2003.
'In general, it seems ...' – Górski & 'Nazar', *Ruska Mafia*.

14. Smuggling is Our Cultural Heritage

'On the one hand ...' – Maringe & Majewski, *Chińczyk: Król Polskiego Narkobiznesu*, p. 142.
'I felt that finally ...' – *ibid.*, p. 143.
'Was pleased such a ...' – *ibid.*, p. 150.
'Like a donut in ...' – *ibid.*, p. 153.
'In the glow of ...' – *ibid.*, p. 157.
'Smuggling is our cultural ...' – Batt (ed.), *Chaillot Paper No. 107: 'Is There an Albanian Question?'* (European Union Institute for Security Studies, 2008), p. 89.
At least 14,000 employees ... – *ibid.*, p. 91.
A survey at the ... – Heyns, 'Emerging Inequalities in Central and Eastern Europe', *Annual Review of Sociology*, Vol. 31, 2005.
'I've never hidden the ...' – Maringe & Majewski, *Chińczyk: Król Polskiego Narkobiznesu*, p. 210.
'My life had become ...' – *ibid.*, p. 170.

15. I'm the King Here

'I'm the king here ...' – Czerwiński & Szatkowski, *Pershing: Król Życia*, p. 100.
'He was never my ...' – Pytalkowski, 'Jak Jarek Rósł w Masę', 27 March 2019 (www.polityka.pl/tygodnikpolityka/klasykipolityki/1786214,1,jak-jarek-rosl-w-mase.read).
'We went looking through ...' – Górski & Sokołowski, *Masa o Porachunkach Polskiej Mafii* (Prószyński i S-ka, 2015).
'I go to the ...' – Latkowski, *Polska Mafia*.
'Felt like Christmas in ...' – Czerwiński & Szatkowski, *Pershing: Król Życia*, p. 126.
'I found myself among ...' – Szostak, *Słowik: Skazany na Bycie Gangsterem* (Harde, 2020), p. 20.
'They rebuilt my value ...' – *ibid.*, p. 31.
'He was a genius ...' – Szostak, 'To "Bolo" Stworzył "Słowika"', 21 November 2020 (crime.com.pl/25577/to-bolo-stworzyl-Słowika/).
'[Y]ou don't wake up ...' – Pytalkowski & Banasiak, *Królowa Mafii* (Rebis, 2016).
'When we were a ...' – Górski et al., *Słowikowa i Masa: Twarzą w Twarz* (Prószyński i S-ka, 2017).
'Don't run, you motherfuckers ...' – *ibid.*
'Pershing was a very ...' – Czerwiński & Szatkowski, *Pershing: Król Życia*, p. 198.
'The [Pruszków management board] ...' – Szostak, *Słowik: Skazany na Bycie Gangsterem*, p. 199.

16. Planet Masa

'Techno music pumps from …' – Ehrlich, 'Food & Drink: Out with the Vlads', *The Independent*, 27 September 1998.
'Cave of debauchery …' – Szostak & Sokołoski, *Bandyci i Celebryci*.
'In the restrooms, Masa …' – Zieliński, *Skarżyłem się Grobowi* (Grafik, 2001), p. 107.
'The customers had never …' – Ehrlich, 'Food & Drink: Out with the Vlads', *The Independent*, 27 September 1998.
'This brought to mind …' – Górski & Sokołowski, *Masa o Kobietach Polskiej Mafii*.
'A wife is a …' – *ibid*.
'No government office ever …' – Górski & Sokołowski, *Masa o Żołnierzach Polskiej Mafia*.
'Some of the ladies …' – Górski & Sokołowski, *Masa o Porachunkach Polskiej Mafii*.
'It's like a game …' – Górski & Sokołowski, *Masa o Bossach Polskiej Mafii*, p. 14.
'I remember that at …' – Sokołowski, *Protokół Przesłuchania Podejrzanego*.
'I appeal to all …' – Bednarczuk, 'Simon był Rezydentem Pruszkówa na Śląsku: Został Postrzelony i Zmarł', 30 January 2022 (tvs.pl/informacje/simon-byl-rezydentem-mafii-pruszkowskiej-na-slasku-zginal-od-strzalu-w-plecy/).
'Did you invite them …' – Górski & Sokołowski, *Masa o Porachunkach Polskiej Mafii*.
'I gave Malizna a …' – *ibid*.

17. Who Killed Pershing?

'[Gołota] will beat him …' – 'Andrzej Gołota Przegrał z Michaelem Grantem w 10. Rundzie', 22 November 1999 (archiwum.rp.pl/artykul/251752-Andrzej-Golota-przegral-z-Michaelem-Grantem-w-10-rundzie.html).
'Pershing suggested …' – Ornacka & Pytlakowski, *Nowy Alfabet Mafii*, p. 102.
'Like horses fighting …' – Czerwiński & Szatkowski, *Pershing: Król Życia*, p. 149.
'After Bedzio's phone call …' – Sokołowski, *Protokół Przesłuchania Podejrzanego*.
'Personally I was a …' – Maringe & Majewski, *Chińczyk: Król Polskiego Narkobiznesu*, p. 53.
'I started receiving calls …' – Sokołowski, *Protokół Przesłuchania Podejrzanego*.
'He looked like he …' – Ornacka & Pytlakowski, *Nowy Alfabet Mafii*, p. 108.
'I think it was …' – Sokołowski, *Protokół Przesłuchania Podejrzanego*.
'I was too weak …' – Maringe & Majewski, *Chińczyk: Król Polskiego Narkobiznesu*, p. 54.
'He was a really …' – Ornacka & Pytlakowski, *Nowy Alfabet Mafii*, p. 100.
'The Don Corleone of …' – Górski & Sokołowski, *Masa o Bossach Polskiej Mafii*, p. 20.

18. Interpol Red Notice

In the five years … – Barclay et al., 'International Comparisons of Criminal Justice Statistics 1999', *Home Office Statistical Bulletin*, Issue 6/01, 2001.
'A vegetable in a …' – Maringe, *Chińczyk: Przemytnicza Odyseja*, p. 16.
'I never wanted to …' – *ibid.*, p. 15.
'The pattern of each …' – *ibid.*, p. 31.
'I remember watching the …' – *ibid.*, p. 89.
'Fucking weather …' – *ibid.*, p. 25.
'The darker, the poorer …' – *ibid.*, p. 162.
'Pure evil, pure hatred …' – *ibid.*, p. 226.
'You won't meet a …' – *ibid.*, p. 237.
'I didn't like the …' – Pytalkowski & Banasiak, *Królowa Mafii*.
'Do not expect to …' – Zieliński, *Skarżyłem się Grobowi*, p. 4.
'Political prisoner of the …' – Niewiadomski, *Świat Według Dziada* (privately published, 2002), p. 4.
'If a dish for …' – Pytalkowski & Banasiak, *Królowa Mafii*.

19. A Moveable Beast

'We talked and I …' – Pytlakowski & Wróbel, *Mój Agent Masa*.
'Keep going [and] be …' – *ibid.*
'Lined with dick where …' – *ibid.*
'Soon you'll be fucking …' – *ibid.*
'I have understood the …' – Sokołowski, *Protokół Przesłuchania Podejrzanego*.
'[A]fter so many years …' – Górski & Sokołowski, *Masa o Życiu Świadka Koronnego* (Prószyński i S-ka, 2017).
'We agreed that we …' – Sokołowski, *Protokół Przesłuchania Podejrzanego*.
'I received alcohol in …' – *ibid.*
'601 940 XXX: Bedzio …' – *ibid.*
'I also financially supported …' – *ibid.*
'If someone did not …' – *ibid.*
'Something between gibberish and …' – Górski & Sokołowski, *Masa o Procesie Polskiej Mafia*, p. 75.
'When we started dismantling…' – 'Cienka Niebieska Linia', *Policja 997*, August 2007.

20. Here Come the Mutants

'I didn't know they …' – 'Po Bitwie w Magdalence', 8 March 2003 (www.zw.com.pl/artykul/164854.html).
'The Mutants were motherfuckers …' – Szostak, *Komando Śmierci* (Harde, 2019).
'We hired a seer …' – Górski & Sokołowski, *Masa o Kilerach Polskiej Mafii*.

In 2001, Poland saw ... – 'Murders Fell 19 per cent in Poland in 2022, "The Largest Decline On Record"', 25 January 2023 (notesfrompoland.com/2023/01/25/murders-fell-19-in-poland-in-2022-largest-decline-on-record).

The price of a ... – Pytalkowski, 'Nieobliczalni, brutalni, źli', 14 December 2002 (www.polityka.pl/archiwumpolityki/1847094,1,nieobliczalni-brutalni-zli.read).

'We were just pieces ...' – 'Cd. Sprawa o zabójstwo Jacka Dębskiego', 11 April 2003 (wyborcza.pl/7,75248,1423285.html).

'While in the early ...' – Pytalkowski, 'Nieobliczalni, brutalni, źli', 14 December 2002 (www.polityka.pl/archiwumpolityki/1847094,1,nieobliczalni-brutalni-zli.read).

'If the ransom is ...' – Szulc, '"Okup W Kawałkach, Człowiek Też W Kawałkach": Tak Działała Grupa Mokotowska', 26 January 2023 (wiadomosci.onet.pl/kraj/byli-postrachem-warszawy-grupa-Mokotówska-slynela-z-brutalnosci/jgnrbwq).

'From now on ...' – Szostak, *Gangsterskie Egzekucje*.

'People were getting hit ...' – Borowiec, 'Relacja Policjanta, Uczestnika Strzelaniny w Magdalence', 7 March 2003 (warszawa.wyborcza.pl/warszawa/7,34862,1360913.html).

'Distinguishing marks: left forearm ...' – Załuski, 'Obława na Mordercę', 1 April 2002 (www.dziennikwschodni.pl/lublin/oblawa-na-morderce,n,1000021357.html).

21. The Eagle Versus the Octopus

'As for the charge ...' – Latkowski, *Polska Mafia*.

'I am a victim ...' – 'Oskarżony: "Pruszków"', 19 September 2002 (dziennikpolski24.pl/oskarzony-pruszkow/ar/2346534).

'There are no political ...' – Wiadomości, 'Polityczne Reperkusje Zeznań Świadka Koronnego w Prociesie, Pruszkowa', 15 July 2003 (wyborcza.pl/7,75248,1574202.html).

'We didn't even think ...' – Maringe & Majewski, *Chińczyk: Król Polskiego Narkobiznesu*, p. 157.

'Inarticulate screams ...' – Latkowski, *Polska Mafia*.

'It was Sokołowski who ...' – *ibid*.

'The funniest thing is ...' – Pytlakowski, 'Jestem już Jednym z Was', 4 May 2004 (kultura.onet.pl/wiadomosci/jestem-juz-jednym-z-was/lferfez).

'Mexico should not, cannot ...' – Carrillo, 'Pretende Mafioso Refugiarse en Mexico' (*Palabra*, 15 January 2001).

'Don't do it with ...' – 'W Procesie Niemczyka Zeznawali "Malizna" i "Tola"', 16 March 2007 (www.money.pl/archiwum/wiadomosci_agencyjne/pap/artykul/w;procesie;niemczyka;zeznawali;malizna;i;tola,186,0,231098.html).

'It's normal that the ...' – Czerwiński & Szatkowski, *Pershing: Król Życia*, p. 202.

'The gang's bosses did ...' – 'Pruszków do Więzienia!', 29 May 2003 (wiadomosci.wp.pl/pruszkow-do-wiezienia-6036347138638465a).

'The tax police will ...' – Ornacka, 'Matki Chrzestne', 18 April 2004 (www.wprost.pl/tygodnik/58832/matki-chrzestne.html).

'Admitted that the number ...' – 'Poland: Ruling Party to Investigate Allegations of Organized Crime Links', Polish Radio 1, 15 July 2003.

'The standard equipment …' – 'Szlachet', *Miasto Młodych Wilków – Część Druga: Walka z Temidą* (Poligaf, 2018), p. 73.
By 2002, over 2,200 … – Pytalkowski, 'Nieobliczalni, brutalni, źli', 14 December 2002 (www.polityka.pl/archiwumpolityki/1847094,1,nieobliczalni-brutalni-zli.read).
'We locked them up …' – Górski & Sokołowski, *Masa o Procesie Polskiej Mafia*, p. 178.

22. Ashes and Diamonds

'Nonsense …' – Maringe, *Chińczyk: Jak Zamknąłem Masę* (Prawicowe, 2018), p. 19.
'We almost became friends …' – Szostak, 'To "Bolo" Stworzył "Słowika"', 21 November 2020 (crime.com.pl/25577/to-bolo-stworzyl-słowika/).
'Żaba, you fucking prick …' – Maringe & Majewski, *Chińczyk: Król Polskiego Narkobiznesu*, p. 187.
'You could say I …' – *ibid.*, p. 186.
'Stay out of Warsaw …' – Krasnowska-Sałustowicz, 'Smętna Starość Mafiosa', 17 July 2010 (www.newsweek.pl/polska/smetna-starosc-mafiosa/zblcj22).
'They don't even have …' – *ibid.*
'You know, first I …' – 'Jarosław Maringe: Ja, Król Koki, Popieram Ziobrę. Ja Też Mam Dość Układu, Rigamonti', 29 September 2017 (www.gazetaprawna.pl/wiadomosci/artykuly/1074419,wyiwad-magdaleny-rigamonti-z-jaroslawem-maringe.html).
'Thus, at the end …' – Michalik, 'Bezwzględny i Tajemniczy Git-Człowiek: "Parasol", czyli "Stary Pruszkowski", Który Nigdy nie Poszedł na Współpracę', 23 November 2022 (wiadomosci.onet.pl/kraj/tajemniczy-i-bezwzgledny-boss-prawdziwa-historia-parasola/gv2c6zo).
'Village idiot …' – Maringe, *Chińczyk: Jak Zamknąłem Masę*, p. 114.

23. Triumph of the Swill

'I received an offer …' – Szostak & Sokołoski, *Bandyci i Celebryci*.
'I've been used …' – *ibid.*
Poland's crime rate had … – 'Poland Crime Rate & Statistics 1990–2024' (www.macrotrends.net/countries/POL/poland/crime-rate-statistics).
'I know that if …' – Dudek, 'Mafia nie Jest Kobietą: Masa Opowiada o Kobietach W Polskiej Mafii', 20 March 2014 (natemat.pl/95669,mafia-nie-jest-kobieta-masa-opowiada-o-kobietach-w-polskiej-mafii).
'I don't consider myself …' – Czop, 'Pruszków Oczami Jarosława "Masy" Sokołowskiego cz. II', 10 July 2014 (www.pruszkowmowi.pl/2014/07/pruszkow-oczami-jaroslawa-masy-sokolowskiego-cz-ii/).
'I must have missed …' – 'Boookster', 24 September 2018 (lubimyczytac.pl/ksiazka/4823794/masa-o-porachunkach-polskiej-mafii).
In 2016, the Górski … – 'Pisarzu, Chcesz Zarobić? Pisz o Przestępcach. "Gangster Masa" Magnesem na Czytelników', 30 May 2016 (wgospodarce.pl/

informacje/26076-pisarzu-chcesz-zarobic-pisz-o-przestepcach-gangster-masa-magnesem-na-czytelnikow).
'He wrote one thing …' – Maringe & Majewski, *Chińczyk: Król Polskiego Narkobiznesu*, p. 76.
'I am a creator of …' – Rakosza, 'Był Królem Polskiego Narkobiznesu. Wyjaśnił Nam, Jak Kokaina z Ekwadoru Znalazła się w Stokrotce', 5 December 2018 (natemat.pl/256963,kokaina-w-bananach-w-stokrotce-Chińczyk-krol-narkobiznesu-wywiad).
'Shortly after writing this …' – Szostak & Sokołoski, *Bandyci i Celebryci*.
'Gangster obsessives at sites …' – pruszkownews.pl is run by former Masa bodyguard Grzegorz Łubkowski, aka 'Mięśniak'; the few rare sightings of Masa after his 2018 arrest have been on this site.

24. Might is Right

'The strong must ever …' – Redbeard, *Might is Right* (Loompanics, 1984), p. 151.
'These people go around …' – Thompson, 'Novel Lifts the Lid on Secrets of Gangland', *The Guardian*, 21 February 2004.
'That was when we …' – Łubkowski, *Kodeks Gangstera* (Fundacja 'Erga Omnes', 2023), p. 51.
In 2015, record seizures … – 'Poland: Country Drug Report 2017', European Monitoring Centre for Drugs and Drug Addiction, 2017, p. 16.
Despite this, native drug … – *ibid.*, p. 20.
'[He] said after his …' – 'Polish Ultra Still Roaming the Streets of Madrid', 20 October 2016 (www.marca.com/en/football/real-madrid/2016/10/20/58090359e2704ebe1b8b465f.html).
'We were cannon fodder…' – Gnauck, 'Polen Bringt seinen Bürgern das Schießen bei', *Die Welt*, 9 December 2017.
'If you dig well …' – Górski & Sokołowski, *Masa o Kilerach Polskiej Mafii*.

Bibliography

Batyr, Tadeusz, *Spowiedź Nikosia zza Grobu* (Zona Zero, 2018).
Czerwiński, Filip, *Śladami Polskich Gangsterów: Miejsca Mafijnej Warszawy lat 90* (Mafia.PL, 2020).
Czerwiński, Filip, & Piotr Szatkowski, *Pershing: Król Życia* (Mafia.PL, 2020).
Górka, Marek, & Grzegorz Tokarz (eds), *Teoretyczne i Praktyczneaspekty Polityki Bezpieczeństwa Publicznego* (Politechnika Koszalińska, 2015).
Górski, Artur, *Gang* (G & J, 2013).
Górski, Artur, et al., *Słowikowa i Masa: Twarzą w Twarz* (Prószyński i S-ka, 2017).
Górski, Artur, & 'Nazar', *Ruska Mafia* (Prószyński i S-ka, 2019).
Górski, Artur, & Jarosław Sokołowski, *Masa o Kobietach Polskiej Mafii* (Prószyński i S-ka, 2014).
Górski, Artur, & Jarosław Sokołowski, *Masa o Pieniądzach Polskiej Mafii* (Prószyński i S-ka, 2014).
Górski, Artur, & Jarosław Sokołowski, *Masa o Bossach Polskiej Mafii* (Prószyński i S-ka, 2015).
Górski, Artur, & Jarosław Sokołowski, *Masa o Porachunkach Polskiej Mafii* (Prószyński i S-ka, 2015).
Górski, Artur, & Jarosław Sokołowski, *Masa o Kilerach Polskiej Mafii* (Prószyński i S-ka, 2016).
Górski, Artur, & Jarosław Sokołowski, *Masa o Żołnierzach Polskiej Mafii* (Prószyński i S-ka, 2016)
Górski, Artur, & Jarosław Sokołowski, *Masa o Procesie Polskiej Mafia* (Prószyński i S-ka, 2017).
Górski, Artur, & Jarosław Sokołowski, *Masa o Życiu Świadka Koronnego* (Prószyński i S-ka, 2017).
Gureczny, Krzystof, *Jak Zostałem Gangsterem: Historia Prawdziwa* (Wydawnictwo Agora, 2019).

Latkowski, Sylwester, *Polska Mafia* (Świat Książki, 2011).
Latkowski, Sylwester, & Piotr Pytlakowski, *Koronny nr 1: Pseudonim Masa* (Rebis, 2017).
Łubkowski, Grzegorz, *Kodeks Gangstera* (Fundacja "Erga Omnes", 2023).
Maringe, Jarosław, *Chińczyk: Jak Zamknąłem Masę* (Prawicowe, 2018).
Maringe, Jarosław, *Chińczyk: Przemytnicza Odyseja* (Wydawnictwo Prawicowe, 2018).
Maringe, Jarosław, & Aleksander Majewski, *Chińczyk: Król Polskiego Narkobiznesu* (Zona Zero, 2017).
Niewiadomski, Henryk, *Świat Według Dziada* (Privately published, 2002).
Ornacka, Ewa, *Kombinat Zbrodni* (Rebis, 2017).
Ornacka, Ewa, & Piotr Pytlakowski, *Alfabet Mafii* (Prószyński i S-ka, 2004).
Ornacka, Ewa, & Piotr Pytlakowski, *Nowy Alfabet Mafii* (Rebis, 2013).
Pichaske, David R., *Poland in Transition: 1989–1991* (Ellis Press, 2017).
Pytalkowski, Piotr, & Monika Banasiak, *Królowa Mafii* (Rebis, 2016).
Pytlakowski, Piotr, & Piotr Wróbel, *Mój Agent Masa* (Rebis, 2015).
Redbeard, Ragnar, *Might is Right or The Survival of the Fittest* (Loompanics, 1984).
Roberts, Andrew, *Napoleon* (Penguin, 2016).
Schom, Alan, *Napoleon Bonaparte* (Sharpe, 2018).
Sumliński, Wojciech, *Czego Nie Powie Masa o Polskiej Mafii* (WSR, 2015).
Sumliński, Wojciech, *Niebezpieczne Związki Bronisława Komorowskiego* (WSR, 2015).
Sumliński, Wojciech, *To Tylko Mafia: Historia Nieprawdopodobnie Prawdziwa i Gorsza Niż Samo Piekło* (WSR, 2018).
Szostak, Janusz, *Byłam Dziewczyną Mafii* (Harde, 2018).
Szostak, Janusz, *Gangsterskie Egzekucje* (Harde Wydawnictwo, 2019).
Szostak, Janusz, *Komando Śmierci* (Harde, 2019).
Szostak, Janusz, *Słowik: Skazany na Bycie Gangsterem* (Harde, 2020).
Szostak, Janusz, & Jarosław Sokołowski, *Bandyci i Celebryci* (Harde, 2018).
Szostak, Janusz, & Jarosław Sokołowski, *Masa: Jak Stałem Się Bestią – Od Pakera do Gangstera* (Harde, 2018).
'Szlacheť, *Miasto Młodych Wilków – Część Pierwsza: Chłopcy z Pruszkowa* (Poligaf, 2018).
'Szlacheť, *Miasto Młodych Wilków – Część Druga: Walka z Temidą* (Poligaf, 2018).
Teresa, Vincent, & Thomas C.Renner, *My Life in the Mafia* (Facwett, 1973).
Zieliński, Andrzej, *Skarżyłem się Grobowi …* (Grafik, 2001).

Index

Page numbers in bold denote images.

Adam (bank robber) 203–4
Adamski, Ludwik 'Lutek' 70, 155–6
Agnieszka (Pershing's girlfriend) 77, 79
alcohol smuggling 42–4
Alfabet Mafii TV series 220
Art-B 49, 65

Banasiak, Andrzej 'Słowik' 68, 116, **130**, 147–50, 169, 178–80, 200, 211–6, 227
Bazar Różyckiego, Warsaw 33
Bączek (drug dealer) 93–4
Bednarczyk, Robert 'Bedzio' 65, **131**, 165–9
Bemowo, Warsaw 199–215
Białołęka prison 143–4
Bogdan 29
Bogucki, Ryszard **130**, 157, 166–7, 203–5, 216
Bonaparte, Napoleon 19–20
books by and about gangsters 221–7
Borowski, Czesław 'Dzikus' 30, 213
bribery of officials 114–5
Brodowski, Jerzy 'Mutant' **131**, 190–1, 196
brothels 55–8
Budziszewski, Wojciech 'Budzik' 30, 84, 89
Bytniewski, Dariusz 'Bysiu,' 101

Centralne Biuro Śledcze (CBŚ – Central Investigation Bureau) 183–4, 206
Cieślak, Robert 'Cieluś' **131**, 189–92, 196–7
Ciężczyk, Andrzej 'Szarak' 30
Clairvoyants 75–6
cocaine 48
'Czaja' (Klub Park bouncer) 45, 47
Czarnecki, Marek Janusz 'Rympałek' 26, 56–7, 102–10, 214–5, 225
Czerwiński, Tomasz 'Czerwus' 231–2
Czetyrko, Andrzej 'Kikir' 70, 78, 190–3

Danielak, Leszek 'Wańka' 34, 37, 41–2, 48, 54, 70, 168
Danielak, Mirosław 'Malizna' 33–4, 58–9, 110–2, **127**, 157–8, 168–9, 199–206
Dąbrowski, Apoloniusz 'Poldek' 118
Dekadent nightclub 114
Dębski, Jacek 115, 191–2
Disco Polo 146
Dr Witt fruit juice company 104
Dresz, Cezary 88–9

economy, Poland's 85
Edlinger, Andy 152–3
European Union 213

Fiszman, Wiktor 61, 113
Florowski, Andrzej 'Florek' 8–9, 64, 71, 77–9, 165–6

Gama restaurant 155–6
gaming machines 145–6
gangsters, rise of Polish 7–16
Gävle, Sweden 174–5
Gdańsk 119–20
George Hotel, Warsaw 26–31, 43
Git-Ludzie 28
'Golden' (gangster) 107
Gołota, Andrzej 161–3, 226
Górski, Artur 221–2
Grant, Michael 161–3, 226
Grzybowska computer market 21, 25

Holmes, Jimmy 230

inflation 41
Isaev, Andrei 113

Jackowski, Krzysztof 9, 75–6, 162
Jarmark Europa 59
Jaruzelski, Wojciech 22
juma (thieving abroad) 23–4
Jurata (ship) 95–6
Jurek, Gruby 24–5

Kamiński, Czesław 'Ceber' 70, 78, 82, 86–7
Kapuściński, Piotr 'Broda' 232
'Kartofel' (crook) 174
Kasprowy hotel 109–12
Kassandra café, Warsaw 33
Kiełbiński, Wojciech 'Kiełbacha' 29, 31, 48, 101–6, **128, 129**
'Klajniak' (gangster) 193
Klepacki, Jacek 'Klepak' 193–4
Klepacki, Marian 'Maniek' 70, 86–7, 155–6
Klimas, Kazimierz 'Kazik' 30, 48–52
Klub Park nightclub 45–7
Klub Planet nightclub 151–4
Kolikowski, Andrzej 'Pershing' 7–10, 52, 63–6, 75–84, **126, 128**, 143–4, 158–65

Kolorowe Lata 90 (colourful 90s) 7, 11, 14, 221
Kołodziejek, Adrian 25–6
'Korek' (gangster) 194–5
Kowalczyk, Tadeusz 115
'Kręciłapka' (drug trafficker) 116
Krzysztof 'Kozioł' 136
'Kuba Gwałciciel' (drug supplier) 93, 96–8
Kujawsk, Zbigniew 'Ali' 32–3, 43–4, 48, 51–2
Kwaśniewski, President Aleksander 158

Łódzka Ośmiornica (Łódź Octopus) gang 122
Łubkowski, Grzegorz 'Mięśniak' 230–1

management board, Pruszków 110–6, 199–206
Maringe, Jarosław 'Chińczyk' 14–6, 20–6, 55–62, 93–100, 125, **128, 132**, 135–8, 169–77, 209–15
Mariusz 'Szlachet' 38, 49, 51, 206
Markov, Georgi 138–9
'Matyś' (gangster) 93–4, 191
Mazur, Małgorzata 45–6
Medvesek, Marek 'Oczko' 68–9, 136
Might is Right (Ragnar Redbeard) 229–30
Mikołajewski, Zbigniew 'Carrington' 121–2
Milicja paramilitaries 28
Miller, Leszek 113
Miller, Paweł 'Małolat' 65
Mirek 28–30
Młode Wilki 35
Mokotów gang 194–5, 197
Multipub bar explosion 67–9, 77
'Mutants' (gang) 190–7

nicknames 31–2
Niewiadomski, Henryk 'Dziad' 43, 69–71, 78, 118–9, **131**, 213
Niewiadomski, Wiesław 'Dziad'/'Wariat' 31, 69–71, 75, 78–9, 117–9, **129**

Index

Odwróconych TV series 220
Ornacka, Ewa 219–20
Ożarów (town) 8

Papała, General Marek 123–4, **130**, 211
Patrycja (Pershing's girlfriend) 8–9, 11, 159, 164–6
'Patyk' (thief) 215–6
Pawlik, Krzysztof Ryszard 'Krzyś' 30, **127**, 200, 231
Pawłowski, Michał 191
Perestroika 21, 23, 46
Pikus, Igor 'Aleksander' 189, 191–2, 196–7
Piłsudski, Marshal Józef 11
Piszczałkowski, Ireneusz 'Barabasz' 31–2, 48–50
Poland, history of 7, 11–4
Polska Rzeczpospolita Ludowa (PRL – Polish People's Republic) 12–3
Prasol, Janusz 'Parasol' 14–6, 27–31, 51, 88, **127**, 158, 168, 200
prison conditions 115
Pruszków (town) 11–5
Pruszków Mafia 10, 14–5, 74–5, 199–215
Pytlakowski, Piotr 219–20

Rakiet (gangster) 210
Raźniak, Zygmunt 'Bolo' 31, 85–6, 168, 225
'Remek' (gangster) 110
Russian Mafia 59–61

Sarna, Karol 'Karolek' 156
'Schnappsgate' 43, 47
Second World War 12, 73
Sekuła, Ireneusz 115, **131**, 167–8
Skatulski, Rafał 'Szkatuła' 194
Skotarczak, Nikodem 'Nikoś' 13, 81–2, 120–2, **130**
Służewiec racetrack 63–4
Sofia, Bulgaria 138–9
Sojusz Lewicy Demokratycznej (SLD – Democratic Left Alliance) 146, 158, 200–1

Sokołowski, Ela 153–4
Sokołowski, Jarosław 'Masa' 14–6, 31, 37–40, 48, 61–2, 101–18, **132**, 144–5, 151–5, 219–23
  as crown witness 182–8, 201–3
Solidarność (Solidarity) 21–2, 120
Sopot (town) 81–2
Stockholm, Sweden 173–4
Suga, Tomasz 'Komandos' 194
Szczepaniak, Zbigniew 'Simon' 157
Szwarc, Ryszard 'Kajtek', 74–5, 77, **129**, 168–9, 213–4
Świadek Koronny film 220

Taj Mahal hotel, Atlantic City 161–3
Teresa, 'Fat' Vinnie 15–6
Trump, Donald 162

vodka consumption 42
vory ('thieves-in-law') 60

Wałęsa, Lech 83, 120
Warsaw 12, 19–20
Wieczorek, Jerzy 'Żaba' 94–100, **128**, 140–1, 211–3
Wilimberg, Jarosław *see* Maringe, Jarosław 'Chińczyk'
Wołomin gang 10, 74–5
Wprost magazine 206
Wróbel, Piotr 181–4, 223–4

Zacharzewski, Daniel 'Zachar' 122
Zakopane (town) 7–9
Ząbki (town) 70, 78
'Zbynek' (gangster) 45, 86
Zemek, Grzegorz 49
Zielińska, Monika 148–9, 178–80
Zielone Bingo 115
ZOMO riot police 28

Żak, Mirosław 192
Życie Warszawy newspaper 73–4